AF574634

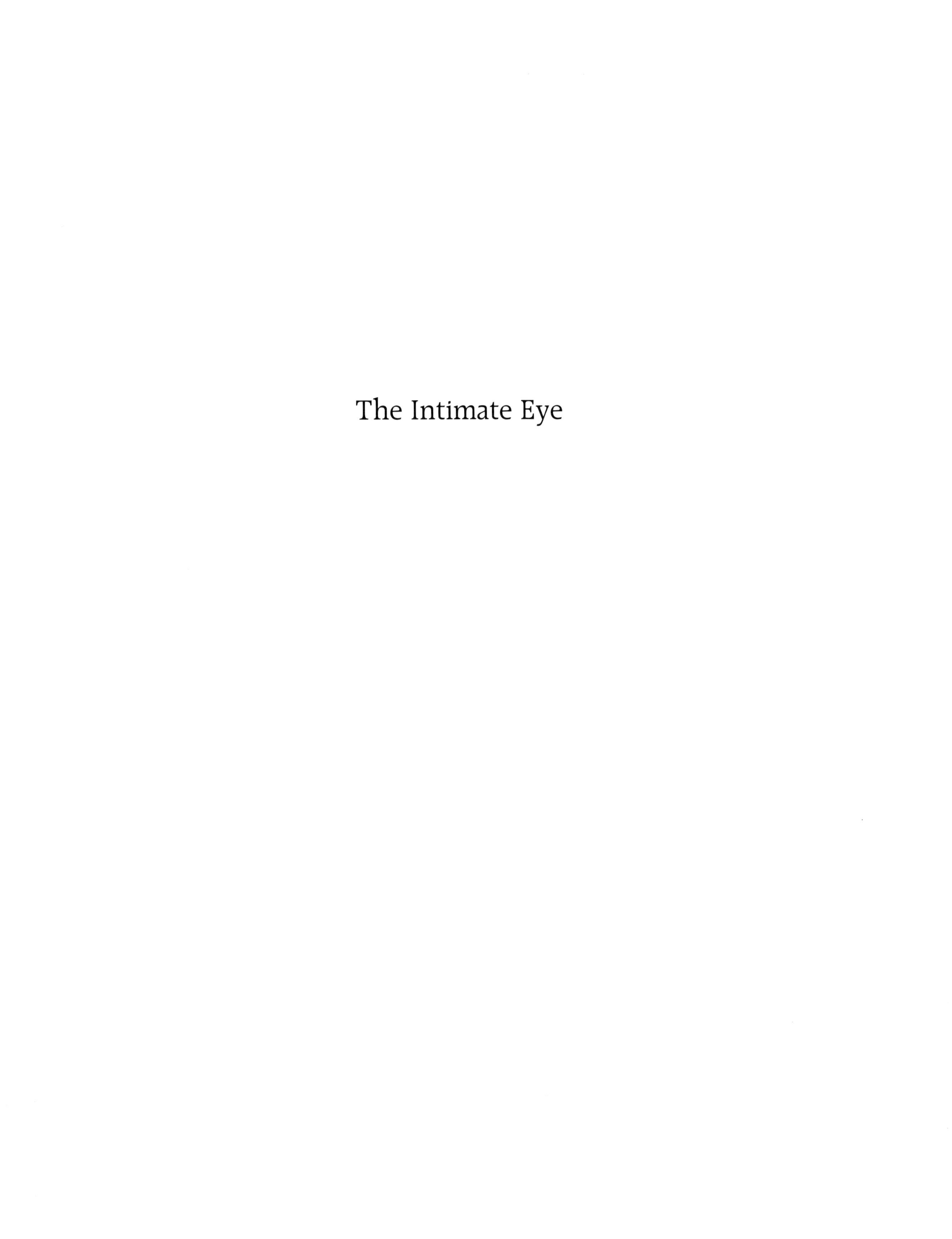

The Intimate Eye

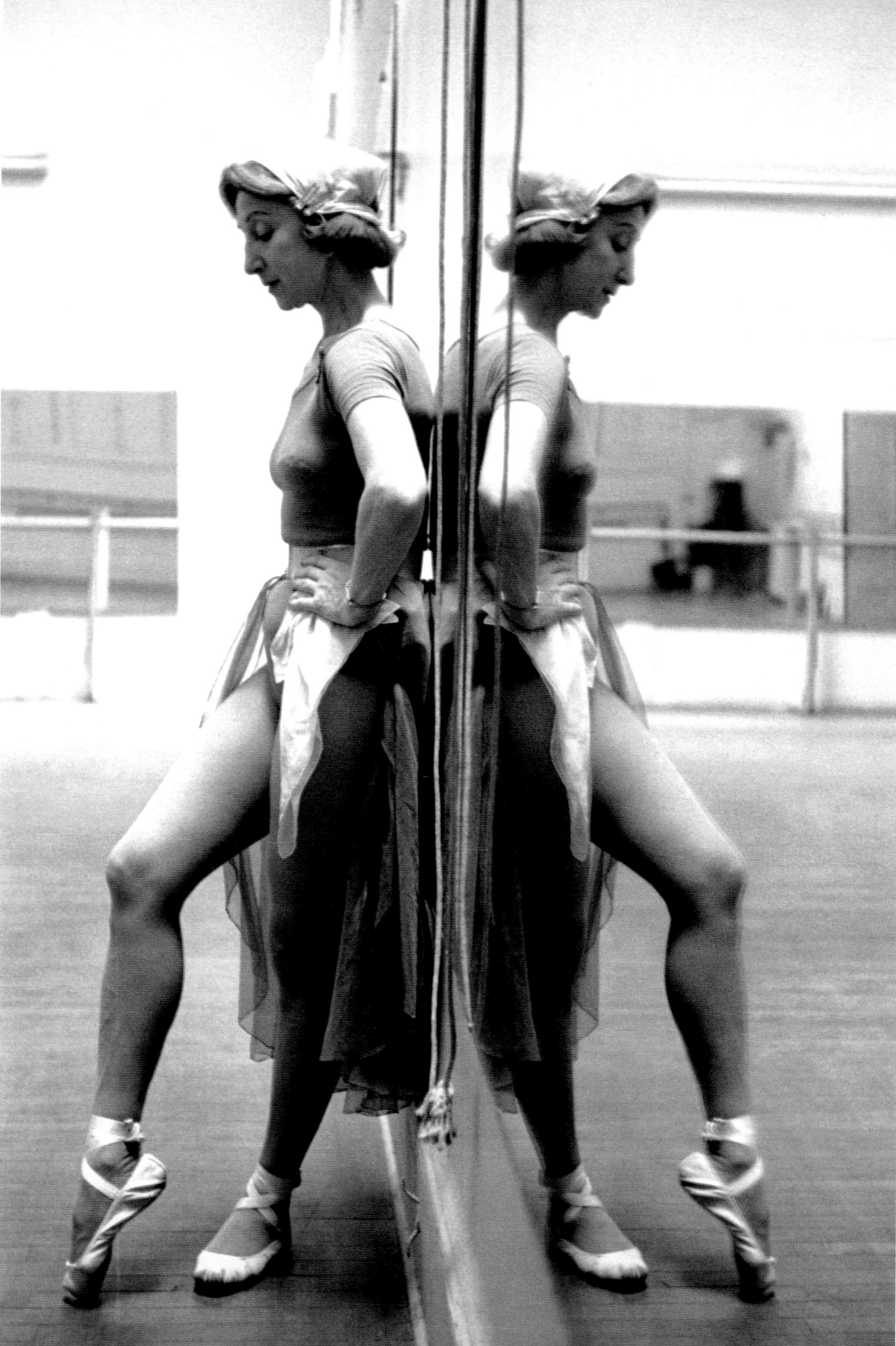

THE

Intimate Eye

PORTRAITS BY BERNARD GOTFRYD

Riverside Book Company, Inc. / New York

To my wife Gina, who encouraged me and inspired me.

This book and the portraits it contains would not have been possible without the cooperation of the current photo editors of *Newsweek* magazine, and of their predecessors, who, over the years, provided the choice assignments and opportunities the evidence of which appears on these pages.

For information, please address the publisher:

Riverside Book Company, Inc.
P.O. Box 237043
New York, NY 10023
www.riversidebook.com
info@riversidebook.com

ISBN-13: 978-1-878351-63-0
ISBN-10: 1-878351-63-x

Design by Lascaro Design

Manufactured in the United States of America.

CONTENTS

INTRODUCTION

IN A CAREER WHICH SPANNED MORE THAN THREE DECADES, from the mid-1950s through the late 1980s, my father Bernard Gotfryd created a portfolio of portraits of many famous figures spanning two generations who had a part in shaping the second half of the 20th century. On assignment for *Newsweek* magazine, he had the opportunity to focus his lens on many of the most influential people of the day. He was able to meet popes, presidents, mayors, union workers, composers, musicians, choreographers, dancers, playwrights, actors, novelists, and rock-and-roll stars, not to mention acid heads and Good Humor men.

Equipped with just a couple of 35mm cameras, a few lenses, and several rolls of black-and-white film, my father would analyze each situation on the spot, and somehow managed to capture the character, physical nature, and sometimes even the soul of his subjects. Occasionally adding a prop, such as a hat, a cigar, or a cherished pet, to lend meaning or add gravity to the portrait, he produced images that were filled with intensity, magnetism, and humor.

Frequently told by a subject, or his agent, that he had just "ten minutes," my father did what he had to. He usually shot in natural light only, without the aid of a flash, and without an assistant to help set up any artificial lighting. It is this lack of artificial illumination that gives his portraits their startling, sometimes stark and gritty, very genuine quality. The viewer confronts the subject of each portrait directly, without the need or benefit of technological enhancement.

My father's subjects often heard his own remarkable tales of surviving the several Nazi concentration camps in which he was incarcerated in his native Poland and in Austria. In some cases, he forged friendships with his subjects, and they encouraged him to write his stories.

Throughout his career, it was not unusual to find him speaking on the phone with people like the composer-performer Nina Simone, the novelist John Cheever, and the Philadelphia radio personality Claude Lewis, or to find literary luminaries such as Edward Dahlberg at the dinner table. My father kept up a correspondence with the novelist and fellow Holocaust survivor Primo Levi until just before Levi's tragic and untimely death. Levi was the friend who gave my father the greatest amount of encouragement to put his stories on paper. My father took his advice and published the stories in 1990. The present publication is the first time that my father's photographs have appeared in book form. Levi would have been pleased by this as well.

It was because of the personal connection that my father made with many of his subjects that he was able to transform the veneer of fame into something that was almost transparent, revealing the essence of each sitter. This is the core of his style and the way in which he approached his subjects, with candor, sincerity, respect, a disarming manner, and a charming smile, all of which allowed him to render some of the most iconic faces of our time in a very human, honest way. Here they are, at moments that may be frenetic or calm, but always illuminated from within by the dignity, integrity, pain, and joy that was captured by the camera along with their physical appearance.

Howard Gotfryd
Brooklyn, NY, February 2006

Authors

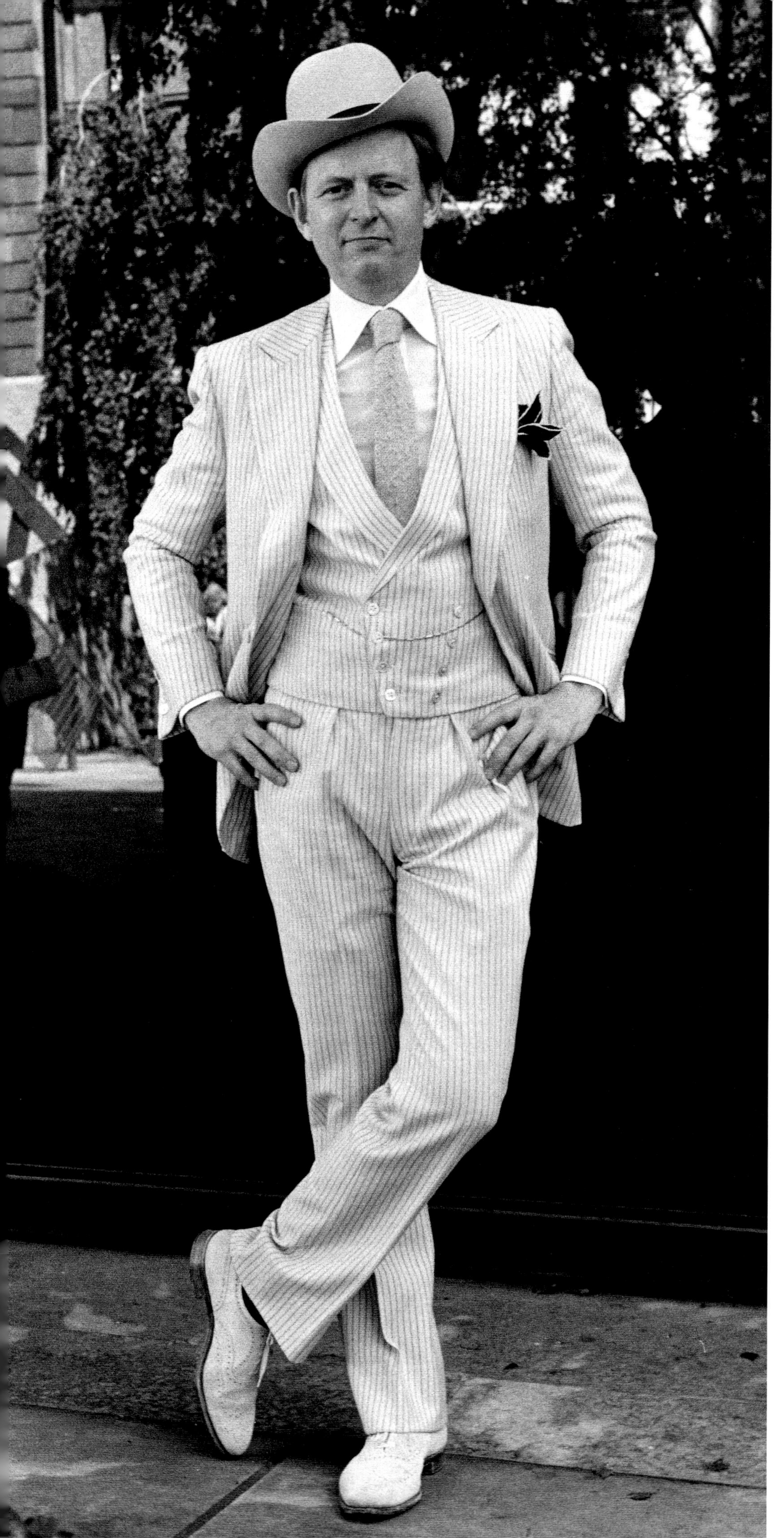

TOM WOLFE

I WAS ALWAYS UNDER THE IMPRESSION that Tom Wolfe might be related to Virginia Woolf, perhaps a nephew. And one day, when we had a photo session, I asked him. "Not that I know of," he said, "we don't even spell our names alike, but if you want to create a nephew, I don't see why you can't, except that it won't be me."

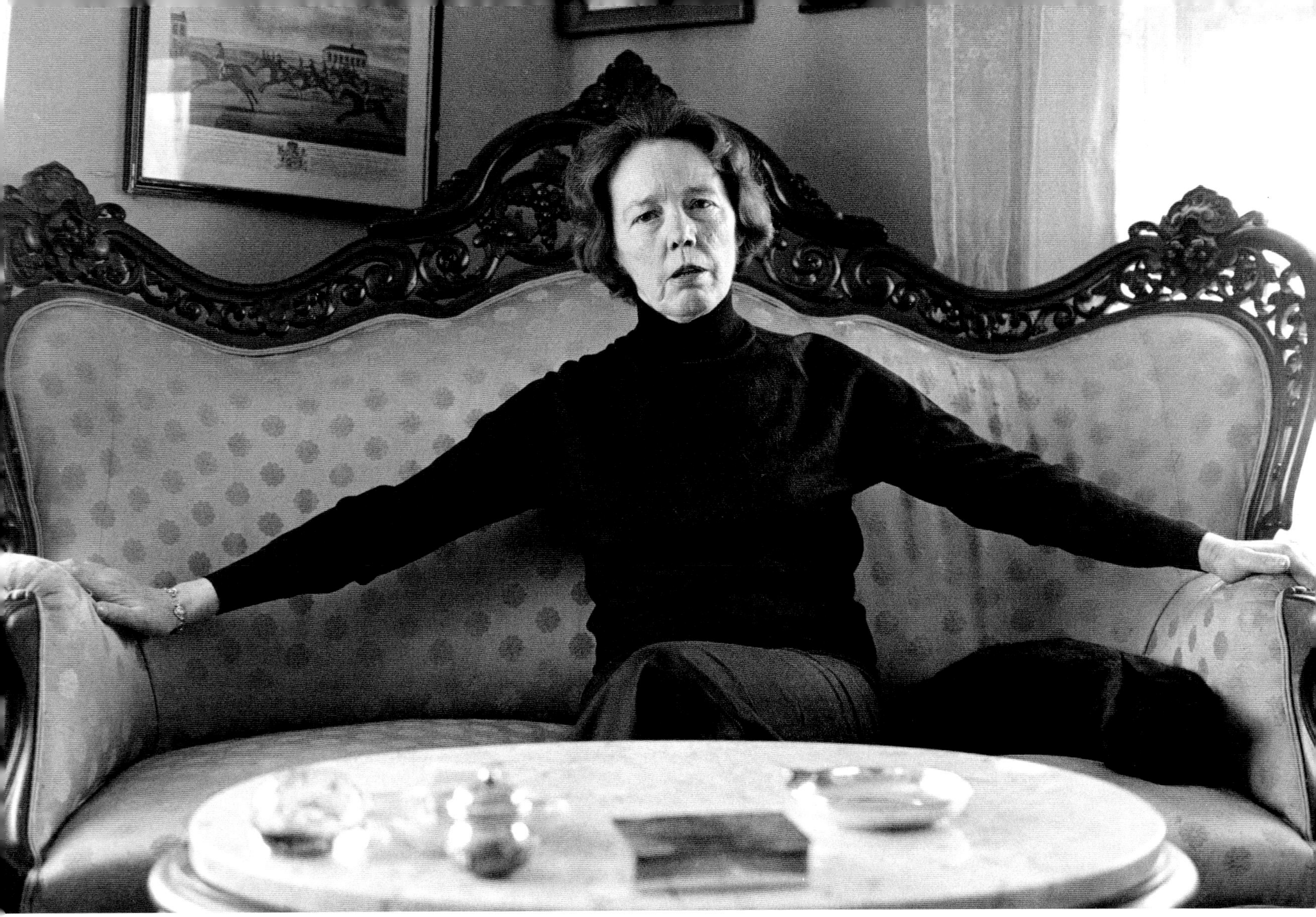

JEAN STAFFORD

ONE MORNING IN THE LATE SIXTIES, near the end of a harsh winter, I drove to East Hampton to photograph Jean Stafford. I didn't know much about her except a few of her short stories, and that she was once married to A.J. Liebling, one of my favorite authors.

She came out dressed in black, as if in mourning. "How was the driving?" she asked. "Not bad at all," I said.

She left the room and soon reappeared with two tall glasses filled with what looked like tea. She put one glass on the table and said, "Well, wouldn't you want to warm up a bit?" I picked up the glass, brought it closer to my mouth, and realized it was alcohol.

"Sorry," I said, "but I must stay in focus, and then I have to drive back to the city."

"I understand," she said, taking a sip from her own glass. After a while she became very giddy, insisting that she be photographed with her cat, which was nowhere to be found. She went outside to look, but to no avail. Eventually, somewhat dishevelled and wet, the cat showed up, with a dead bird in its mouth, and this completed our photo session.

When I was leaving, she gave me a small package. In it were some sugar cookies with a Merry Christmas inscription in chocolate chips. The cookies were hard as rock. When I bit into one, I chipped a tooth. Ever since, around Christmas time, I think of Jean Stafford's hospitality, and my dental bill.

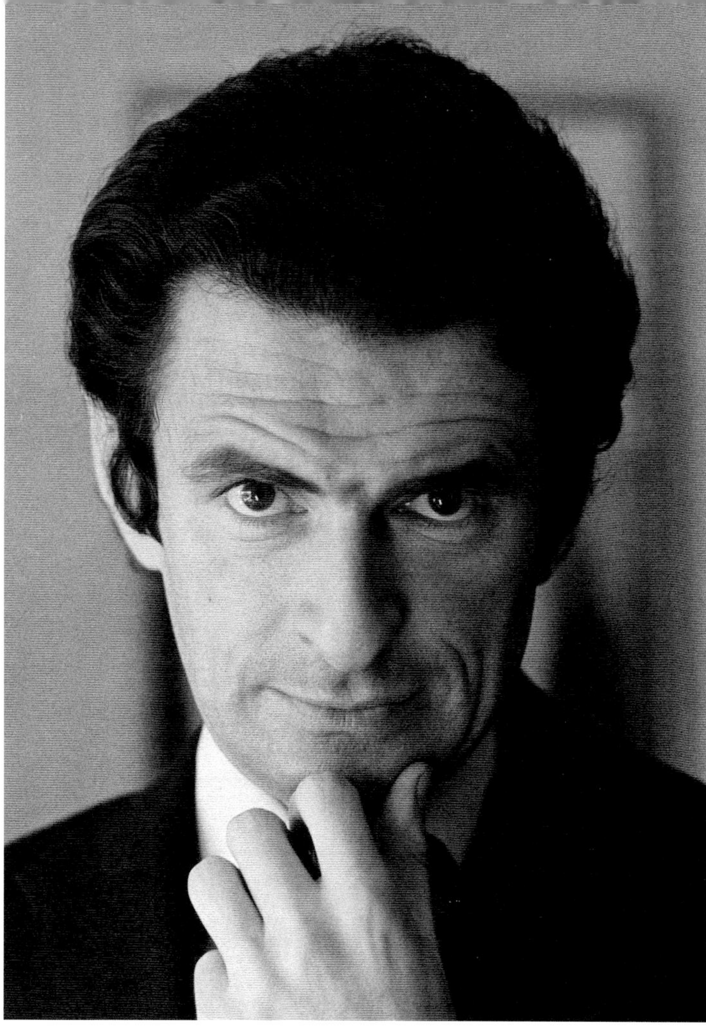

JERZY KOSINSKI

I PHOTOGRAPHED Jerzy Kosinski shortly after *The Painted Bird* was published. Being a survivor myself, I wanted to meet him. I read the book and was enthralled by it.

The first thing I noticed in his office was a display of framed photographs. "Whose photographs are these?" I asked. "They're mine, I've taken them," he said. I complimented him on such professional work.

"Powerful images," I said. "I really would like to talk to you about your book, if I may. I have some questions."

"I hope not too many."

"I assume, as others do, that *The Painted Bird* is autobiographical, and therefore I couldn't understand why the little boy hides his identity."

"The little boy happens to be a Jew, and the book doesn't have to be autobiographical," Kosinski said, somewhat annoyed.

"You're not Jewish, are you?" I said.

"In a way, but let's not discuss that." Although puzzled by his answer, I decided not to pursue it. I took some photos of him, we talked about photography, and I left.

Almost twenty years later, shortly before Chanukah, I went to a Judaica store to purchase a menorah. And there was Jerzy Kosinski. "How strange," I said, "I never thought I would find you in a store like this, looking at menorahs."

"Why not," he said. "Chanukah is coming, and I need a new menorah. And what brings you here? Are you Jewish?"

"In a way," I said.

"But you don't look it," he said, and we burst out laughing. We ended up buying identical menorahs.

MARIO PUZO

BEFORE I WENT to photograph Mario Puzo, I managed to read *The Godfather.* We sat in the kitchen of his new house on Long Island, chatting and drinking coffee. He was smoking a thick cigar, which made me dizzy, and soon I began to sneeze. He must have realized that it was the cigar, and he put it out. I liked Puzo immediately. He was a friendly, modest man with no airs. We spoke about editors and authors I had photographed, some of whom he knew personally. Then he told me how unsuccessful his previous novel was.

"I just finished reading *The Godfather,*" I said, "and I think it would make a hell of a movie." He looked at me and smiled. "Do you want to buy the rights to it?"

"If I were a producer, I certainly would."

Not very long after, *The Godfather* was made into a movie. On the night of its premiere, I photographed the party that the film company threw for the cast and the author. When Puzo saw me, he introduced me to his family and a host of other people. Pointing a finger at me, he said, "Believe it or not, this guy with the camera knew that *The Godfather* would be made into a movie."

I could see lots of doubtful expressions, but then someone asked me, "Is it true? How did you know?"

Without knowing who that person was, I said, "If you had read the book, chances are you would have felt the way I did." As it turned out, I was talking to the executive producer.

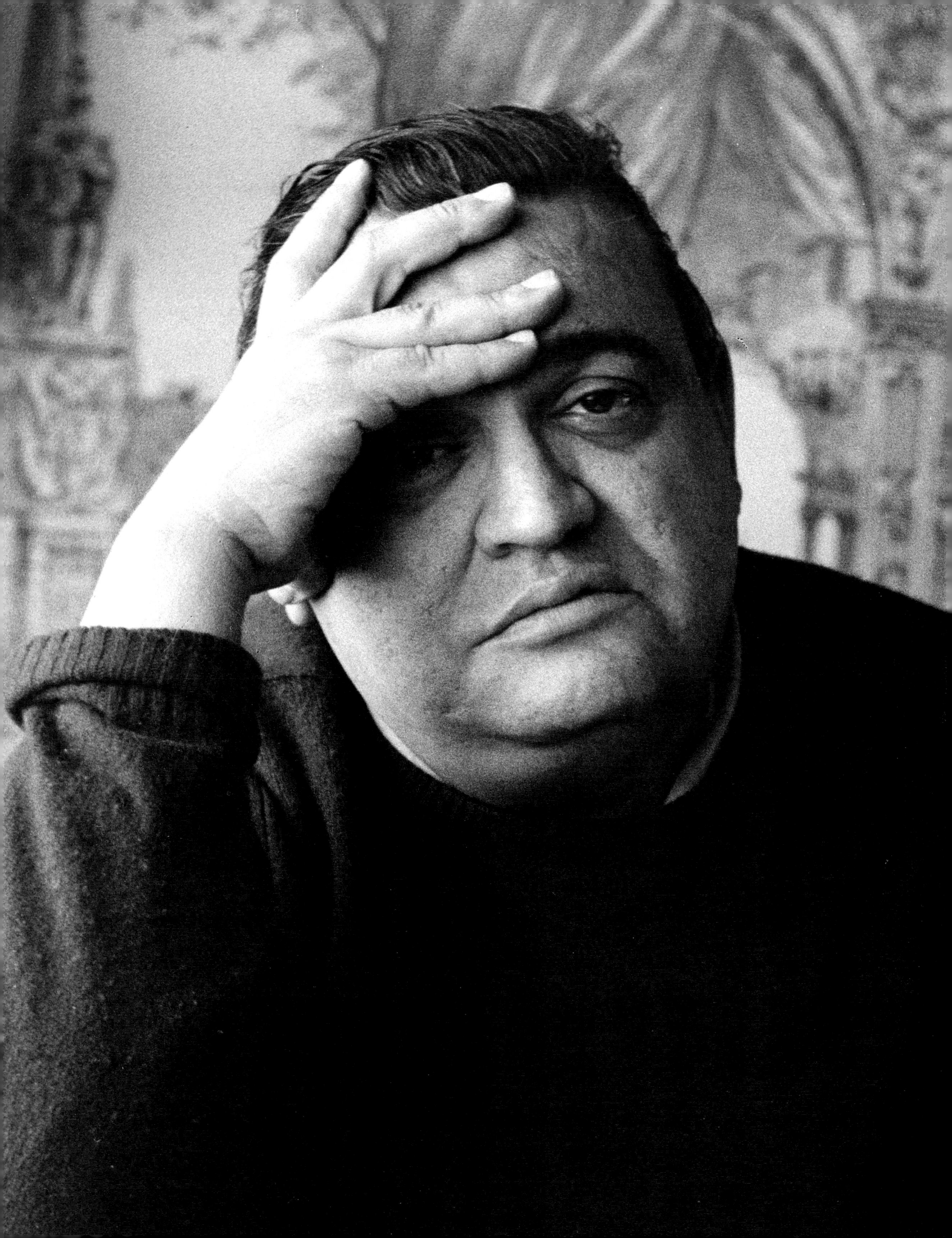

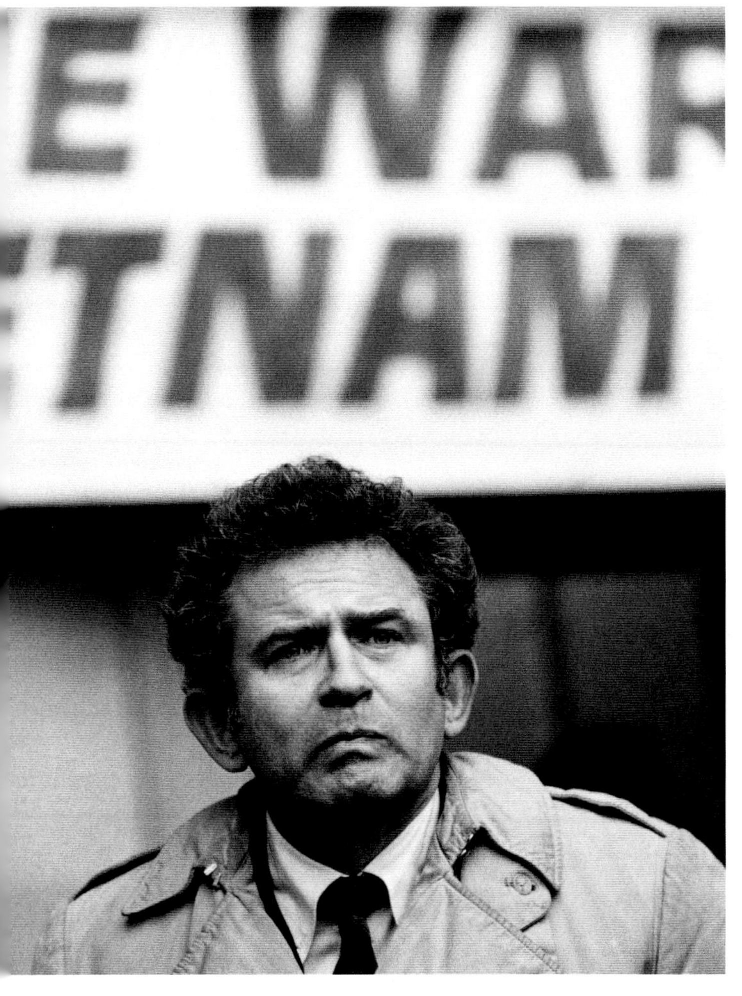

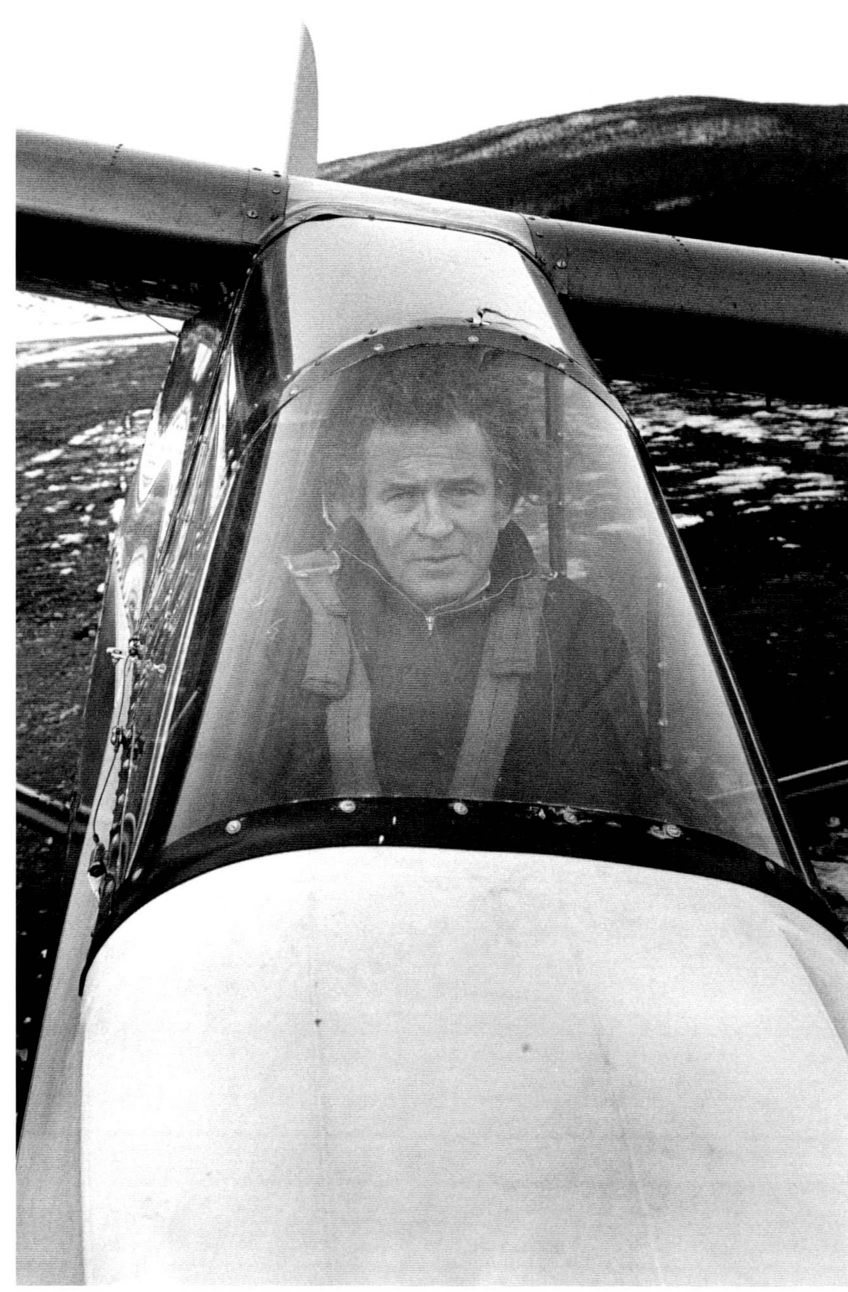

NORMAN MAILER

OVER THE LAST THIRTY YEARS, I photographed Norman Mailer several times, but one session in particular stands out. I don't know how it came about, but, as I recall, a *Newsweek* editor challenged him to go up in a glider. It took a lot of guts, I thought, to do that without any previous experience. We drove together to an upstate New York airfield, and before I knew it, Mailer was strapped into his seat, canopy in place, ready to go. The glider was hitched to a tow plane, and soon he was aloft. I watched the glider circle above me and wondered how and when he would ever be able to land. I had visions of the glider being smashed to bits.

In spite of all this, the landing went smoothly. Mailer scrambled from his seat triumphantly and, reminiscent of Lindbergh after crossing the Atlantic, said "I wouldn't mind trying that again."

When the photo was published, Mailer sent a note saying, "It certainly takes imagination to take a picture of a stationary glider and make it appear as if it were aloft. You're a master of illusion, and I thank you."

NADINE GORDIMER

NADINE GORDIMER, the South African author and Nobel Prize recipient, was attending a PEN meeting in New York City. A photographer who was standing nearby asked me if she was Indira Gandhi. I thought he was being funny.

When I told him who she was, he said, "I could swear she looks just like Indira Gandhi."

"I don't think so," I said, "and furthermore, Indira Gandhi has been dead for twenty years." He was surprised to hear that.

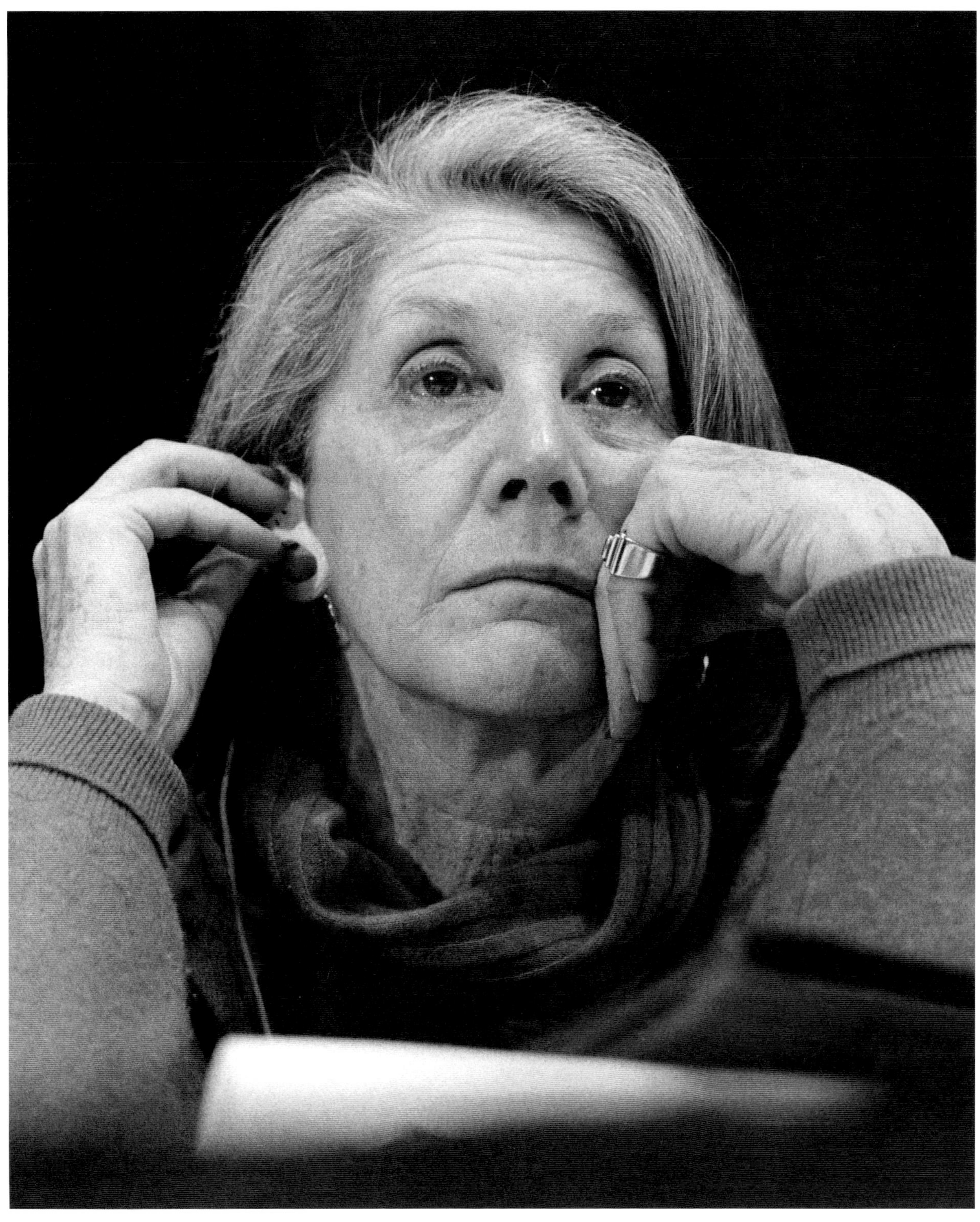

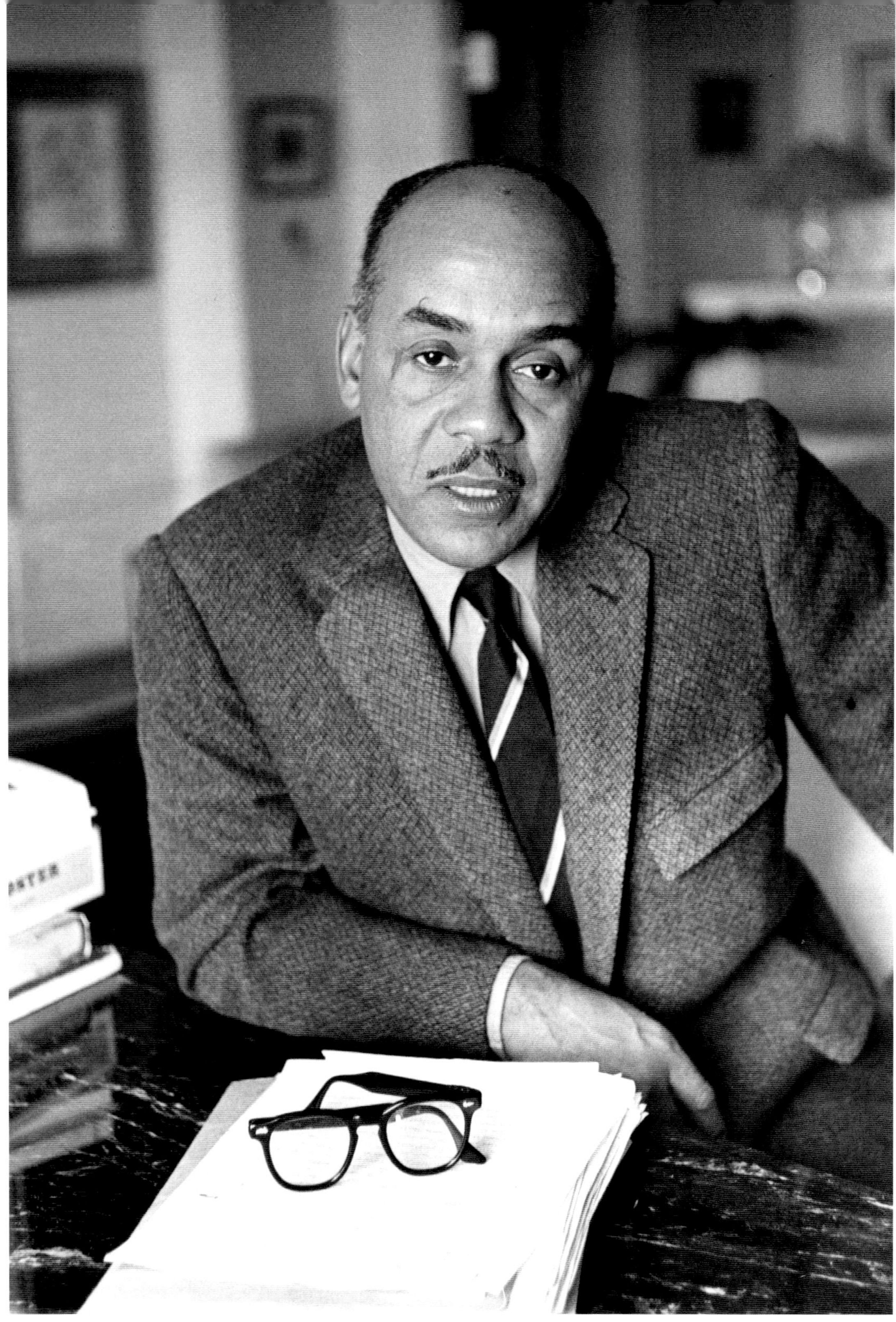

RALPH ELLISON

AFTER A SHORT PHOTO SESSION, Ellison suggested we go to the park. As soon as we arrived, a man walked over and told him how much he admired his writing, especially *The Invisible Man*. Ellison thanked him, and the man asked Ellison if he could spare some change for a cup of coffee. Ellison reached into his pocket, came up with a dollar, and gave it to him. "He certainly doesn't look like a panhandler," I said, after he walked away. "Well, I'm not sure myself who he is, or what he does, but why should it matter?" Ellison said. "I consider him a most polite, well-behaved person, and, mind you, isn't it worth a dollar to hear such a compliment?"

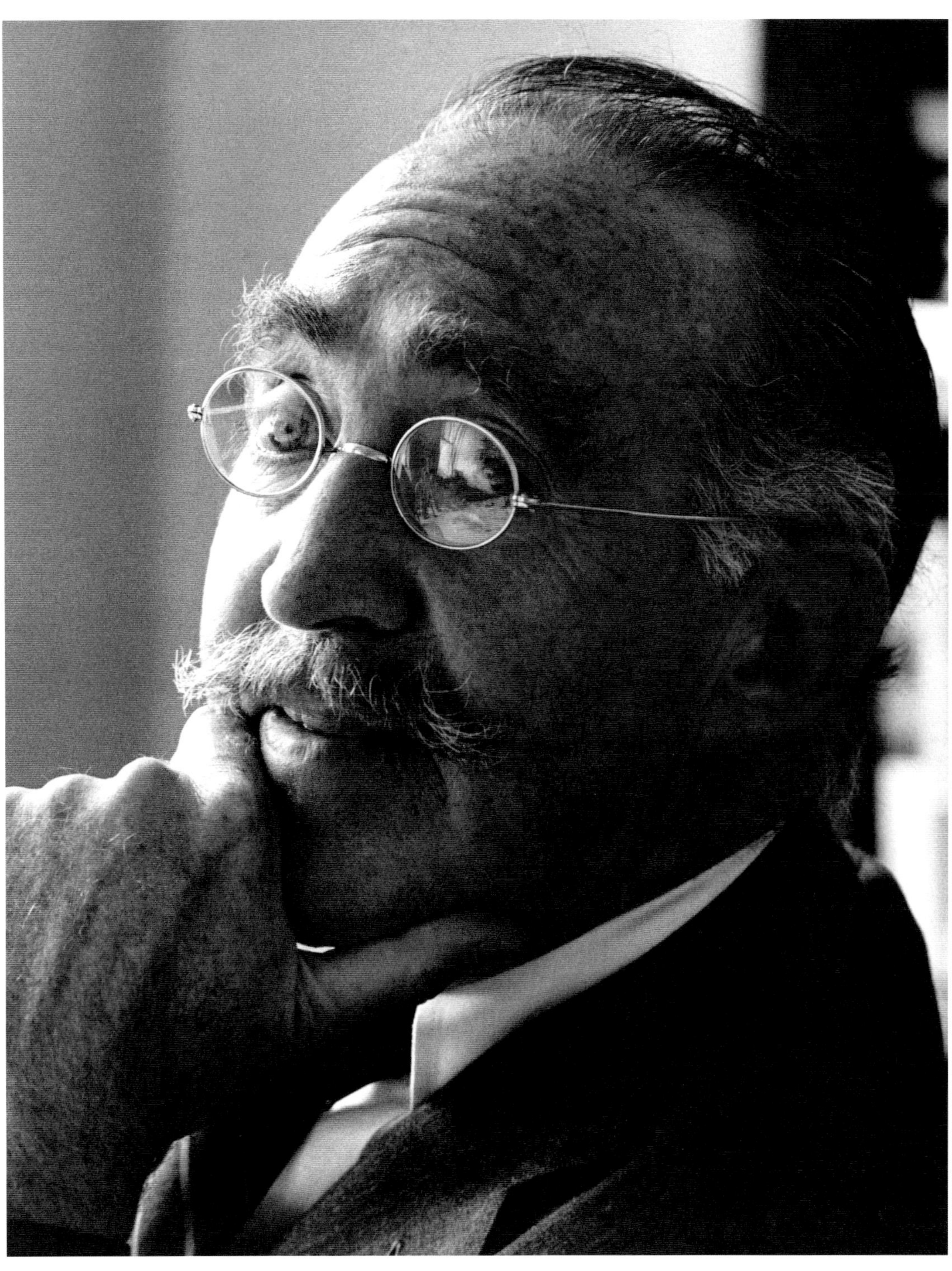

S.J. PERELMAN

IN THE LATE 1960s, I had a photo session with the author and humorist S.J. Perelman. It was during the Vietnam war, and he wasn't saying anything funny. He spoke about war and peace, and was especially critical of the situation in Vietnam. He did not think we should have gotten involved in the first place.

"It's death and destruction all over again," he said. "So many young lives down the drain."

I was very depressed afterward when I thought about my fourteen-year-old son, who in another five years would be subject to the draft.

RUTH PRAWER JHABVALA

I FOUND RUTH PRAWER JHABVALA in her small East Side apartment hard at work, writing. She was modest, talkative, and charming. Considering her features, I asked if she was of Indian descent.

"Not at all," she said. "I married an Indian man and lived in India for some time, but originally I come from Poland."

"I also come from Poland," I said. She didn't seem surprised. "We're all wanderers," she said, "and everyone, or almost everyone, comes from another place."

I asked if she could find time to read some of my short stories. Some weeks later, I received a lovely letter from her praising my work. When my book was published, she gave permission to quote from the letter, for which I have been grateful ever since.

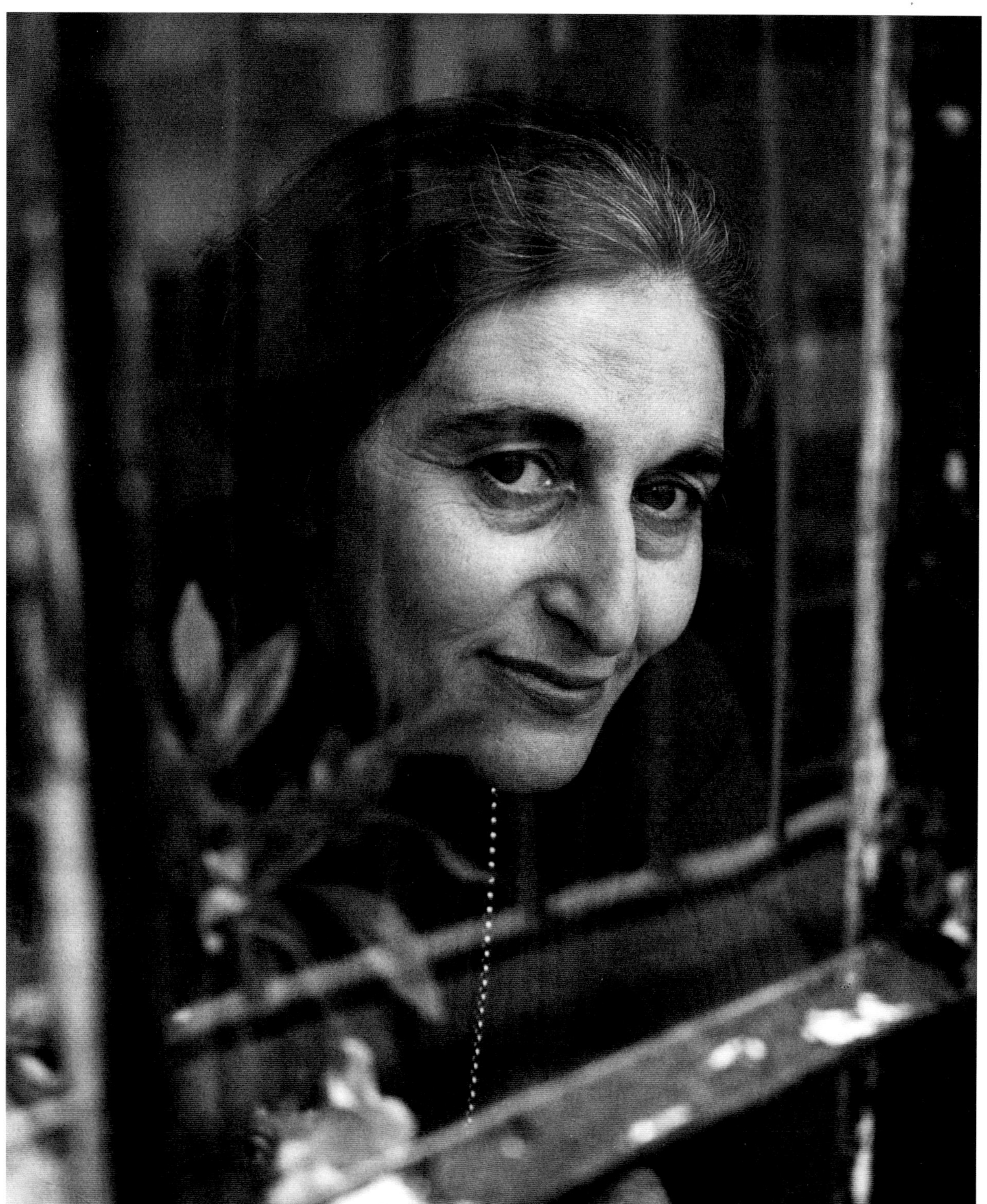

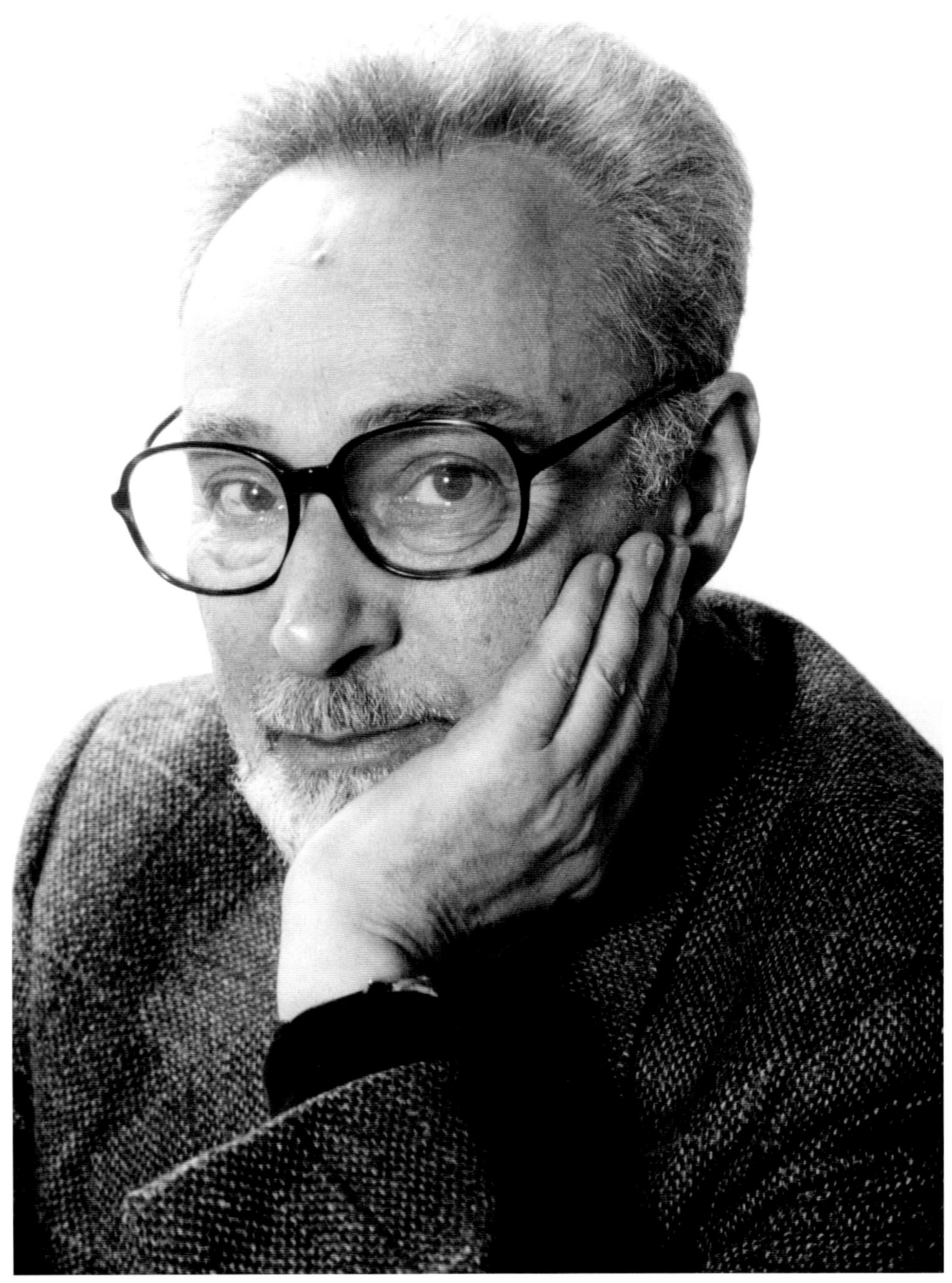

PRIMO LEVI

I WILL ALWAYS REMEMBER PRIMO LEVI, the brilliant writer and survivor of Auschwitz. We first met in 1985, when he came to New York to promote two of his books, recently published in translation. He told me that he had read one of my short stories in a magazine, and complimented my work.

Before he returned to Italy, I gave him some of my published work. Not long after, I received a letter from him urging me to continue writing, and, at the bottom of the letter, he wrote, "I know that one day you'll have a book, and if you will, I would like you to use the enclosed endorsement."

My book was published in 1990, and Primo Levi's endorsement went on the back cover. When I heard about his tragic death in 1987, it felt like a personal loss.

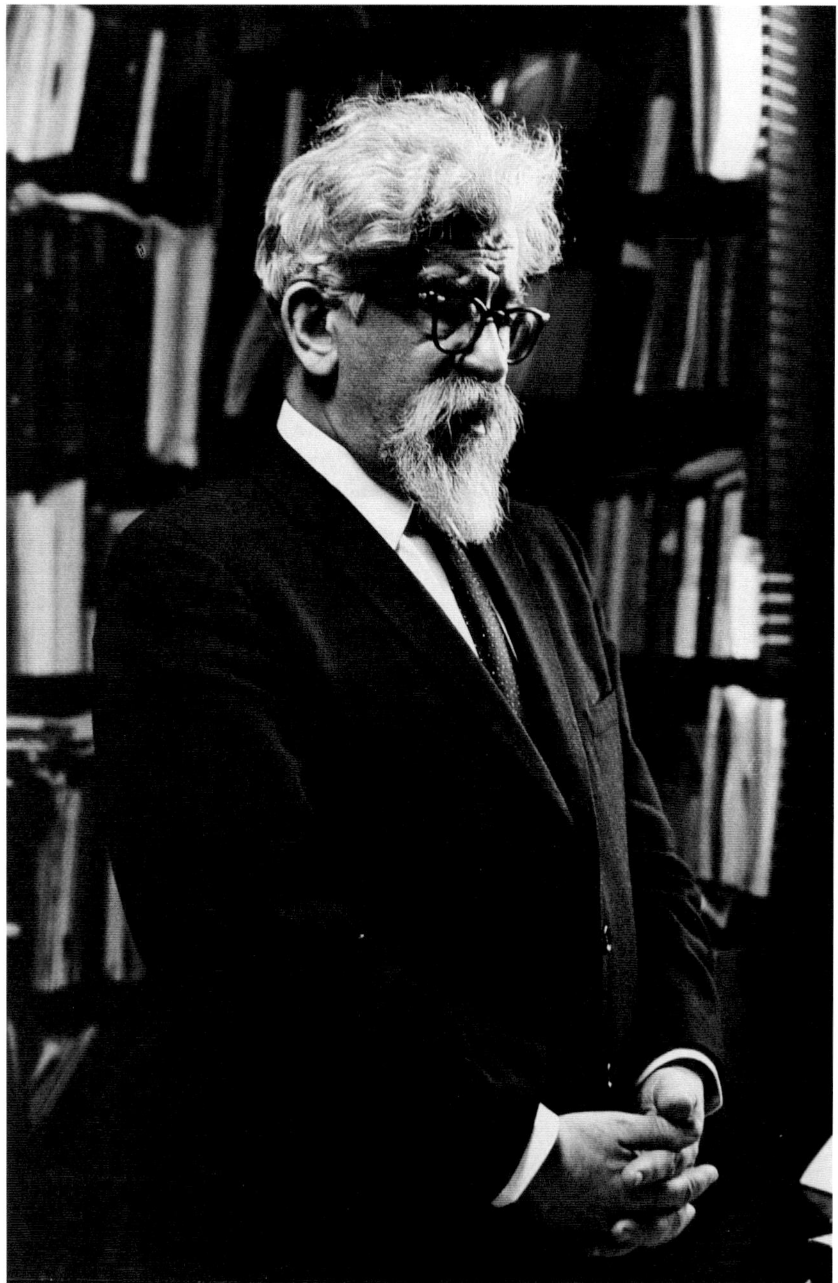

ABRAHAM JOSHUA HESCHEL

DR. ABRAHAM J. HESCHEL, the Jewish theologian, was very attentive to the young reporter who came along with me to interview him. He didn't pay the least attention to the camera, which made things difficult for me. At last, I was able to corner him for several minutes and take some shots. When the photo and article finally appeared, he sent a letter asking if he could have a print. I obliged, and soon received a thank you note, actually more of an essay, praising my generosity. When I saw him again some years later, he gave me a pocket-size prayer book, which I stuck inside my camera bag. Some time later, on one of my trips, the bag was stolen. When I went around the terminal looking for it, I found only the prayer book, in a telephone booth that I was about to use to call the police. The bag itself was never recovered. I called Dr. Heschel the next day to tell him the story. He listened very quietly, and when I finished, he said, "I hope you can see that it was meant for you to pray."

ALDOUS HUXLEY

I PHOTOGRAPHED ALDOUS HUXLEY in the summer of 1957 on one of his visits to New York. When I arrived at his hotel, he was on the telephone. Suddenly, he covered the receiver with his hand, and told me that he was ordering sandwiches for lunch, and would I like to join him. "Well," I mumbled, unprepared for such hospitality, "whatever you'll have, sir, is okay with me."

"You may not like my choice," he said.

"Then, a tuna fish salad on toast, lettuce and no mayonnaise would do."

"How strange," I heard him say, "that is exactly what I'm having."

We spoke about television and its future influence, especially on children. Being the father of two toddlers, I was quite concerned about that. I assured him that my wife and I were able to control the programs our children were watching.

"I wish you luck," Huxley said. "I hope one day you and your wife will succeed in making your children read books, and if you do, you'll deserve a medal."

As it turned out, Huxley needn't have worried. Our children turned out to be avid readers. ▶

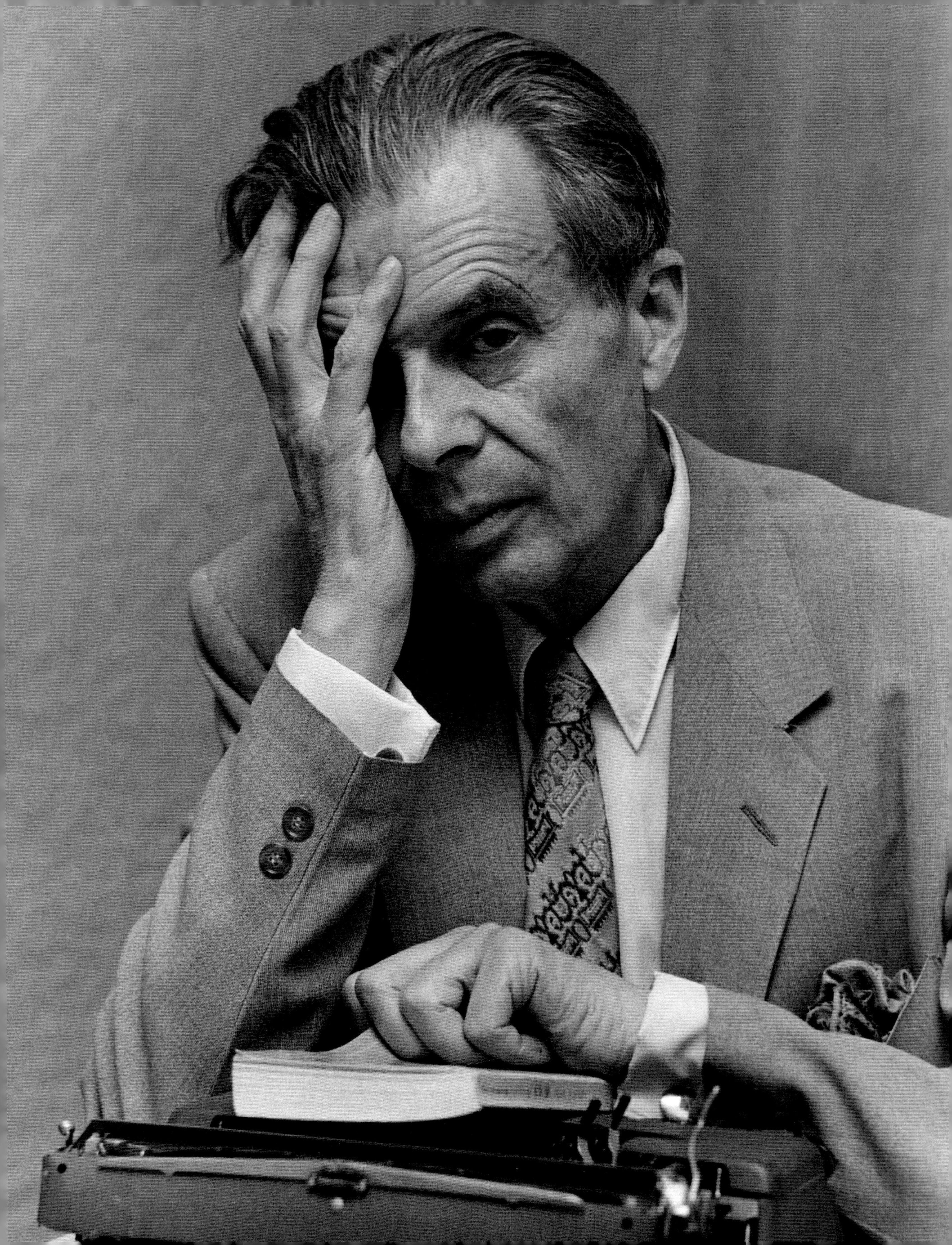

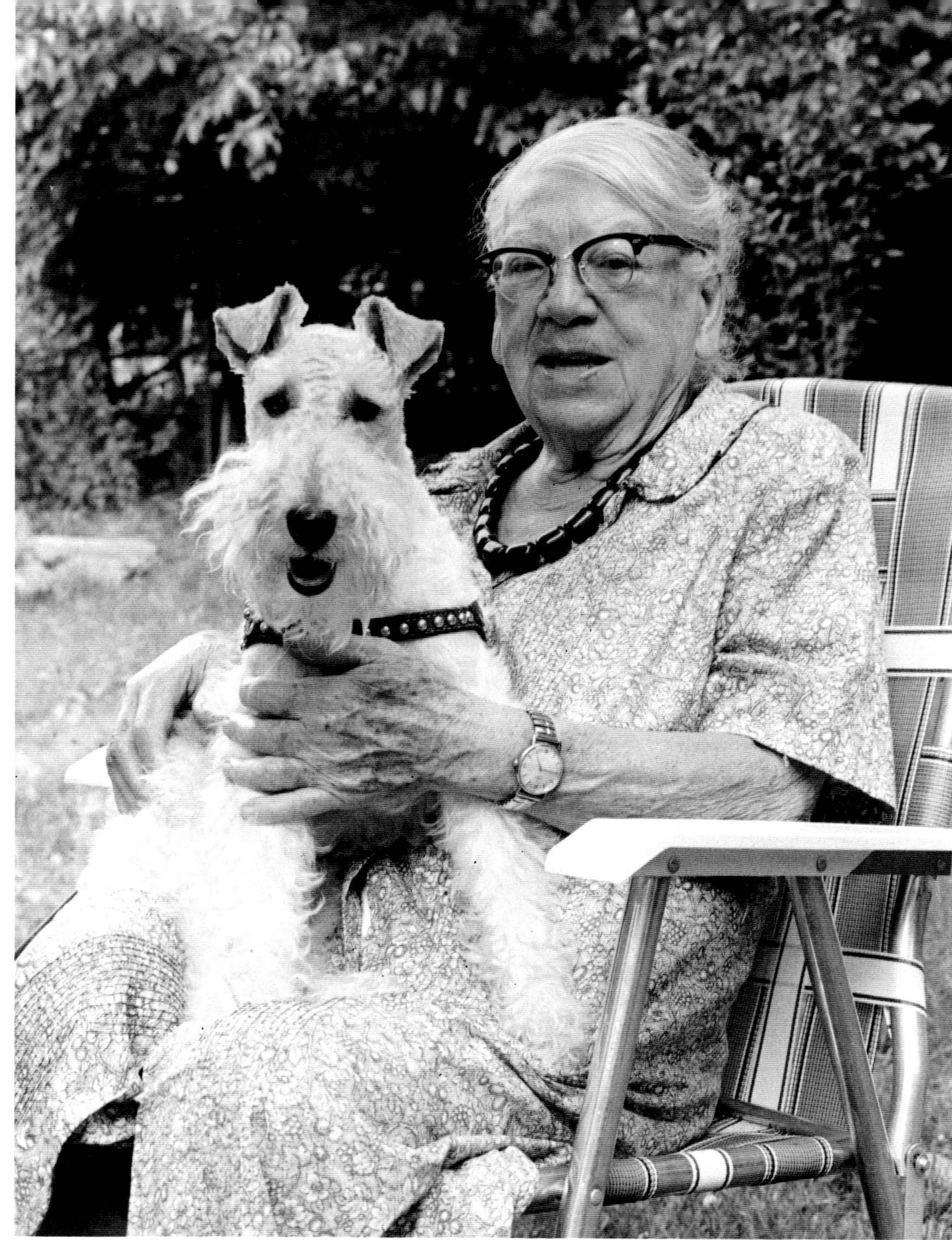

ALEXANDRA TOLSTOYA

ALEXANDRA TOLSTOYA, the daughter of Leo Tolstoy, was about to turn ninety when I photographed her. We communicated in three different languages, English, French, and Russian. I wasn't very fluent in Russian, but she insisted.

She told me that when she was in her teens she acted as her father's social secretary, and that on Sundays her father's friends would come to their house for tea and conversation. Most of them, if not all, knew that she liked raspberry candy, for which they would always receive a kiss on the cheek in exchange.

One day, Anton Chekov came to visit, empty-handed. When Alexandra opened the door to let him in, she noticed his pock-marked face and decided that she didn't like him. Some time later, Chekov came to visit again, but this time he made sure to bring candy. As much as she didn't want to, she kissed him on the cheek. Eventually, she even got to like him.

The story, she told me, is a good example of how easy it is to corrupt a child, even with a small bag of candy.

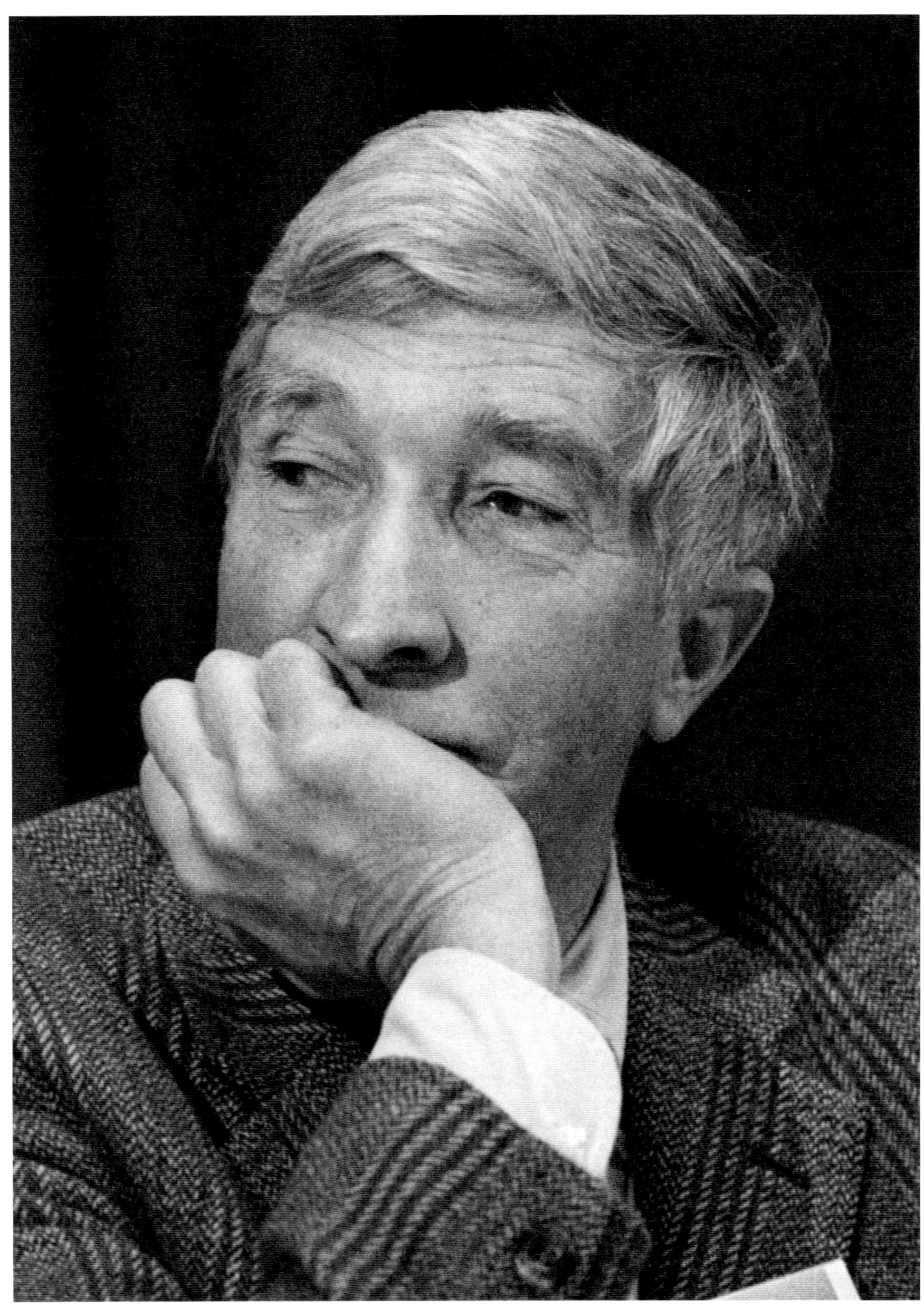

JOHN UPDIKE

WHEN I WAS COVERING A PEN CONFERENCE IN 1986, I spotted the author John Updike on a discussion panel. He was one of the few authors I never had the opportunity to photograph alone. But every time I pointed the camera at him, he would turn around and show his profile. It isn't that I don't like profiles, but not every profile happens to be photogenic. In my opinion, to say the least, his wasn't.

When I finally persuaded him to look at the camera, he closed his eyes and showed me the other side of his face. I didn't have much of a choice. When the panel discussion was over, he turned toward the camera and smiled, but by then I was out of film.

With luck, I did find one exposure with open eyes.

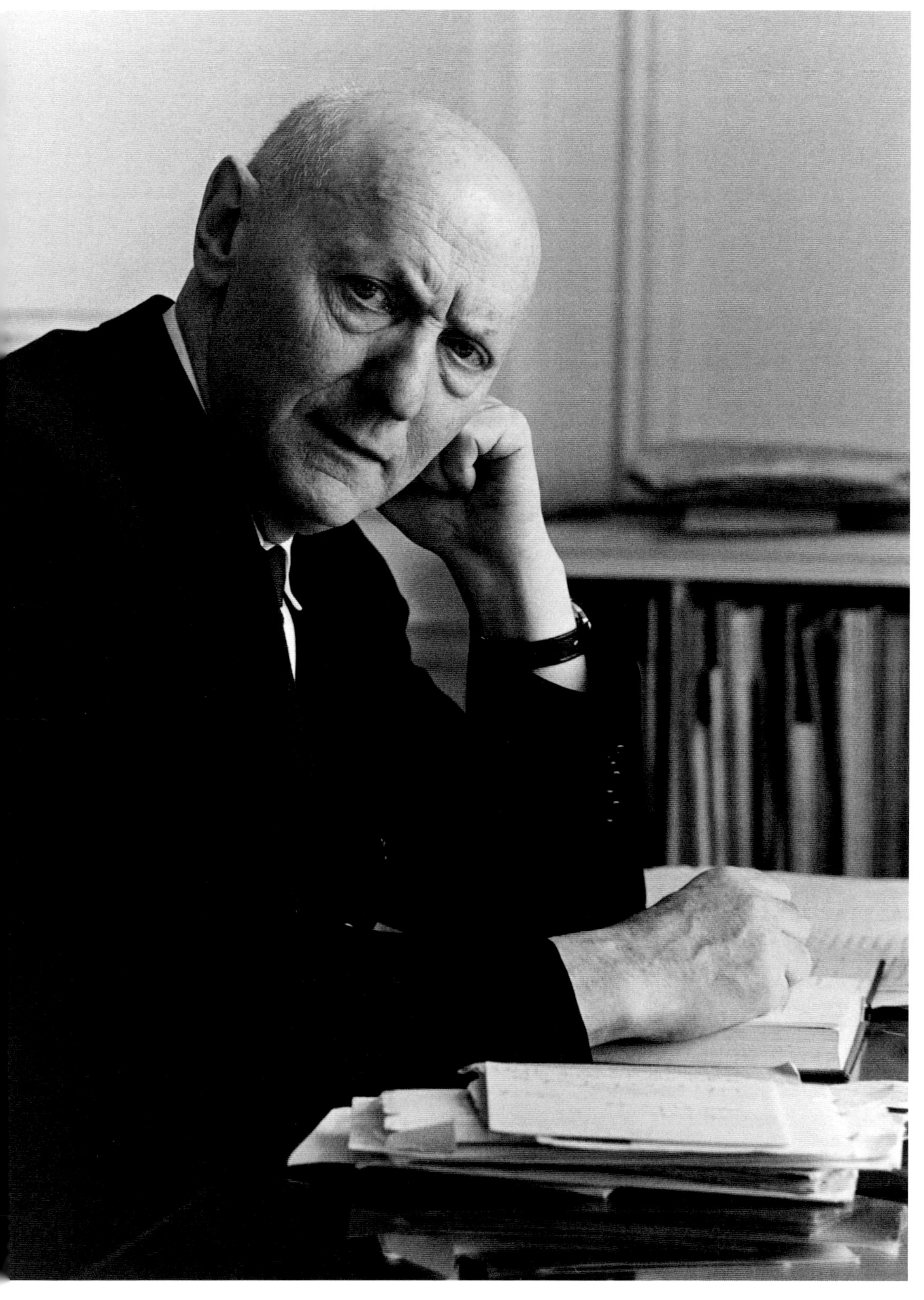

I. B. SINGER

I KNEW AND PHOTOGRAPHED Isaac Bashevis Singer for almost two decades, and I've probably read everything he wrote. After he got to know me, he would occasionally invite me to lunch at his favorite vegetarian restaurant on Broadway, where we would have long conversations in Yiddish. At times, he would compliment my Yiddish, especially my knowledge of idioms.

One day, after a photo session, he gave me a copy of his *The Family Moskat.* That summer, I took the book with me on vacation. When I saw him again the following year, I told him how impressed I was with the book.

"A magnificent story," I said, "how vivid and moving. I could practically smell the gutters of Warsaw, I could see and hear the characters," and so on, until I ran out of words.

When I finally stopped, he smiled and said, "I wish you could be my literary critic."

Some years later, I photographed Singer at a presentation of the Mendelson Award by Mayor Ed Koch at City Hall. After the ceremony, I went to congratulate him. When we shook hands, he looked at me and said, "You look familiar, but I'm not sure if I remember you. Are you the man who owns the cleaning store on Broadway?"

My throat went tight. I couldn't get a word out. I had to move on because there was a long line of well-wishers behind me. That was the last time I photographed and spoke to Isaac Bashevis Singer.

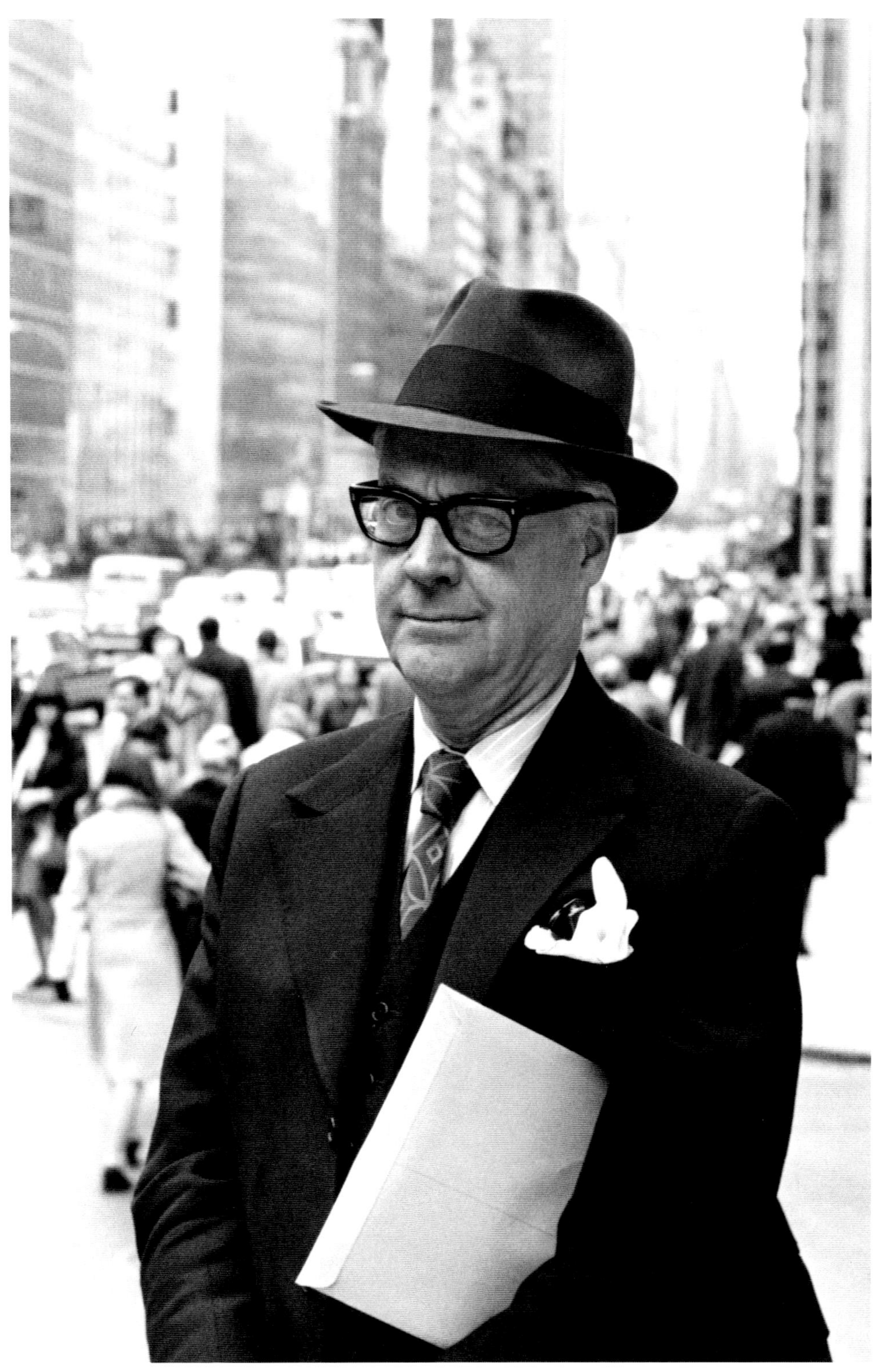

RICHARD CONDON

SOME YEARS AGO, I was taking pictures of Richard Condon in Washington Square Park. As we stood talking, a woman passed by with several dogs, one of them not on a leash. Without any warning, the dog urinated on Condon's shoe. By the time he realized what was happening, it was too late. "It could have been much worse," Condon said, laughing. "Where I come from," I told him, "a thing like that is considered good luck." "No, thank you," he said, "where I come from we like to keep our shoes dry."

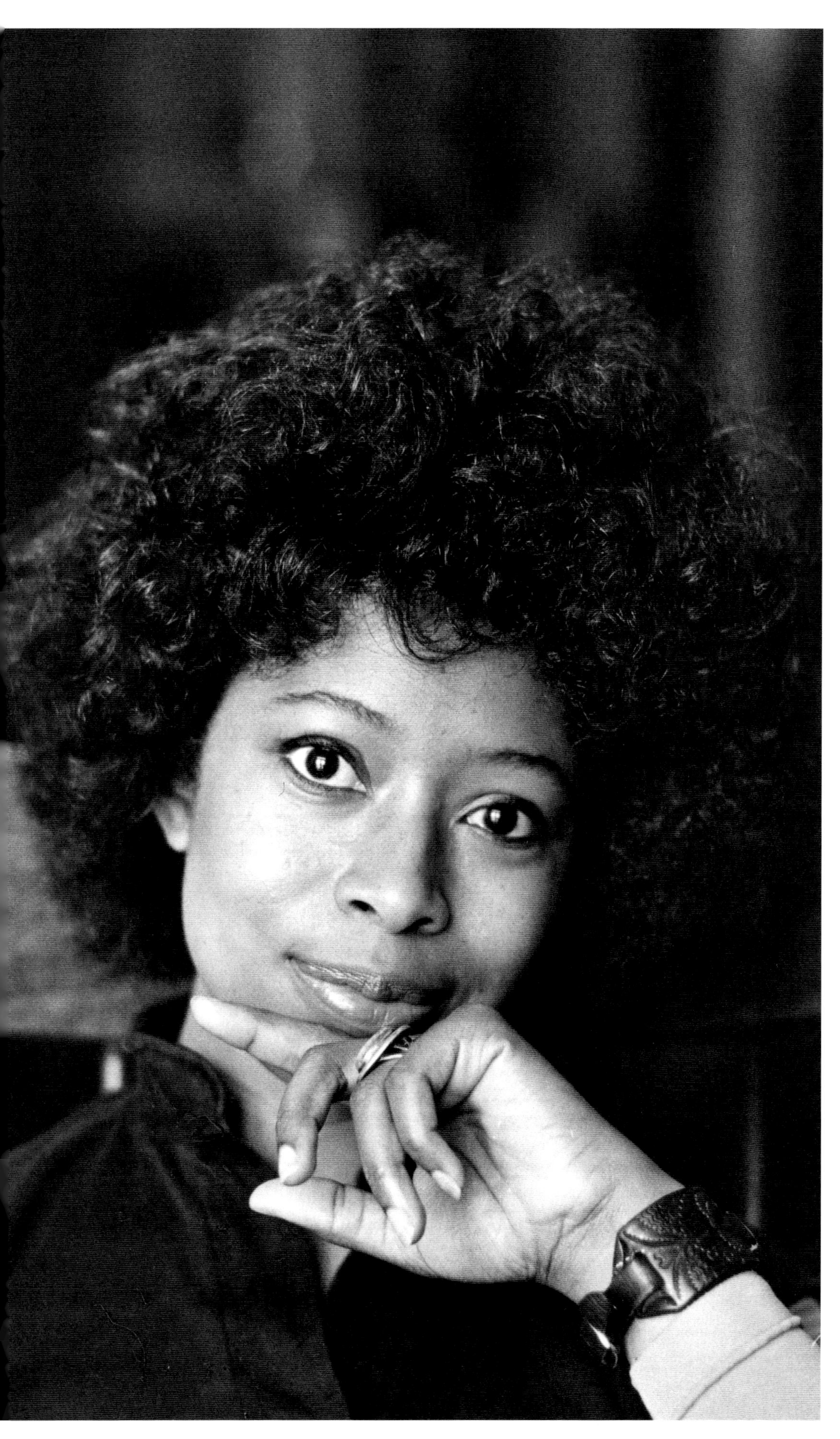

ALICE WALKER

I FIRST PHOTOGRAPHED ALICE WALKER many years ago, and then again some years later. She wasn't very talkative. One could sense that she was intelligent and wise, and she proved it with her books.

ALFRED KAZIN

ALFRED KAZIN WASN'T IN A GOOD MOOD when we met. He complained about back pain and not getting enough sleep. I tried to be understanding and to make the photo session a short one.

During our conversation I mentioned Primo Levi. Suddenly, Kazin came alive, and delivered a short lecture about Levi's work. It was the best analysis I have ever heard.

Ironically, that was the year of Levi's death.

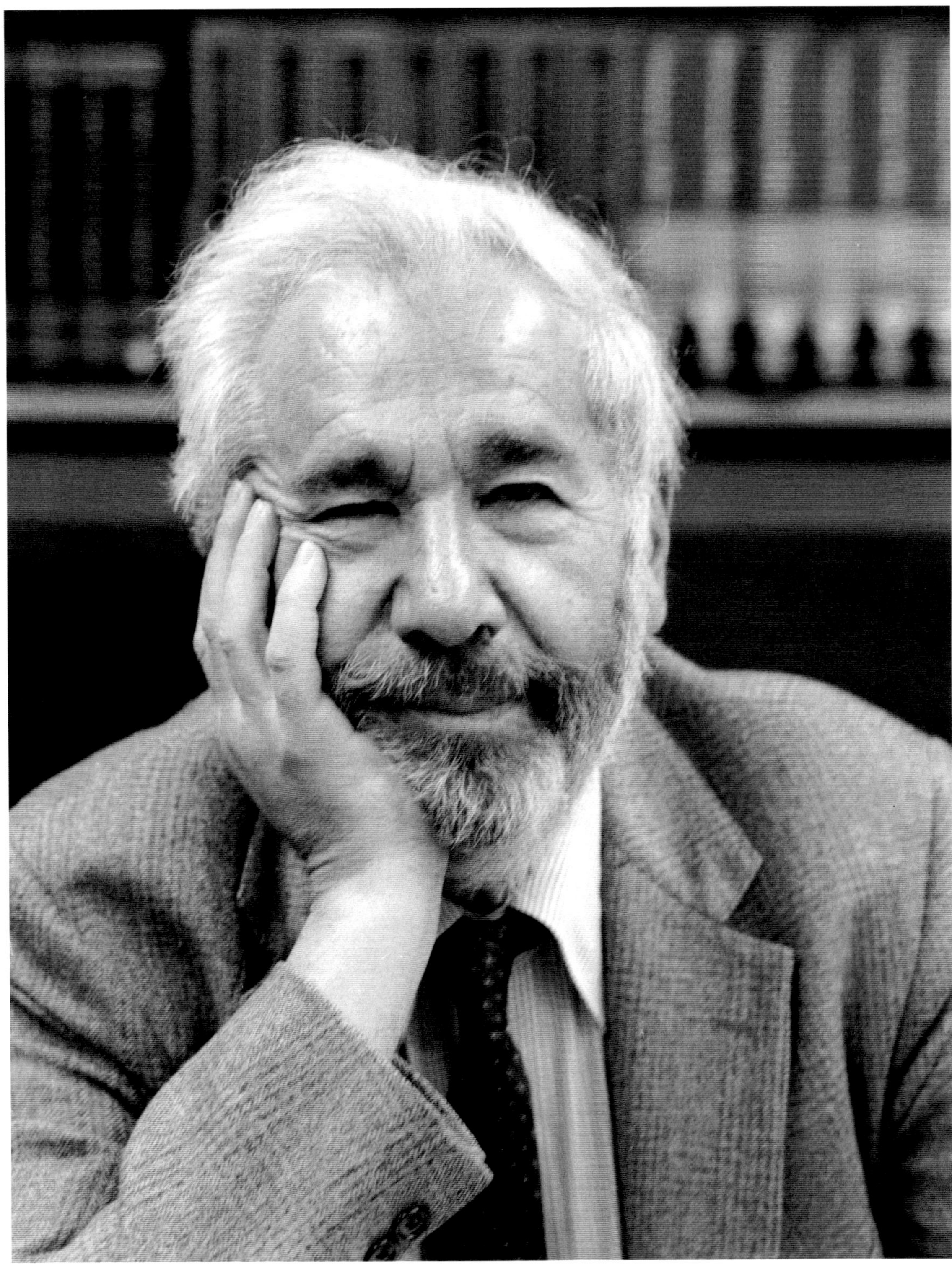

CZESLAW MILOSZ

SOME YEARS AGO, during a lengthy interview, I photographed the poet and Nobel Prize winner Czeslaw Milosz. When I was ready to leave, I went over to him to say goodbye.

Suddenly, a few lines by the 19th-century Polish poet Adam Mickiewicz came to my mind, and without hesitation I recited them. "How do you know this?" he said excitedly.

"I read it in the original when I was twelve years old," I said.

"And you still remember?" He was moved, I could tell. His eyes welled up, and so did mine. When I was at the door, I heard him say to the interviewer, "What a memory, what a memory. . . . "

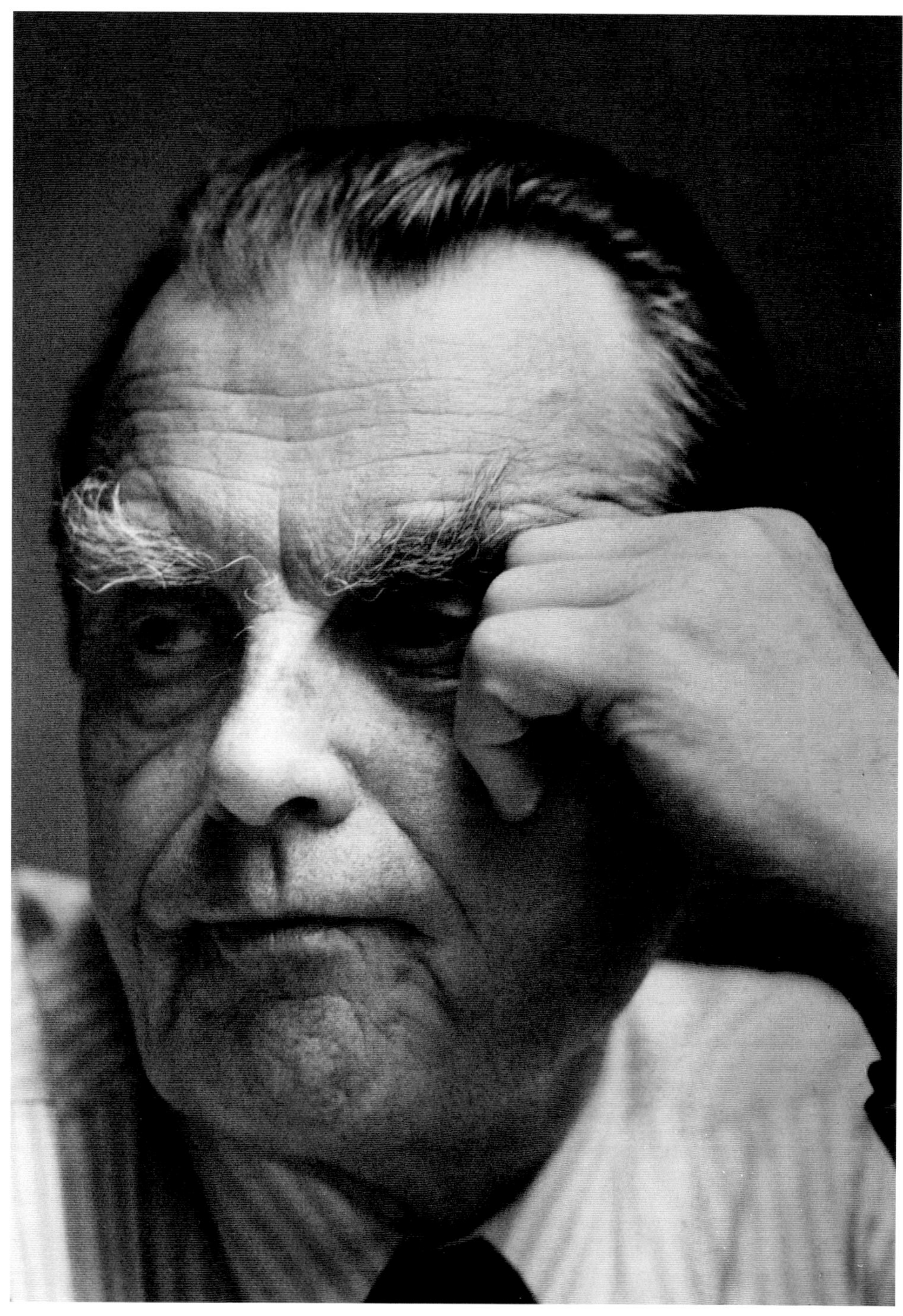

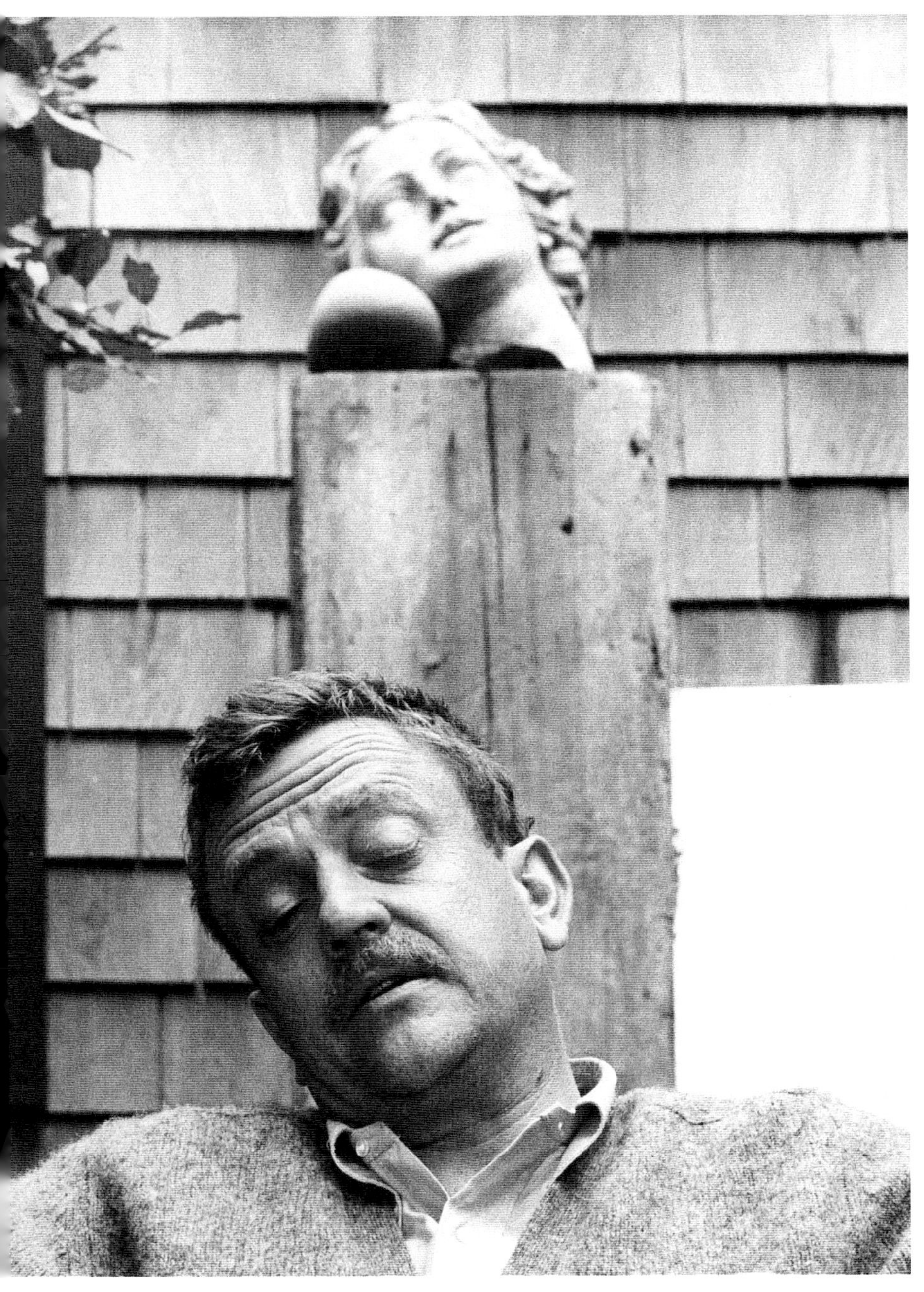

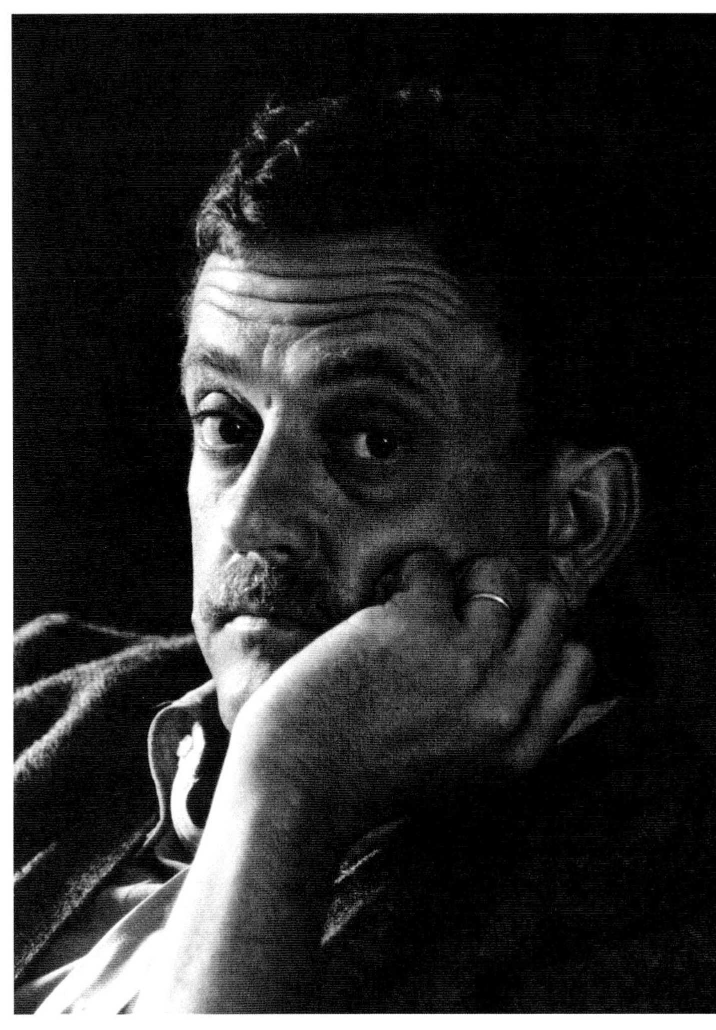

KURT VONNEGUT

I PHOTOGRAPHED KURT VONNEGUT in the 1960s when he lived in Barnstable, Cape Cod. He was friendly, pleasant, and very funny. As we sat in his yard chatting, behind him on a tall pedestal was the sculpted head of a woman with her eyes closed. I sat across from him, watching, hoping that at some point he, too, would close his eyes. Suddenly, for a split second, as if in imitation of the sculpted head, he closed his eyes. This was sheer luck. Quickly, I took the picture. Eventually, it appeared on the cover of *The New York Times Book Review*, with the review of his *Slaughterhouse Five*. The next time I saw Vonnegut, I asked what he thought of that picture. "You certainly were quick on the trigger," he said, smiling. I had a feeling that he wasn't crazy about the picture, but never said so. As much as I wanted to photograph him again, I never succeeded. It was difficult to set up another session, and he subsequently married a woman photographer.

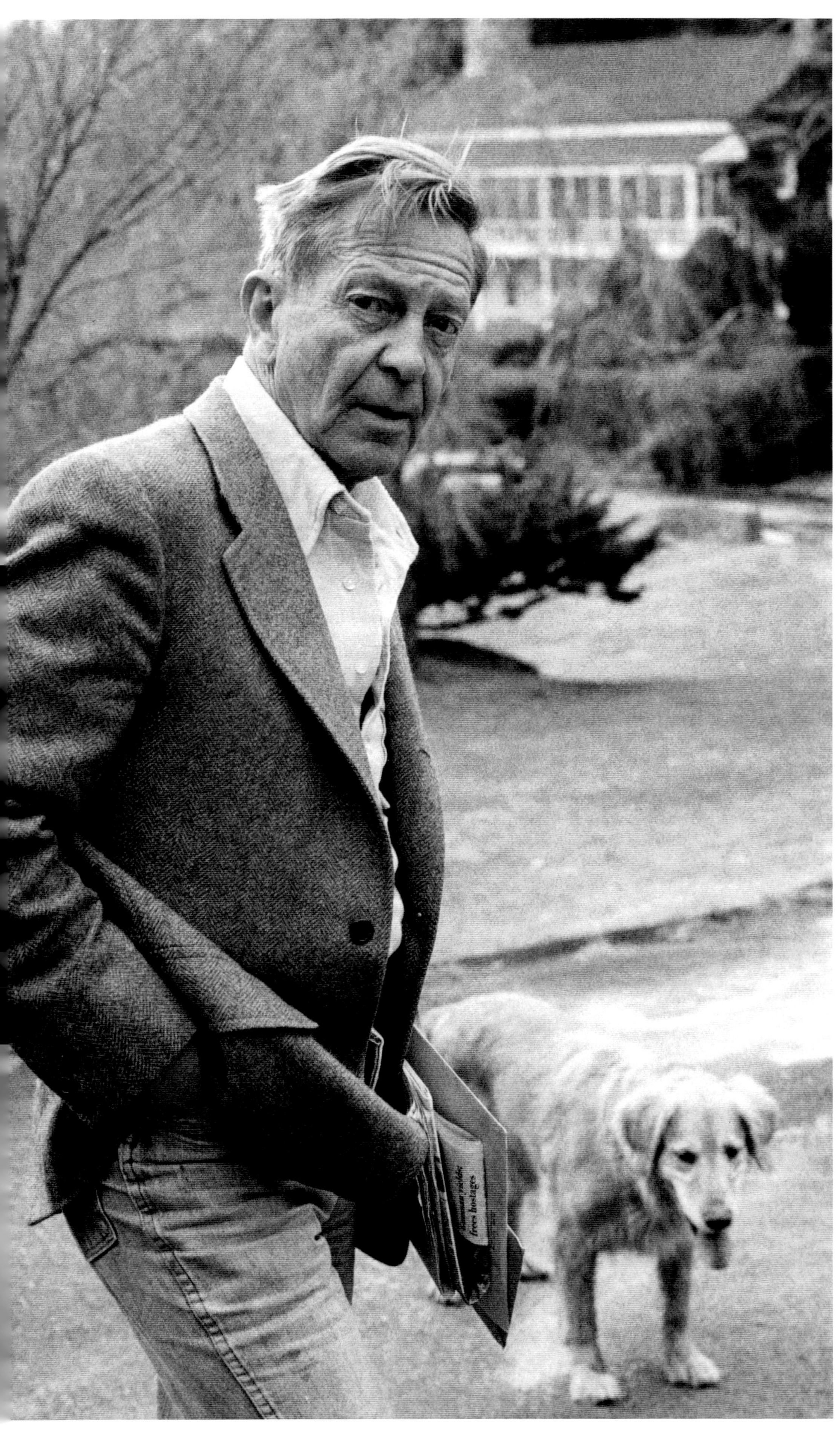

JOHN CHEEVER

I HAD BEEN ACQUAINTED with and photographed John Cheever for more than a dozen years. He was a warm, hospitable individual, and a good listener, always ready for conversation. Cheever lived with his wife in Ossining, New York, in an old Dutch-style house surrounded by acres of beautiful scenery. I liked to listen to him talk about his travels in Europe, especially about some of his more unusual encounters.

When his book *Falconer* was published, I was asked to photograph him with Sing-Sing prison in the background. We walked around outside the prison walls, looking for the appropriate angle. When I stopped to take a picture, a guard appeared at one of the watchtowers. In a loud voice, he told us to move on, unless we had permission from the warden. Cheever shouted back that he had been teaching in the prison and knew the warden personally. The next thing I saw was the guard pointing his weapon at us. With a warning loud enough to scare the birds off the roof, he said, "You click that camera shutter and I'll squeeze the trigger."

"He sounds convincing enough," said Cheever, "let's get out of here."

We walked away as fast as we could. It would have taken too much time to get permission from the warden, so a different picture of Cheever was used instead.

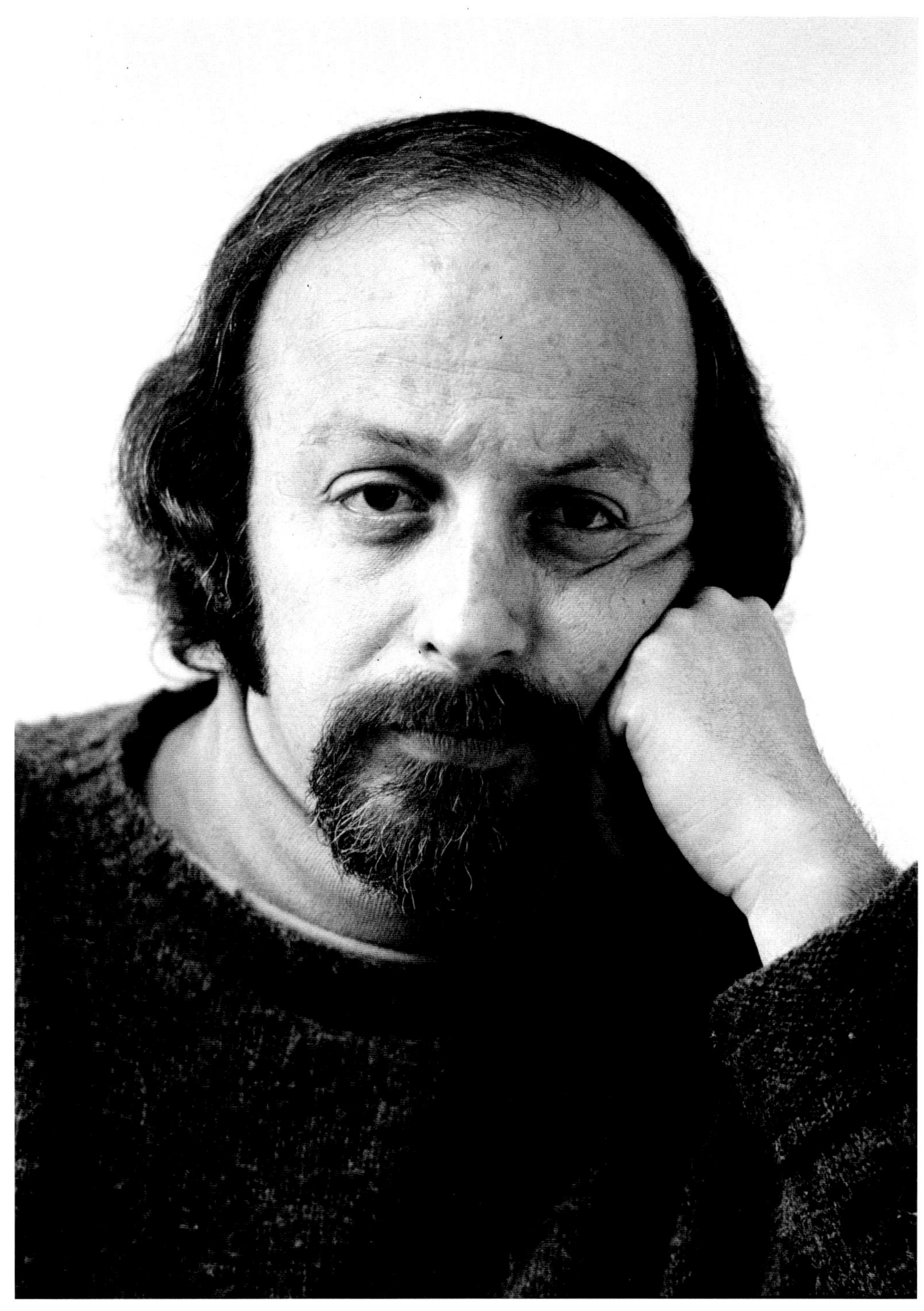

E.L. DOCTOROW

I FIRST PHOTOGRAPHED E.L. DOCTOROW after *Daniel's Book* was published. He was very friendly and cooperative. Some years later, I had to photograph him again. By that time he lived in a big house in Westchester. One day I decided to send a photo of him that I had taken some years before. Frankly, I was hoping for a thank you, but never heard anything. Some fifteen years went by, and I went to hear him speak at the synagogue in Sag Harbor, Long Island. After his talk, I said hello and asked if by chance he had heard about my book. He hadn't, but soon after I received a note asking for a copy. I sent one right away. I hope he received it.

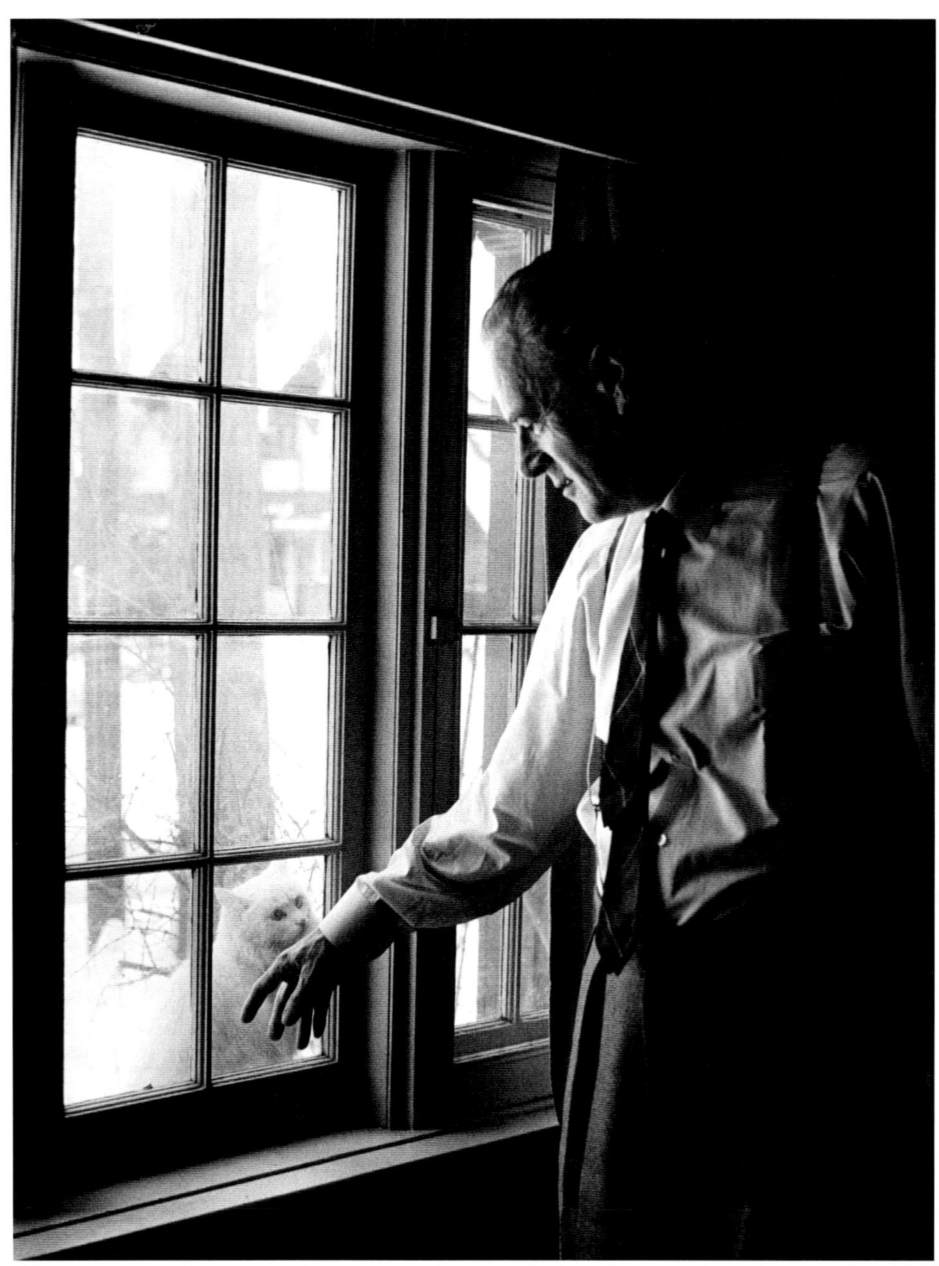

MARSHALL McLUHAN

THE FIVE-DAY SESSION with Marshall McLuhan was the longest I ever experienced, except for those times when I traveled with the president of the United States. I followed McLuhan everywhere, including the several different universities in Toronto where he taught and lectured, on shopping trips, and even to the Chinese laundry. He was very philosophical, always patient, and never complained. Even though I felt that I was a nuisance, he made me feel welcome in a very civilized way. One day, he jokingly told me that once the session was finished, he would likely be the most over-exposed person in Toronto, the only consolation being that I would at least leave him alone for the next twenty years.

One day, during a lecture at the Graduate School of Engineering, a student asked, "Professor McLuhan, how do you foresee the future?"

The professor responded, "There is no future, the future is now." The audience burst out laughing and McLuhan laughed with them.

WILLIAM BURROUGHS

WILLIAM BURROUGHS LIVED in a Bowery tenement above a hardware store, barricaded by an iron gate. As soon as I rang the door bell, a tall, well-dressed man appeared on the staircase. "Is Mr. Burroughs at home?" I asked.

"I'm Mr. Burroughs," he said, opening the gate to let me in. I couldn't believe my eyes. Was this well-groomed man who looked like a bank president the legendary Burroughs of the Beat generation?

After a brief introduction, I followed him to his sparsely furnished, windowless apartment. I didn't know where to begin. I was at a loss for words. At last I located an arm chair, put it in the center of the bare room, and asked him to sit. The fluorescent fixtures mounted on the low ceiling gave off very little light and accentuated the shadows around his eyes.

Since I hadn't read his books, I couldn't possibly talk about his work. But I wanted to know what he could tell me about Jack Kerouac. "I'm sorry," I said, "that I never had the opportunity to photograph Jack Kerouac."

"So am I," he said, and then the door bell rang and he went down to see who was there. After some minutes, he came back carrying a parcel and told me that he had to leave for an appointment right away. There was nothing else for me to do but pack up and leave, too.

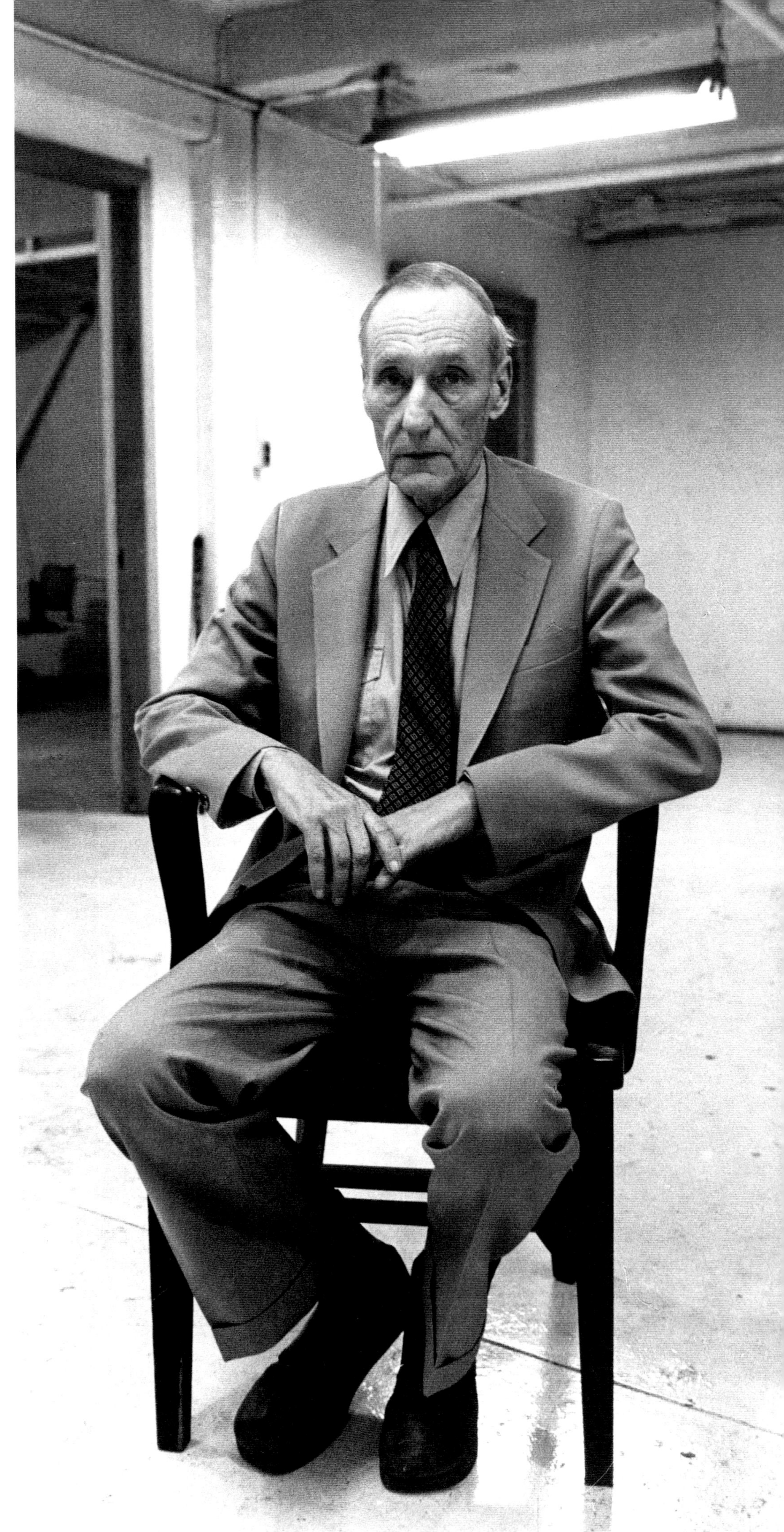

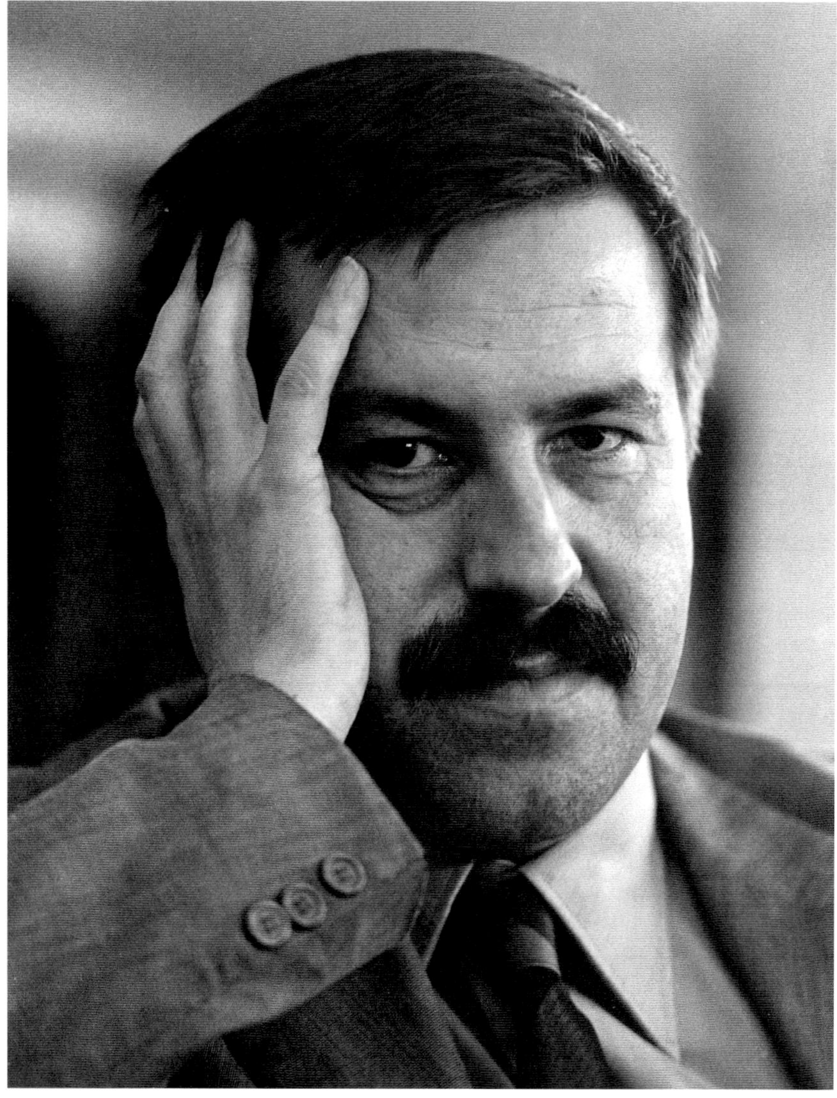

GÜNTER GRASS

I PHOTOGRAPHED GÜNTER GRASS when he spoke at the 92nd Street Y, when his book *The Dog Years* was published. He was very friendly and cooperative. He was born in Danzig, he told me, the free city over which Hitler started World War II. I was born in Radom, a Polish city that was eventually occupied by the German army.

We talked about our respective childhoods. He appeared concerned when I told him that I had been incarcerated by the Nazis during the war. When I tried to inquire if any of his relatives had served in the German army, he quickly changed the subject. I didn't press the issue.

When I saw him years later at a PEN conference in New York, he had difficulty remembering me. He did recall receiving a picture of himself in the mail, the picture I had taken more than twenty years earlier. "It was a good likeness," he said.

LILLIAN HELLMAN

OVER A PERIOD OF FIFTEEN YEARS, I photographed Lillian Hellman on several occasions. I first met her at her East Side apartment in the middle of a hot summer. She was all dressed up, perspiring profusely. "The air conditioner isn't working," she said, wiping her forehead. I suggested she take off her jacket and make herself comfortable.

"This is not a fashion shoot for *Vogue*," I said, "so you might as well relax."

"Frankly," she said, "I didn't know what to expect."

"Nothing very formal, just a few head shots," I told her.

"I like your style," she assured me. We spoke about her book *Julia*, which had recently been made into a play, and I told her briefly about my own World War II experiences under the Nazis. She was all ears.

"You must definitely write about it," she said, with urgency in her voice. "It's important that you do. You're an eye witness, and a survivor."

I also told her how moved I was watching an interview with her on public television. "It was so touching." She looked at me through her thick bifocals, and thanked me.

Some months before she died, I photographed her again, for the last time. "I'm so glad you've come back," she said, shaking my hand. "Have you written anything?"

"I'm still thinking about it."

"Get to it, don't wait," she said. "I still would like to see it before I go." Her eyesight was failing, and she had difficulty walking. When I was leaving, she insisted on walking me to the door. "Next time," she said, "don't wait as long as you did this time, because I might not be here." I kissed her hand, and she rested her head on my shoulders, and wept. ▶

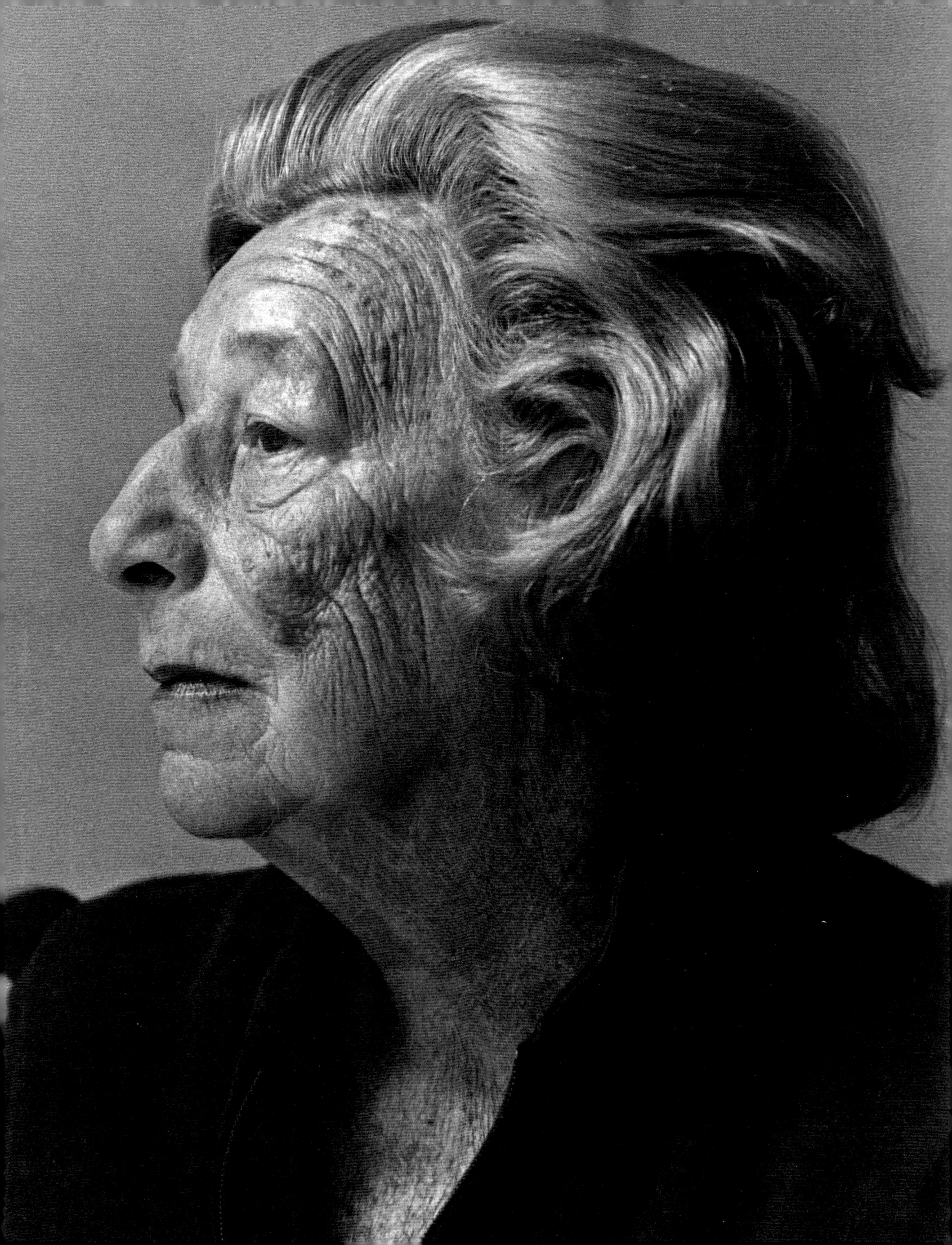

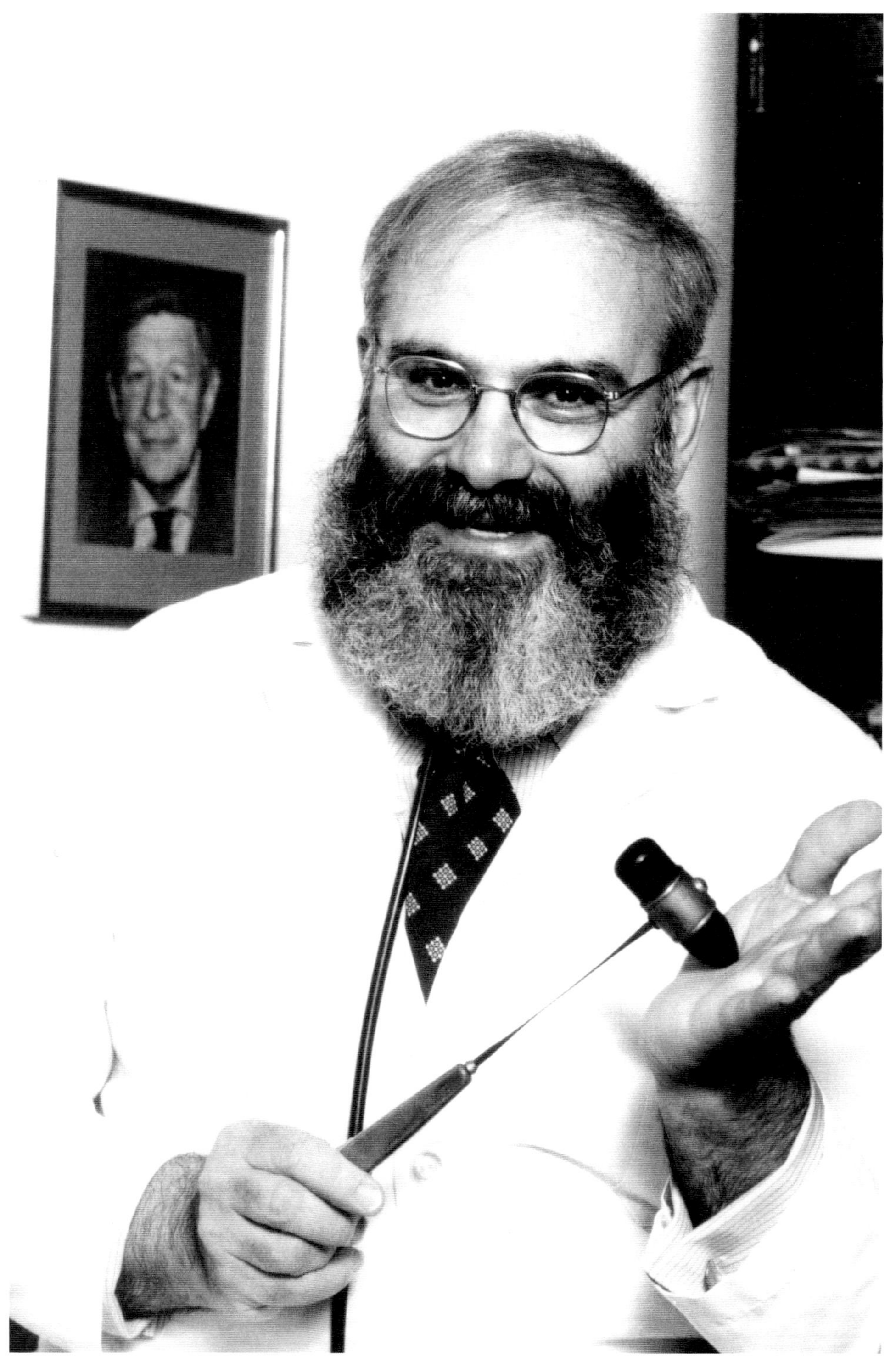

OLIVER SACKS

DR. OLIVER SACKS, the famous neurologist and author, was talking excitedly about W.H. Auden, the poet, whose picture was prominently displayed on his office wall. When I told him that I had met and photographed Auden some years earlier, and that Auden encouraged me to write about my experiences in World War II, he was eager to hear about it.

Some time later, I sent my first stories to Dr. Sacks, and received a very kind letter in response. When my book was published in 1990, a quote from him was on the front cover. Thank you for such a generous gesture, Dr. Sacks.

ELIE WIESEL

VERY FEW PEOPLE had heard of Elie Wiesel when I first photographed him in the early 1960s. I didn't know much about him either, except that he was a survivor of concentration camps. It made me feel a kinship, because I am also a survivor. We compared a few notes and had a very pleasant photo session. Some years later I had to photograph him again. By then, he was well known as a writer. More years had passed when he won the Nobel Peace Prize and I photographed him a third time.

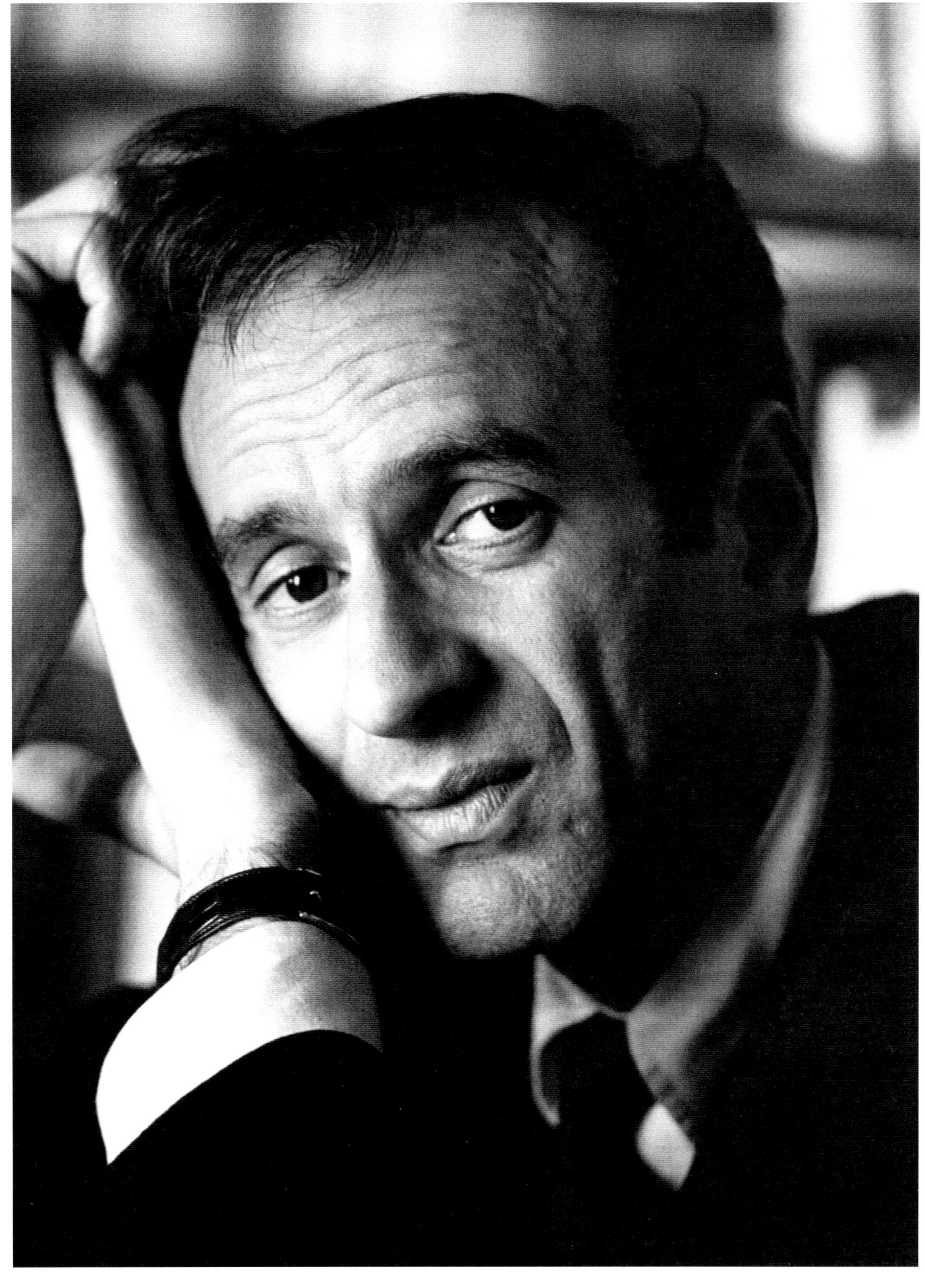

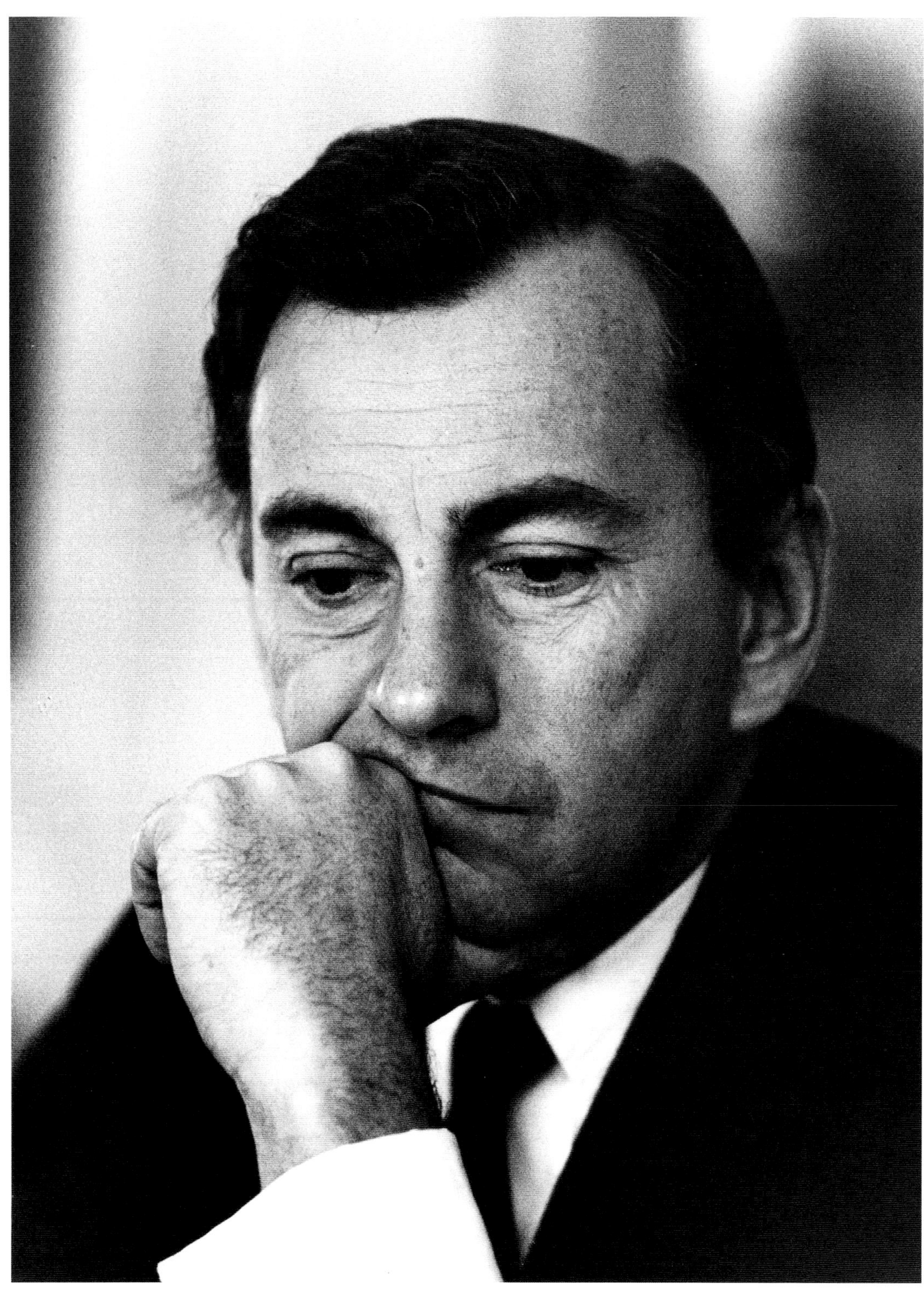

GORE VIDAL

GORE VIDAL IS A CULTURED MAN with good manners. Taking photos of him was very enjoyable. There wasn't much time to talk about anything specific, and I had to rush to my next assignment, but we still managed to have a cup of coffee together. When I told him that he resembled an uncle of mine who disappeared during World War II, he said: "I hope you have pleasant memories of him."

"I certainly do," I said.

"In that case," he said, "I take it as a compliment."

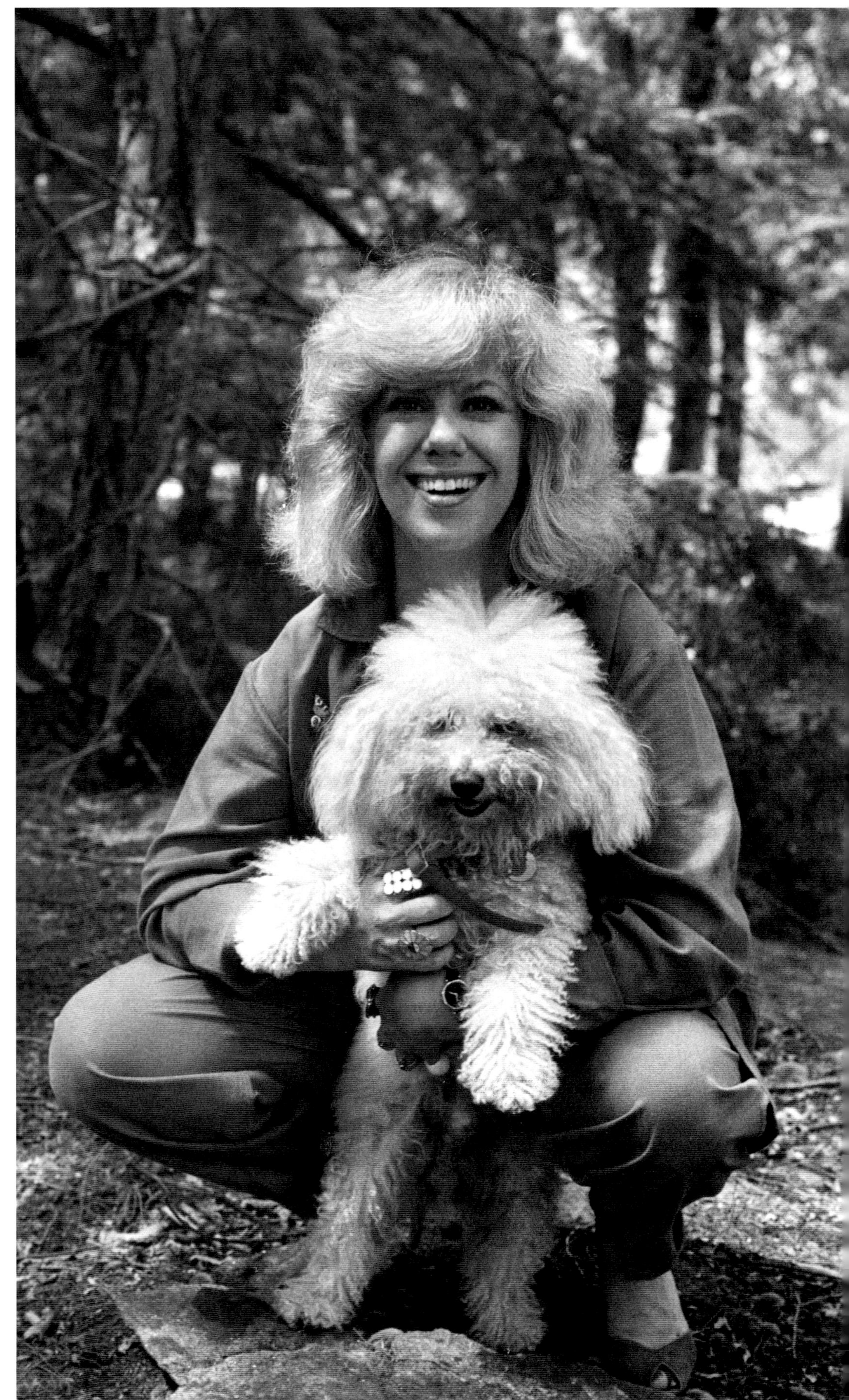

ERICA JONG

I DON'T THINK THAT Erica Jong was at all happy about having to face the camera when her book *Fear of Flying* was published. It was a fairly long session that was part of a lengthy interview, followed by more shots in Central Park.

Some years passed, there was another book, and another photo session. This time, however, it was in Connecticut, where she lived in a house that had a spectacular view. It was early autumn and the leaves were turning. As far as one could see, everything was yellow, gold, and orange. I was mesmerized, and without thinking too much, I began to take pictures. Luckily, I had a telephoto lens with me. I was so taken with the scenery that I forgot to shoot her.

When I drove away, I realized what I had done, and quickly turned around. When I got back to the house and told her about it, she said, "I was sure you only wanted the scenery." I felt pretty stupid. I took a picture of her with her poodle, and realized that she and the poodle had identical haircuts. I hope she has forgiven me.

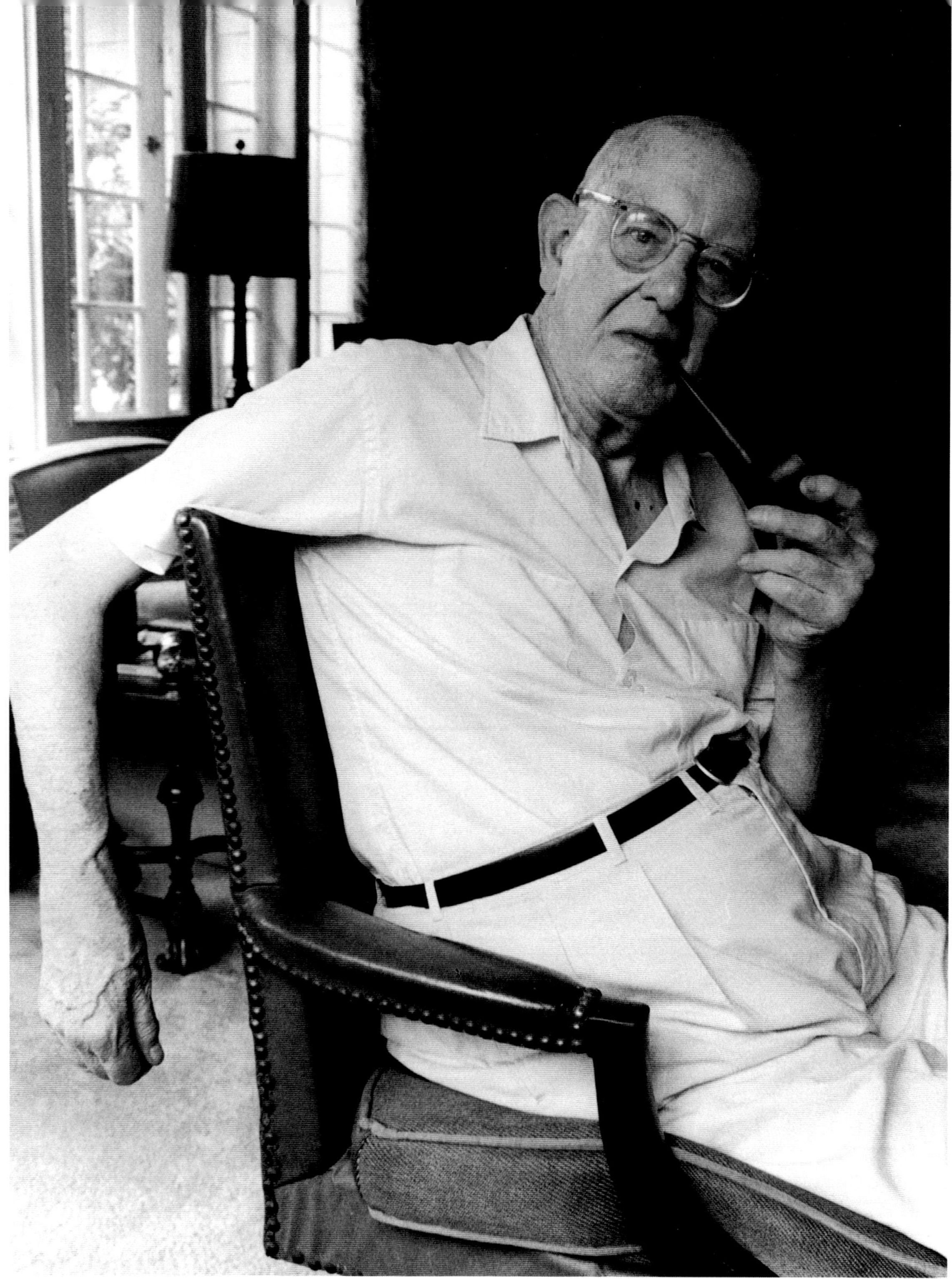

P.G. WODEHOUSE

WHEN I POINTED THE LIGHT METER in his direction, P.G. Wodehouse said, "Good God, that isn't a Geiger counter, is it?"

"No, it isn't," I assured him. "Why would I want to know how radioactive you are, sir?"

"Well," he said, laughing, "with all the atomic testing going on, God only knows." I thought he was only joking, but he was actually very concerned, he assured me.

We walked around his Remsenburg estate, his two dogs following closely. He would stop every now and then to point out certain kinds of trees and plants, or wild flowers. Suddenly he turned to me and said, "Why would men want to destroy all this? Can you tell me?"

ARTHUR MILLER

I HAD ALWAYS WANTED to photograph Arthur Miller, the playwright. Many years ago, at a PEN meeting in New York, I noticed him in the audience. Inconspicuously, I moved closer and pointed the camera at him. I'm not sure if he saw me, but as soon as he heard the shutter, he turned his head away from the camera.

During a break in the meeting, I went over and asked why he had turned away from the camera. He assured me that he hadn't noticed it.

"I only managed to get one exposure," I said.

"All you need is one picture, right?" he replied. And that was it. In a way, I couldn't blame him. He was married to a photographer.

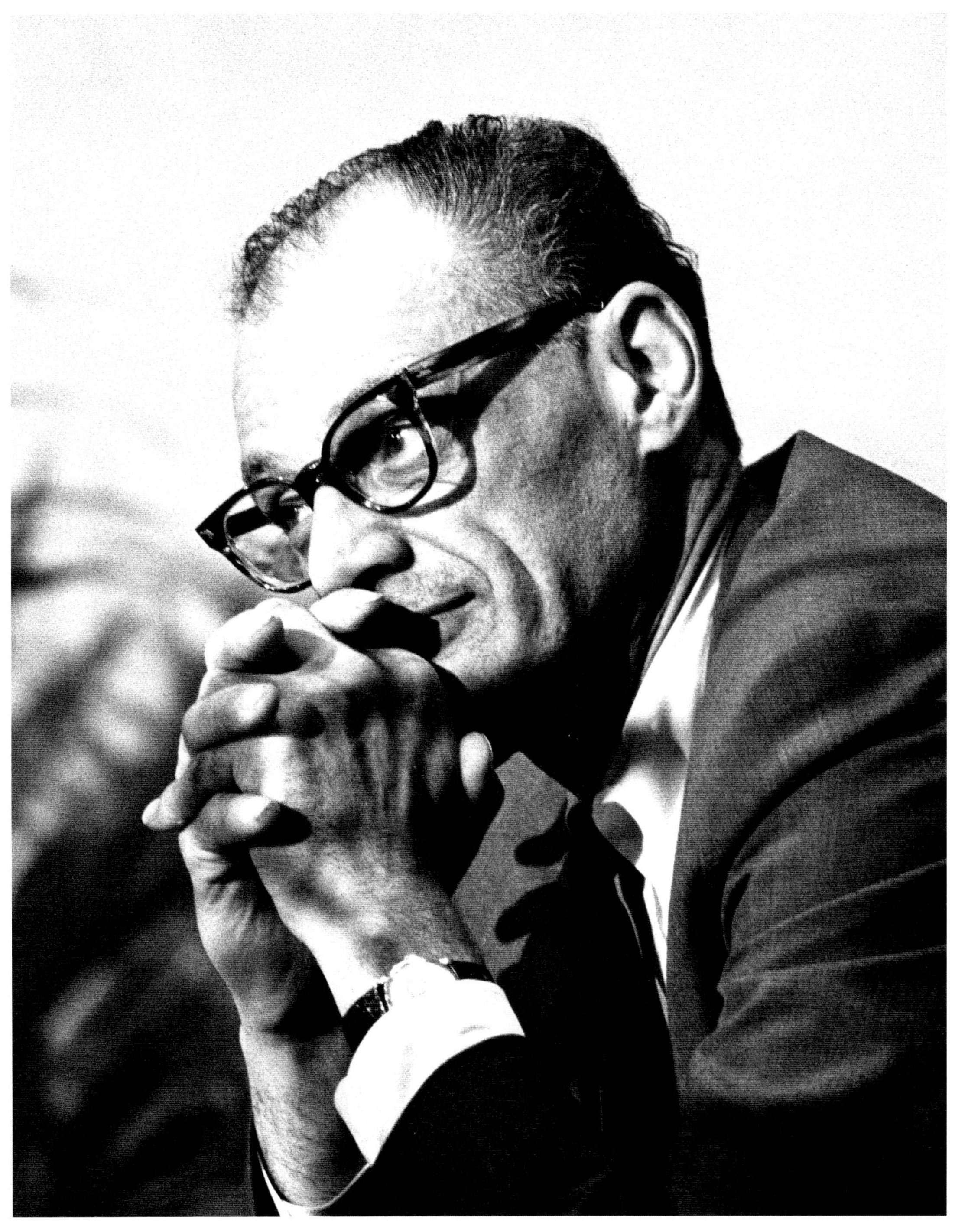

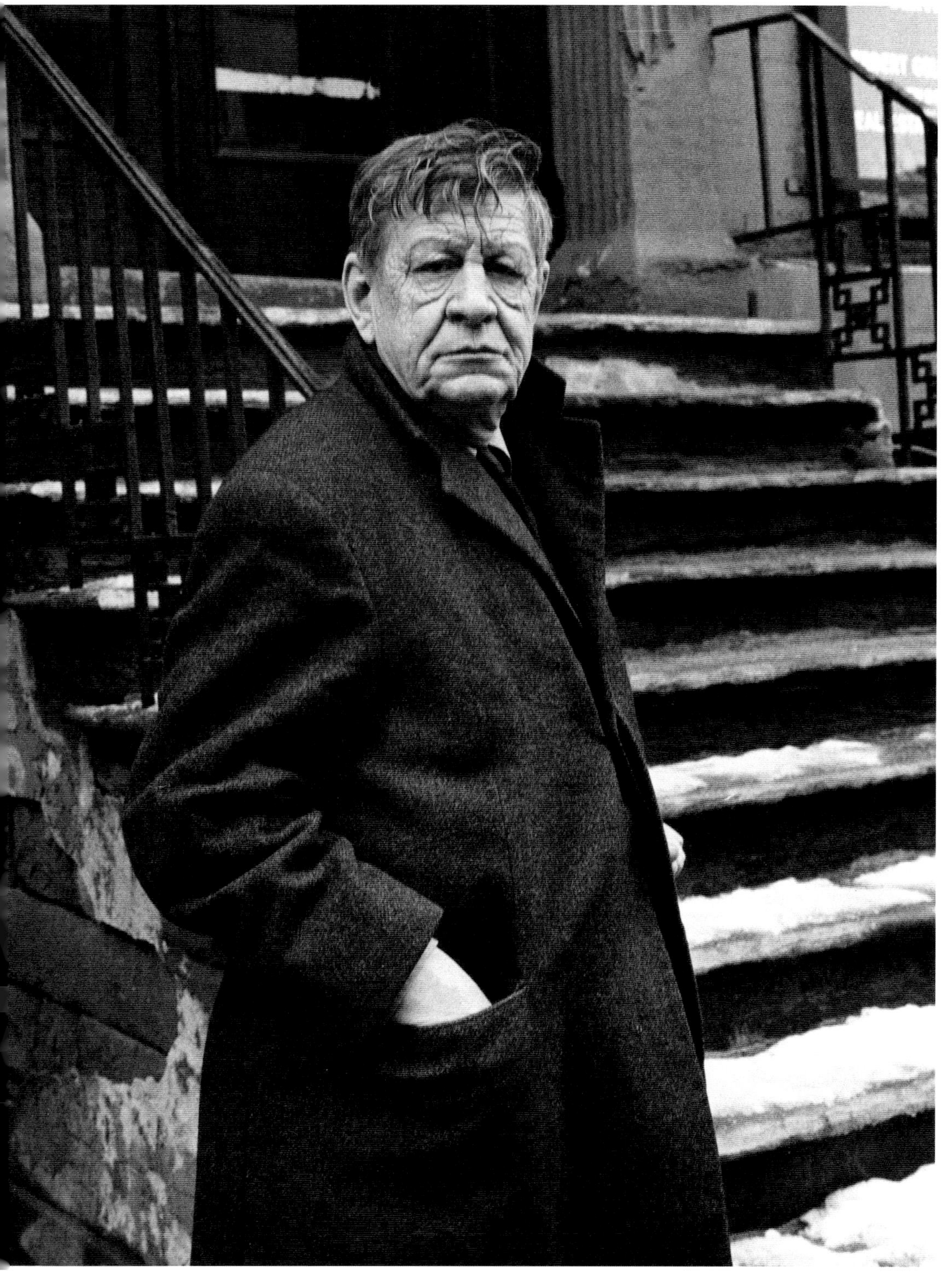

W. H. AUDEN

ALMOST FORTY YEARS have gone by since I photographed W. H. Auden. We sat in his kitchen sipping black coffee—stronger than any coffee I ever drank—which, he told me, he had brewed before I arrived. Suddenly, he said, "Nothing personal, but do I detect an Austrian accent?"

"It's more a mixture of Polish, French, and German," I said, "but I've been to Austria. I'm an alumnus of Mauthausen-Gusen."

"Good God," he said, "what were you doing there? Do you care to talk about it?"

"Why not," I said. When I described what life was like in the camps, Auden said, "Do you ever think of writing about it?"

"I'm not a writer, Mr. Auden."

"You really don't know unless you try and put it on the bloody paper. There are some writers I know who never thought they could write, and somehow they succeeded." He sat there, across from me, puffing away, and thick clouds of cigarette smoke drifted overhead, giving me a headache. I began to see double.

When I was leaving, Auden went out with me to deposit the trash in front of the house. As we descended the steps, the trash bag broke, and lots of empty beer cans came tumbling out. I helped him pick them up.

"Thank you," he said, "you're a gentleman and a scholar, and, by the way, don't forget to send me a copy of your memoir." When my book was published twenty years later, Auden was already gone.

Thank you, Mr. Auden. You were a gentleman and a scholar.

SAUL BELLOW

SAUL BELLOW WAS REHEARSING a play at a Broadway theater. He was not in a good mood, and refused to be photographed. "I can't give you any time right now. I'm in the middle of a rehearsal. I'm sure they can find a photo of me."

"You may be right," I said, "except that you might not like it. In fact, if you were to see it, you might become upset."

His expression suddenly changed. "How much time do you need?"

"Ten minutes at most."

"How about five? All I can spare is five minutes." I agreed.

He stood up, got his seersucker jacket, a fedora, and a cane, and went outside behind the theater. I asked him to lean against a wrought iron fence and hold the cane. I wondered if this was what Herzog looked like. Before I could finish the first roll of film, he said that time was up.

The picture was used in several different places, including the front page of the Sunday *New York Times Book Review* when they reviewed *Herzog*.

Some time later, I wanted to send a print as a thank you, but sent it to Bernard Malamud by mistake. I understand that Malamud was nice enough to give it to Bellow.

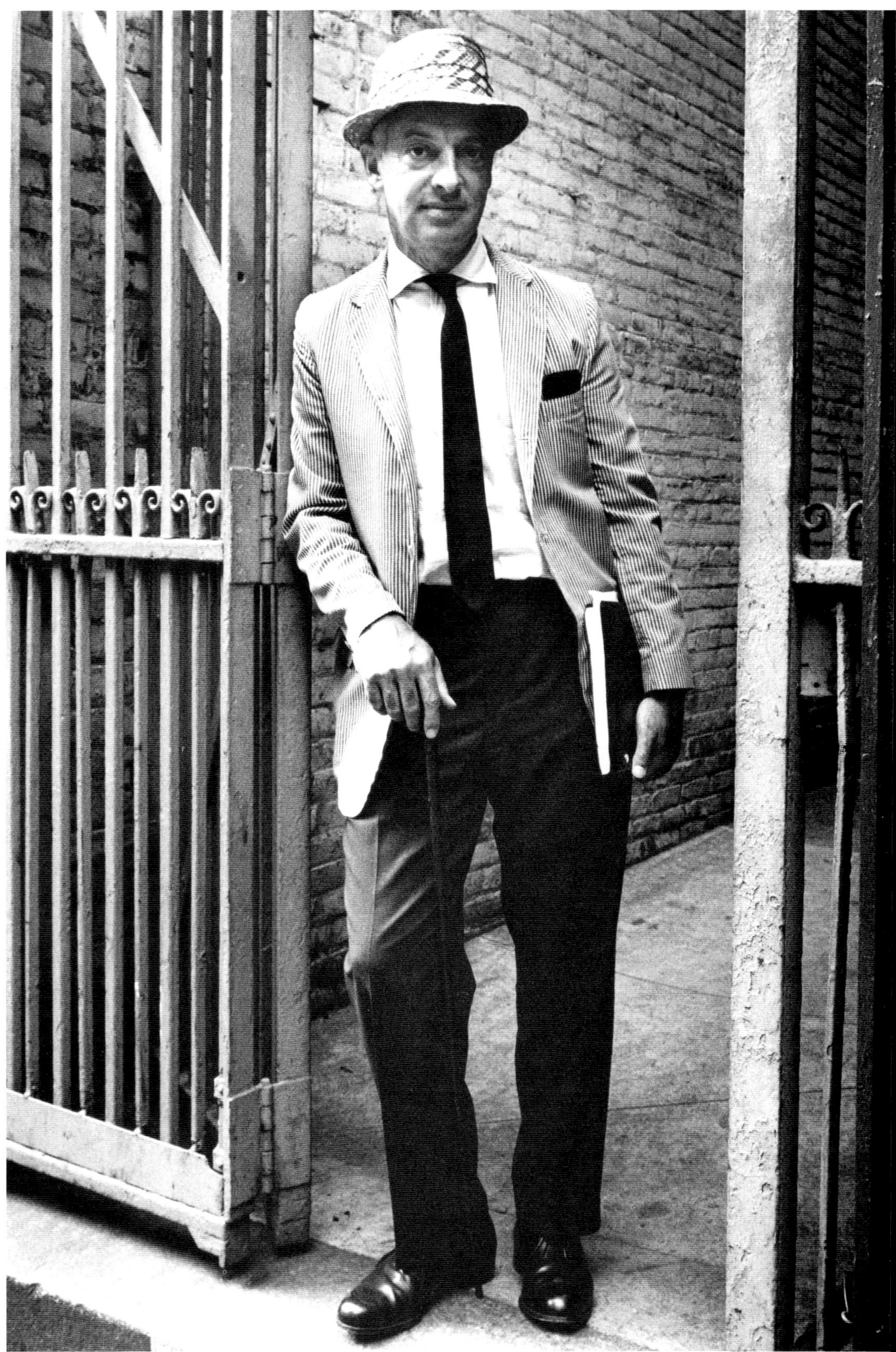

Performing Artists

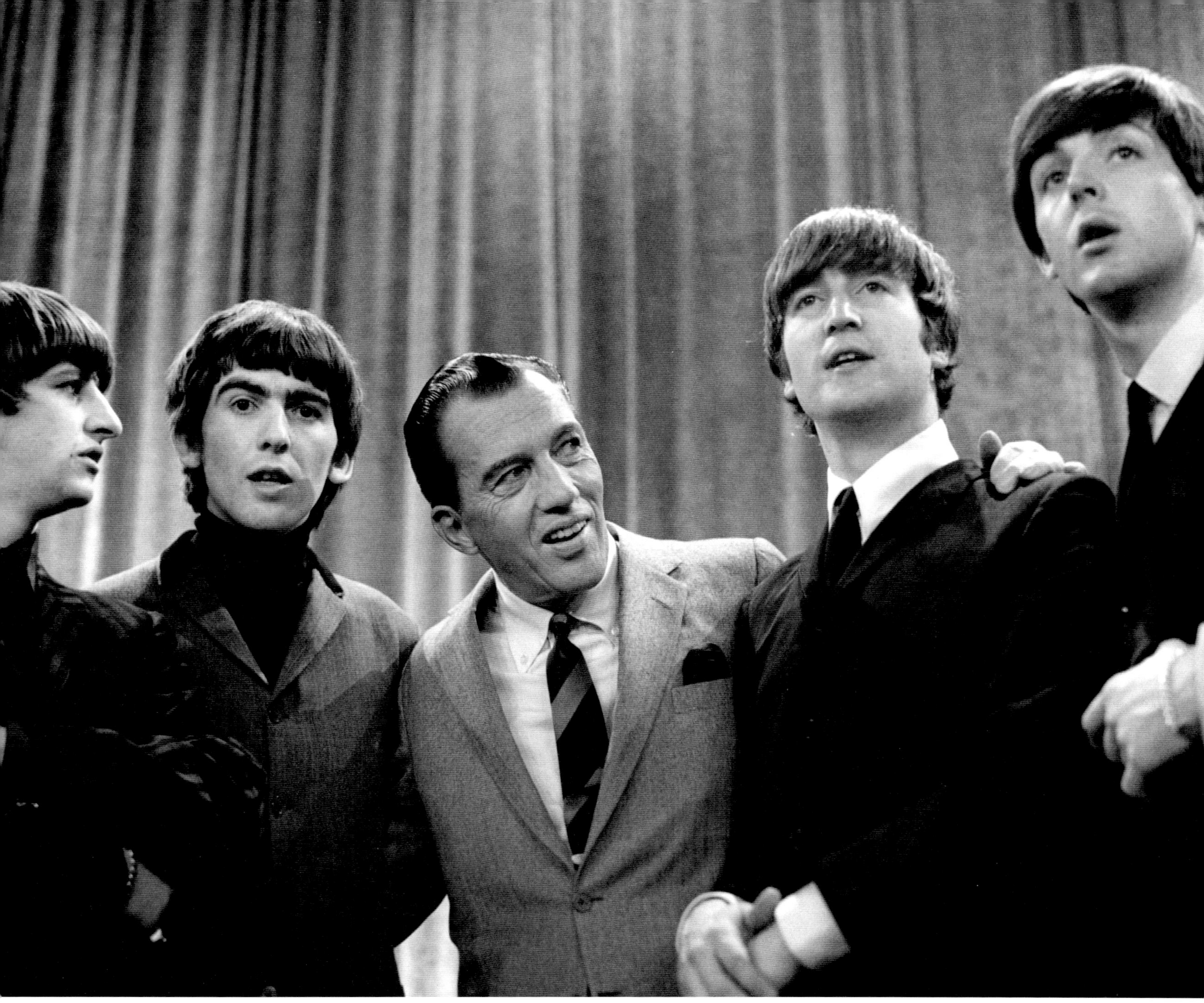

THE BEATLES

WHEN THE BEATLES first came to New York, they appeared on the Ed Sullivan show. As everyone knows, they were a huge hit. I spent an entire weekend photographing every move they made.

I suggested to my nine-year-old son that he might like to send them a gift. He decided on one of his treasured possessions, a Native American peace pipe, and I took it with me on the day of the taping.

I gave it to Paul McCartney before the rehearsal and he was visibly touched. He asked me to thank my son and hid it backstage after showing it to the other Beatles.

When the limo came to take them to lunch, there was a sizeable crowd of young people outside the studio, eager to see them. Just before getting into the car, McCartney turned around and quickly ran back into the studio. The police could hardly control the crowd.

After a few minutes, McCartney reappeared, package in hand, beaming. "I nearly forgot the peace pipe gift," he yelled out.

JAMES EARL JONES

IT WAS 1963 when a little-known actor named James Earl Jones appeared in Jean Genet's play *The Blacks* in a theater on Second Avenue in New York. He was young and handsome and had real presence. I felt that pictures taken on stage would not do him justice, so when the play was over I asked him for a short photo session outdoors. One could tell that he would make it in show business.

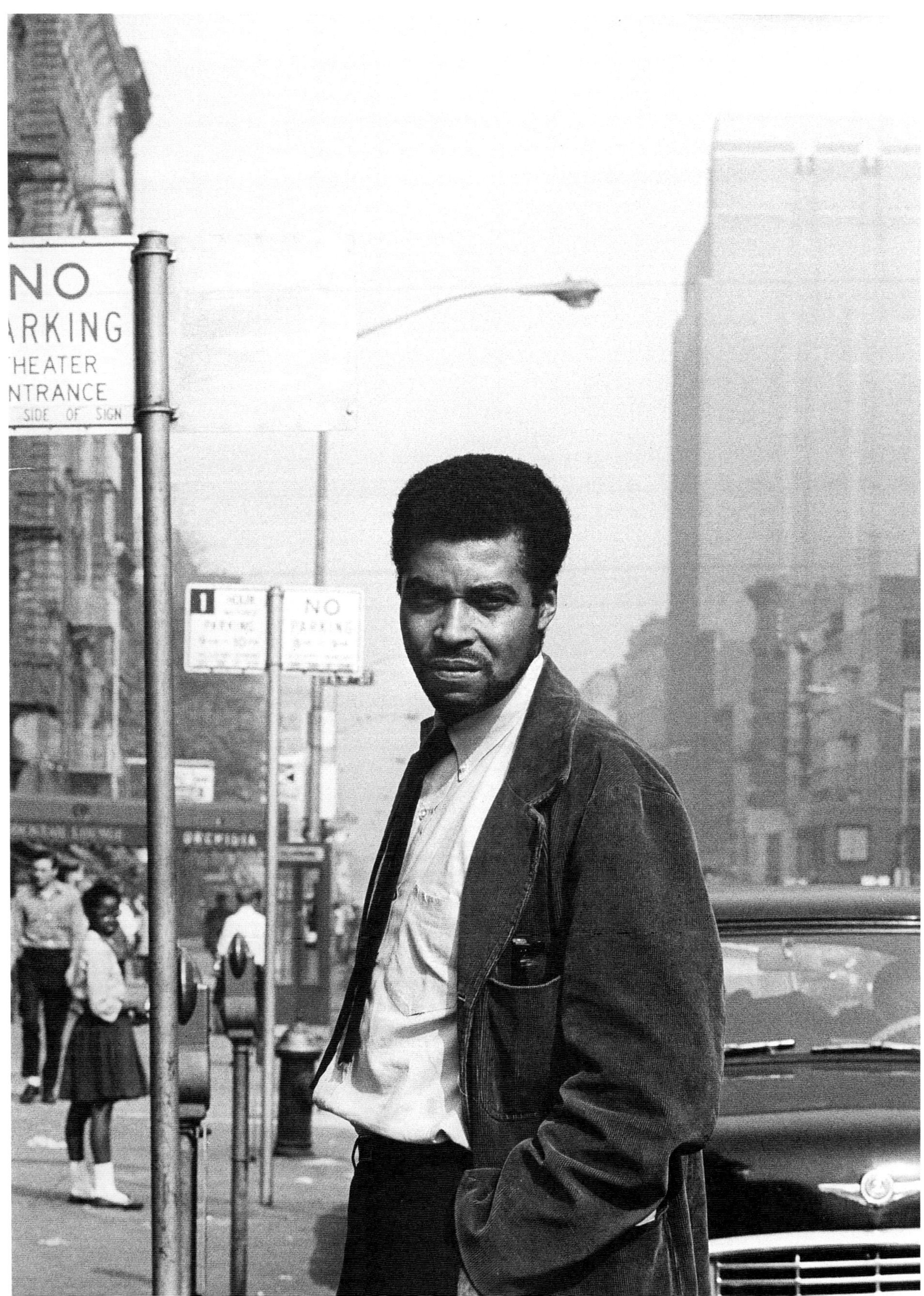

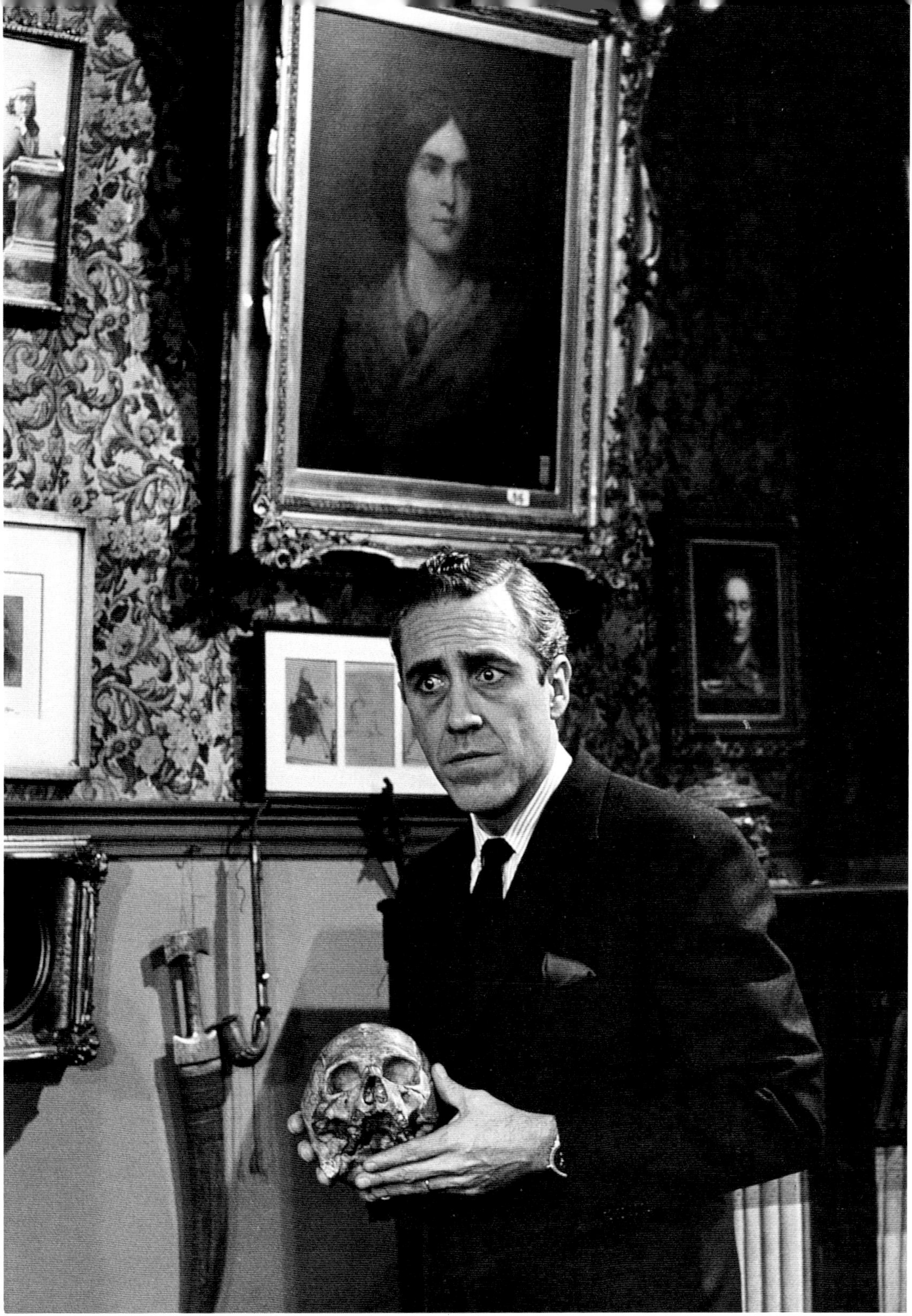

JASON ROBARDS

JASON ROBARDS WAS REHEARSING *Hamlet* at the Players' Club on Gramercy Park in New York City, originally the home of the actor Edwin Booth. This was the first time I had seen Jason Robards in person. Standing so close to him with a camera was a very unusual experience. I could see every line on his face, and admired his rich, deep voice. When it was over, I wanted to tell him how much I enjoyed it, but there were too many people crowding around.

On my way out, I met him on the stairs. "I hope you got some good shots," he said. Before I could answer, a young woman appeared and took him by the arm, the two of them running quickly down the steps. I was left standing there with my mouth wide open.

RUDOLF NUREYEV

THE FIRST TIME I photographed Nureyev was shortly after his arrival in the United States. I later photographed him when he performed in a TV special with Maria Tallchief. One time during a rehearsal at the Metropolitan Opera House, when he was being interviewed while standing in the middle of the aisle, I came a bit too close with the camera.

"Not so close with the camera, not good for my nose," he said, stopping the interview. Of course, I obliged. I had no idea a male dancer could be so vain. That was the only time I took a close-up of him. I never dared get so close again.

When he finally saw the print, he realized that he had over-reacted, and told me that he was sorry. "After all," he said, "my nose is not so big," and we had a good laugh.

Some years later, I photographed him on opening night at the Martha Graham Festival on Broadway, where he appeared as Lucifer. It was an amazing performance.

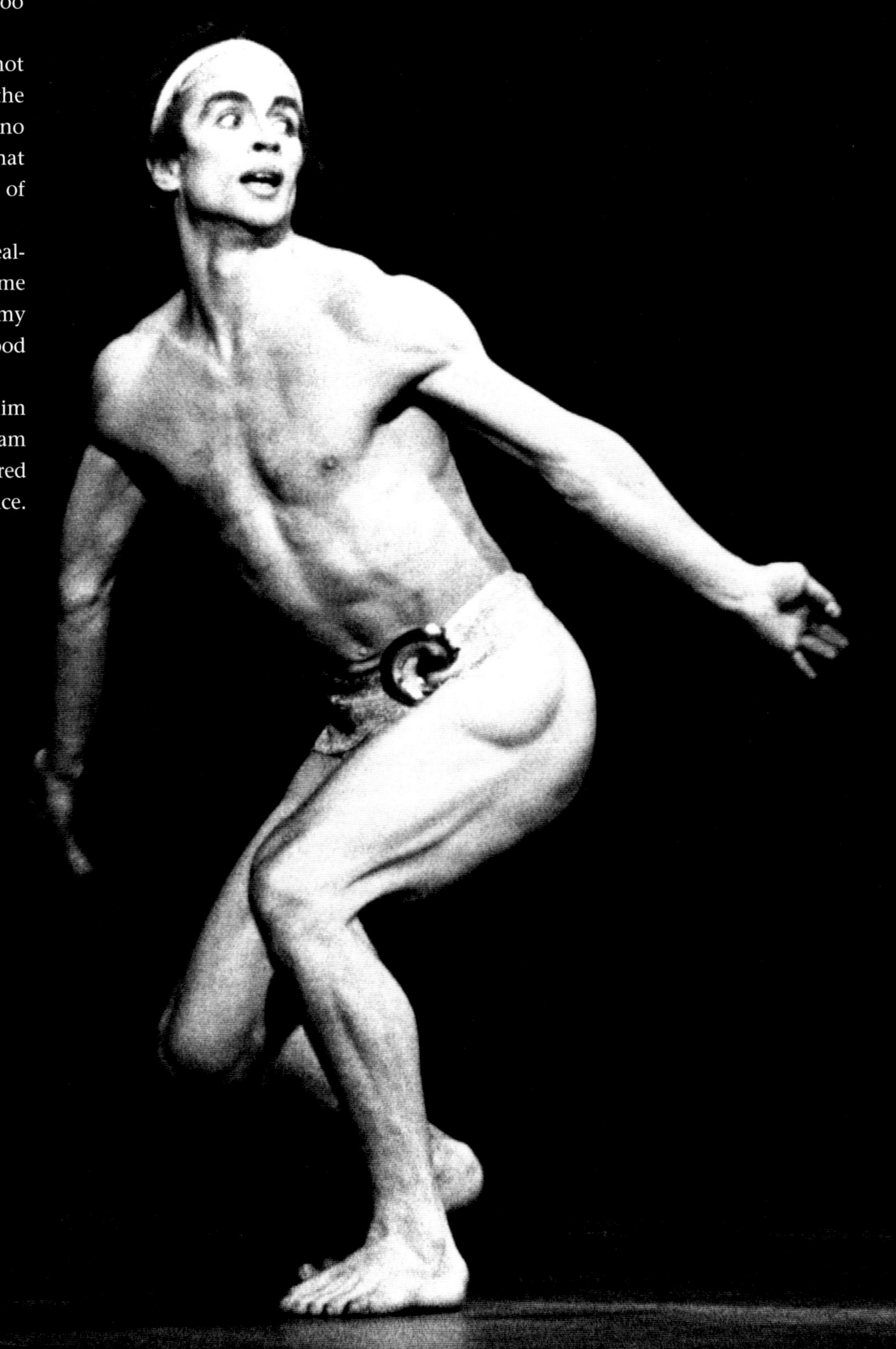

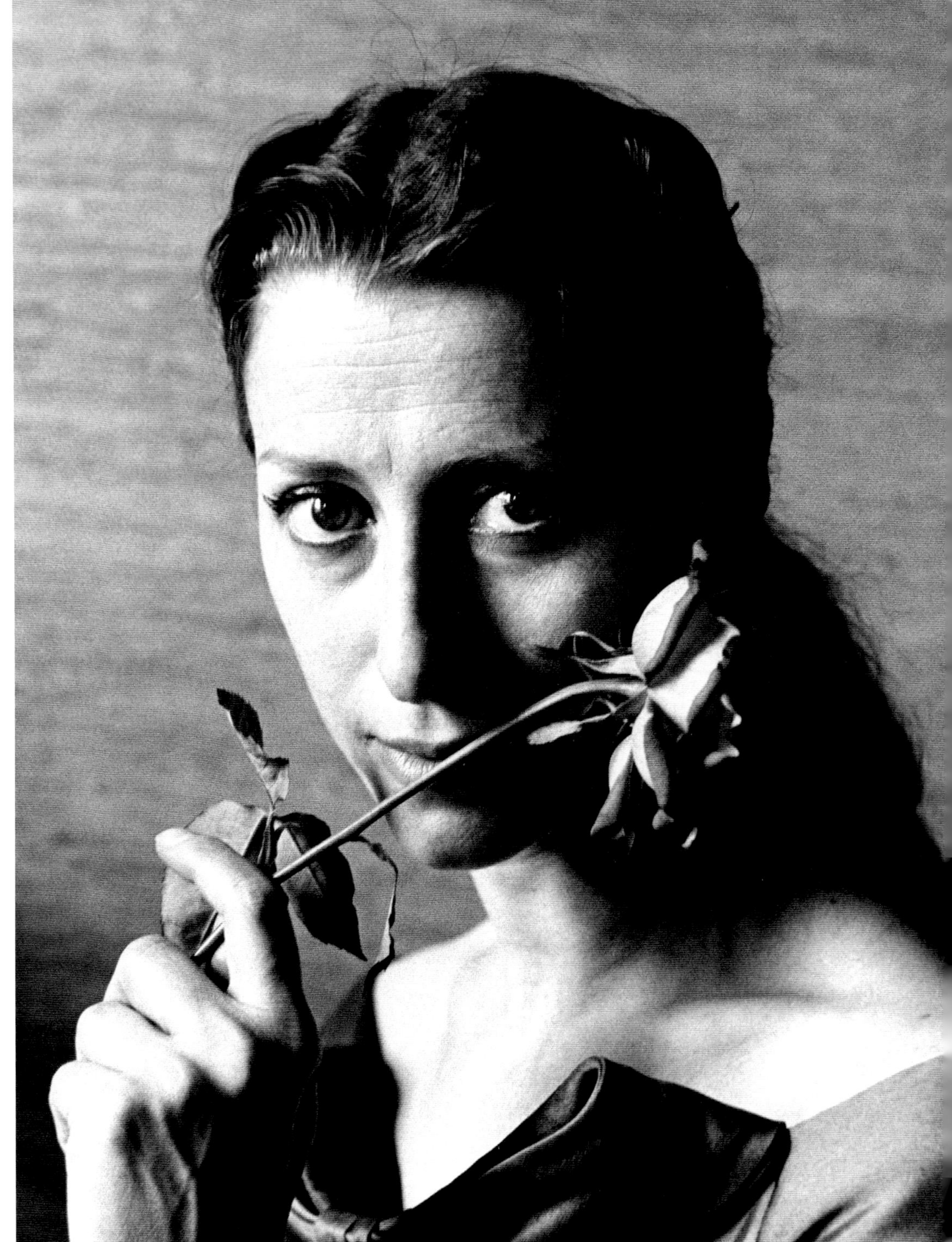

MAYA PLISETSKAYA

I FIRST HEARD about Maya Plisetskaya when she came to New York with the Bolshoi to perform in *Swan Lake* at the old Madison Square Garden on Eighth Avenue. She was very graceful, with a long neck, and the most expressive eyes. I had a second photo session with her at her hotel, this time for informal portraits. On the way there, I bought a rose. When I gave it to her, she caressed it and brought it close to her face and held it there. There was just enough daylight filtering through the window.

After I took the pictures, she asked, "Don't you need reflectors?"

"I prefer available light," I said. "It's more natural."

"One day I must learn how to take pictures with natural light," she said. I gave her a short lesson and she was thankful.

Before her return to Russia, I gave her the photograph of her holding the rose. She was very touched, she said. And I told her how privileged I felt to have photographed the greatest prima ballerina in the world.

"If you ever come to Moscow," she said, "please get in touch. We have plenty of natural light."

I never went to Moscow, and I often wonder if she still has the photograph with the rose.

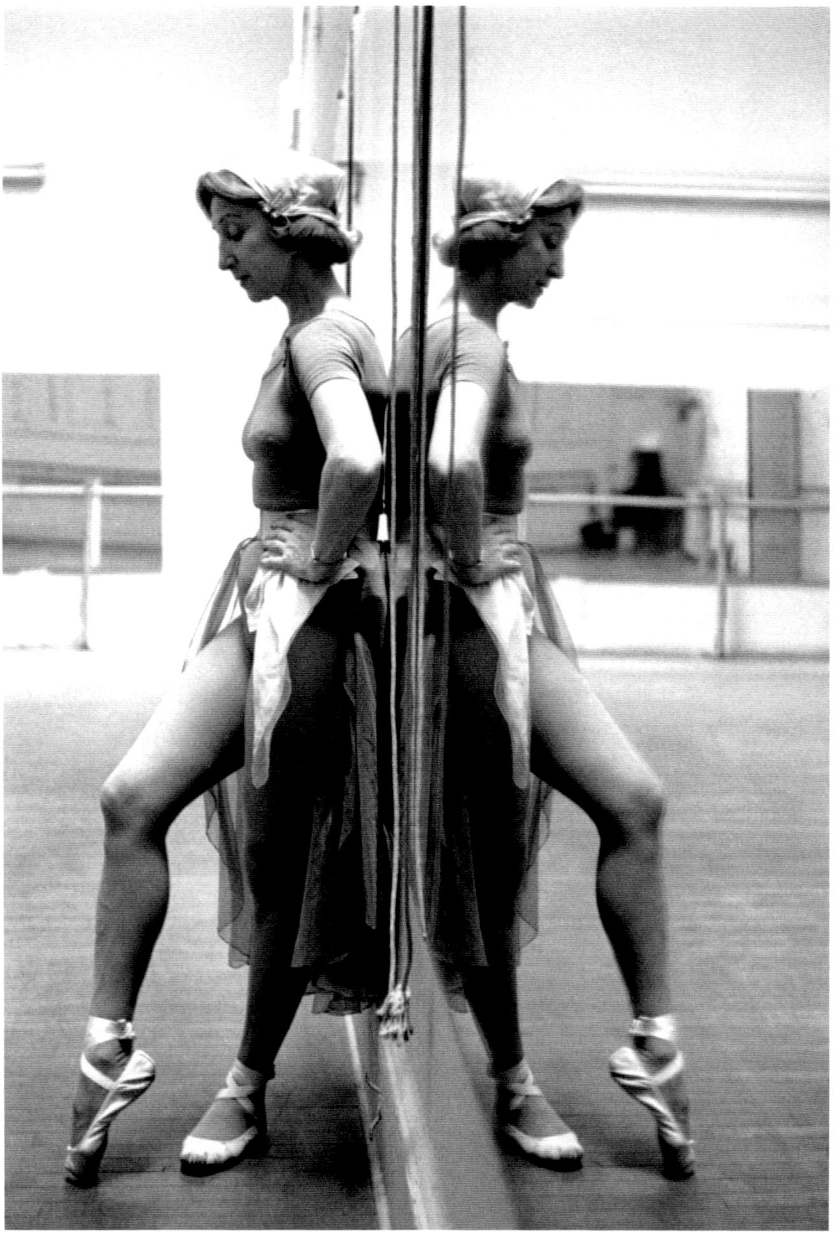

ALEXANDRA DANILOVA

THIS PICTURE OF ALEXANDRA DANILOVA, a ballet dancer, teacher, and choreographer, is thirty-six years old. She was conducting ballet class, and one could feel the tension. I stayed out of her way as much as I could. Suddenly, she stopped to rest, for just a few seconds it seemed, and leaned against a mirror. I managed to get just one exposure. When I gave her a print of the photo some years later, she said, "The Danilova twins. Will the real Danilova get in shape?"

"I thought she was," I said.

"I really love this photo," she said, and gave me a big hug.

Years later, when she died, this photo was used in her obituary in *The New York Times Magazine.*

RUDOLF NUREYEV & MARIA TALLCHIEF

SOON AFTER Rudolf Nureyev arrived in the United States, I photographed him rehearsing with Maria Tallchief for a television appearance. Watching them dance together was a real experience.

As I followed them around, they unexpectedly made a quick turn and bumped into me. I nearly fell to the floor. Nureyev was especially annoyed, and in simple Russian told me to go to hell. He didn't know that I could understand him.

When the rehearsal ended, I went over to apologize, and spoke to him in Russian. When he heard me, he said, "I hope you didn't hear what I said before."

"Of course, not," I said. "I happen to be hard of hearing." I could tell he didn't believe me. ▶

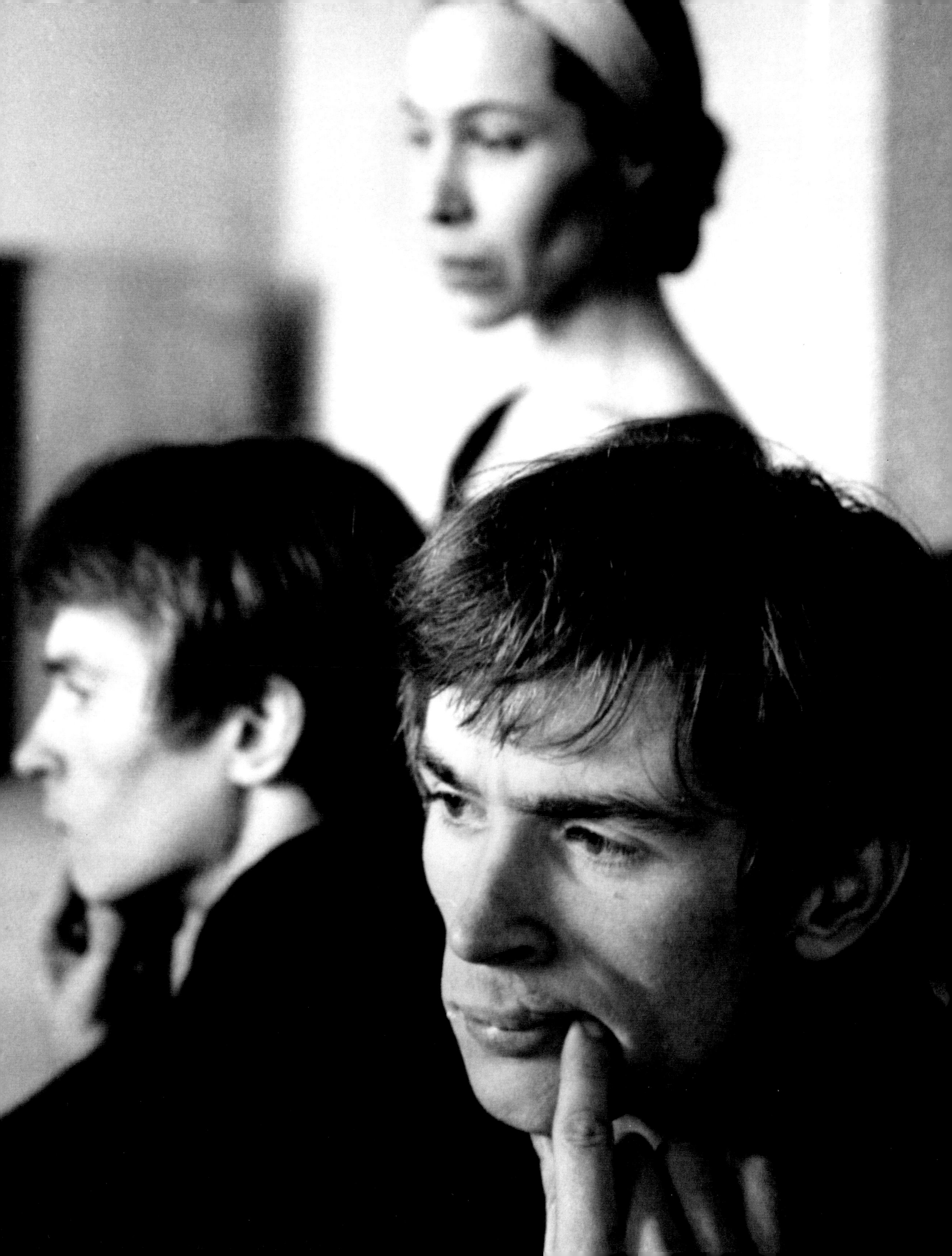

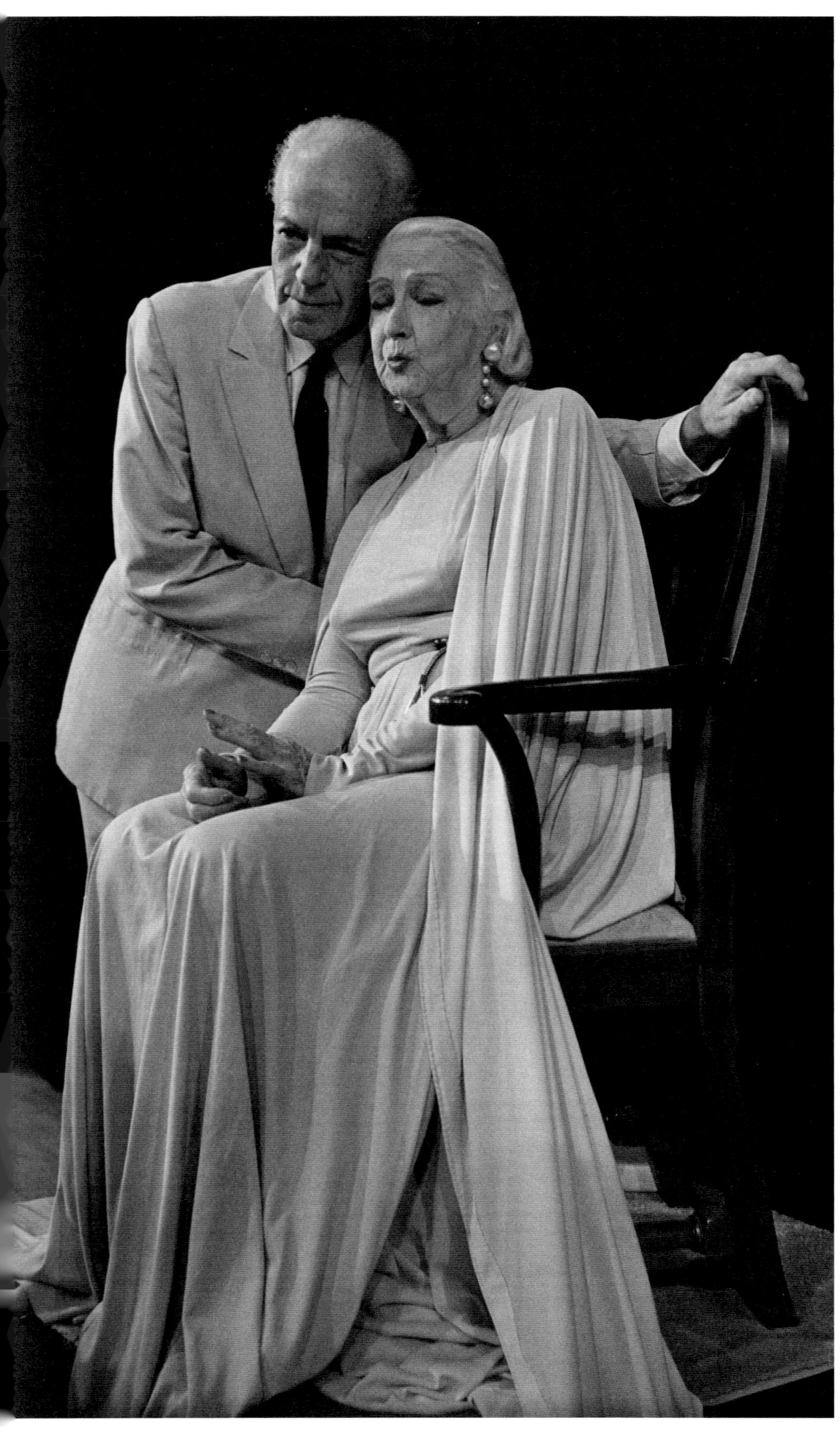

RUTH ST. DENIS & TED SHAWN

I DROVE up to Jacob's Pillow in Massachusetts on a very hot and muggy day to photograph the fiftieth wedding anniversary celebration of Ruth St. Denis and Ted Shawn. After being separated for thirty-seven years, I was told, they had decided to get together and celebrate their fiftieth anniversary with a performance. They danced together in some of the pieces they had choreographed many years before. There was a reception with a big cake and champagne for a room full of guests. She was dressed in a white gown and looked as if she had been cut from marble.

She would allow only five minutes for photos, and when I complained, she said, "If you're good, you can accomplish a lot in five minutes."

"That good I'm not," I said, but it was no use.

During the press conference, a reporter asked about her name. Without hesitating, she said, "There must have been a saint in my ancestry, I suppose." Everyone laughed. The reporter seemed a bit confused, and said, "I certainly admire your sense of humor, Miss St. Denis."

"Thank you," she replied, "how else can you get through life? You have to laugh once in a while. Don't you think so?"

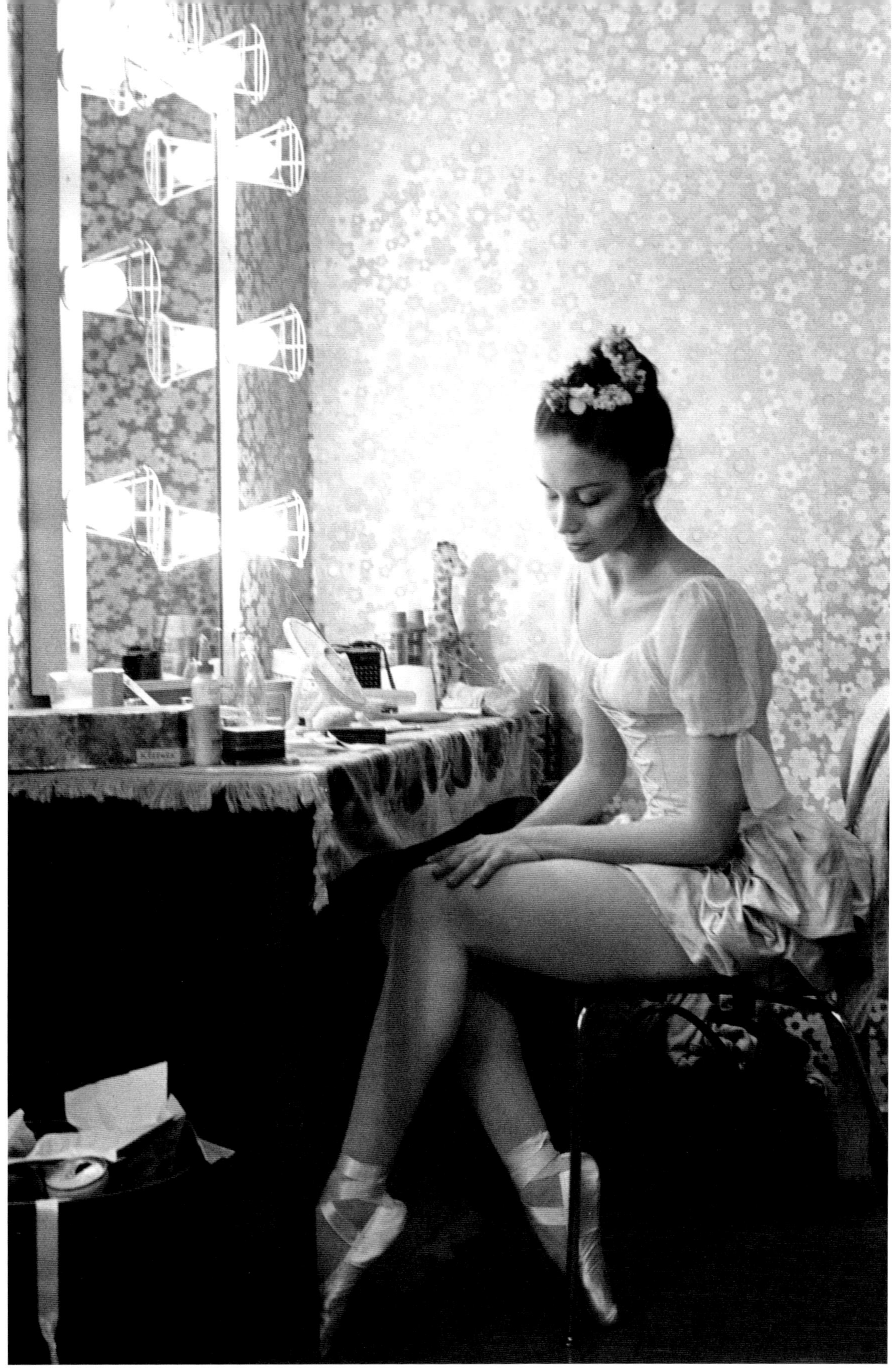

KAY MAZZO

I USED TO PHOTOGRAPH the New York City Ballet quite frequently. One day, wandering backstage, I noticed Kay Mazzo, one of the principal dancers, in her dressing room, resting, or perhaps meditating. The door was wide open. I couldn't resist, and took one exposure. As far as I could tell, she didn't hear me, or the sound of the camera.

GEORGE BALLANCHINE

WHEN I ARRIVED to photograph George Ballanchine and his dancers, I was told that I would have five minutes, and not a minute more. I was also told not to order him around. I had no idea what Mr. B. was like, but I had heard from others that he was very impatient with photographers. As I stood there anticipating the worst, he walked on stage, introduced himself, and asked me point blank: "What do you want me to do?" Without hesitating, I said, "Please, sit down on the floor in front of the dancers." The public relations woman covered her face with her hands and moved to the other end of the stage.

I quickly climbed a chair and began to shoot. More than ten minutes went by and I was still up there, shooting and telling him what to do: sit on a high stool, lean against the stool, stand up, hands in pocket, out of pocket. . . . He followed my instructions without a single complaint. As I was ready to wind it up, he said to me, "Take all the time you need, maestro. I really enjoyed this session."

"Thank you, maestro," I said, "but I'm all finished." When I was about to leave, he came over and asked, "Wasn't the lighting too harsh?" Without giving it a thought, I said, "We'll soften it in the processing," and bid him goodbye. In order to save time, I had used the existing stage lights, which do have a tendency to be somewhat harsh. Mr. B. was right. The lighting *was* harsh.

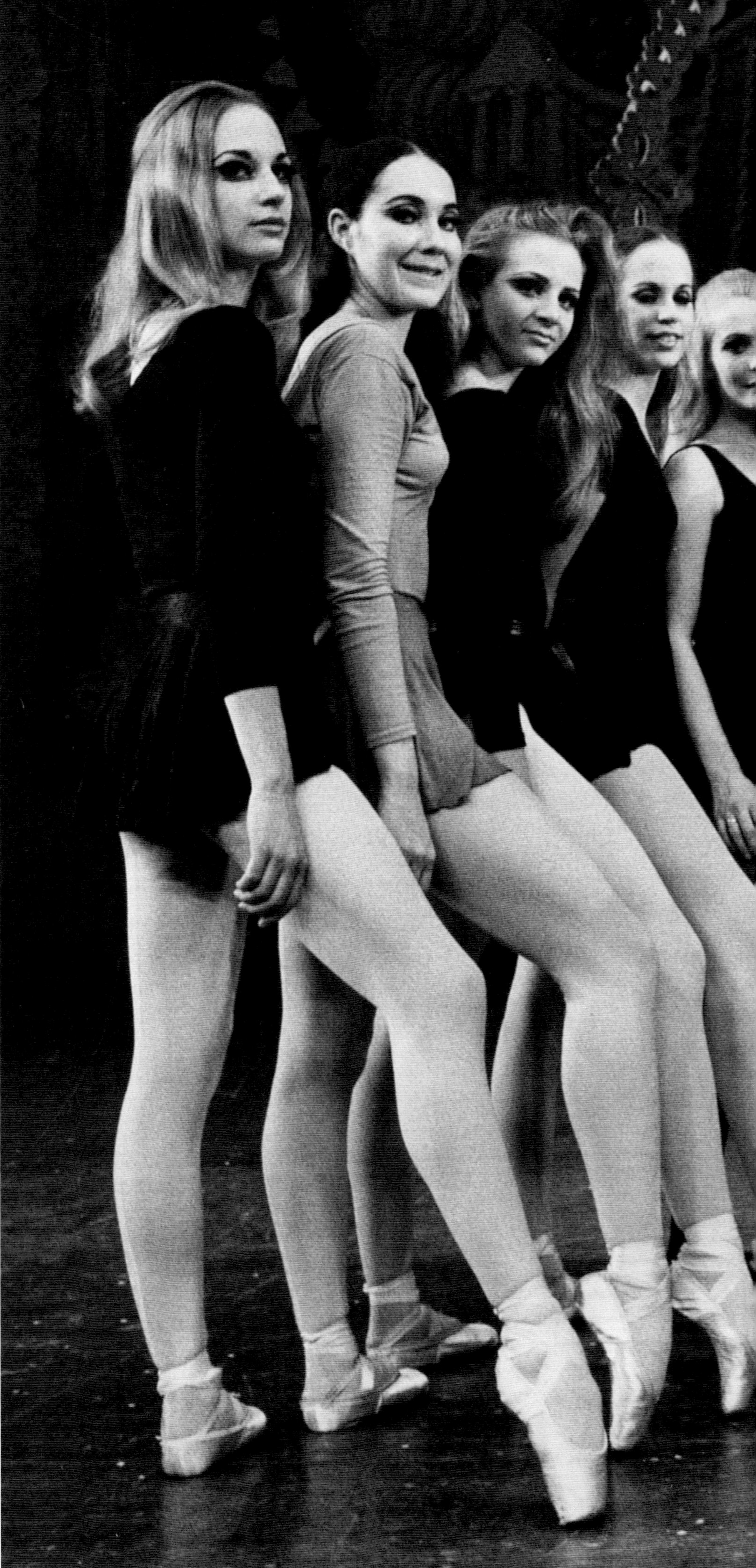

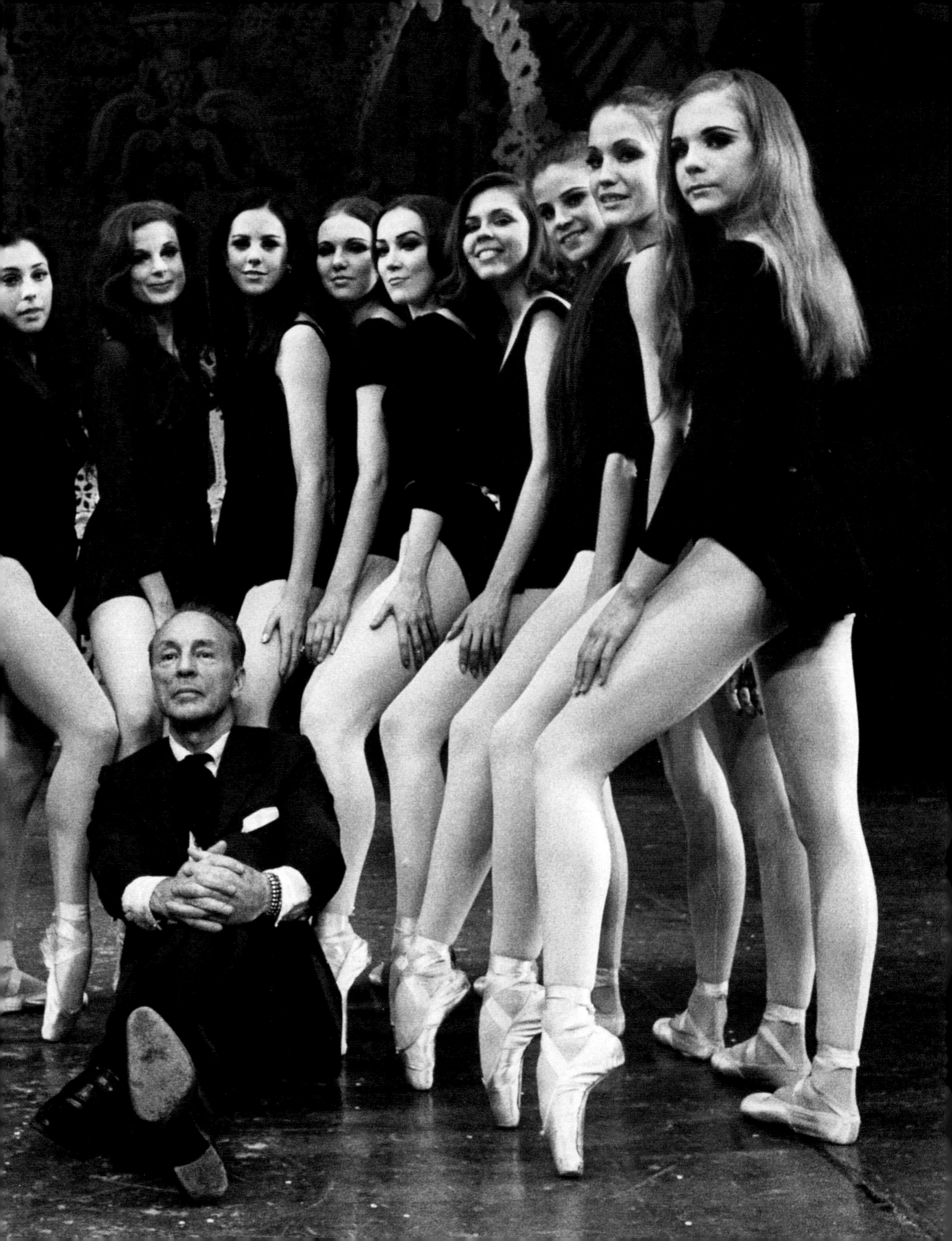

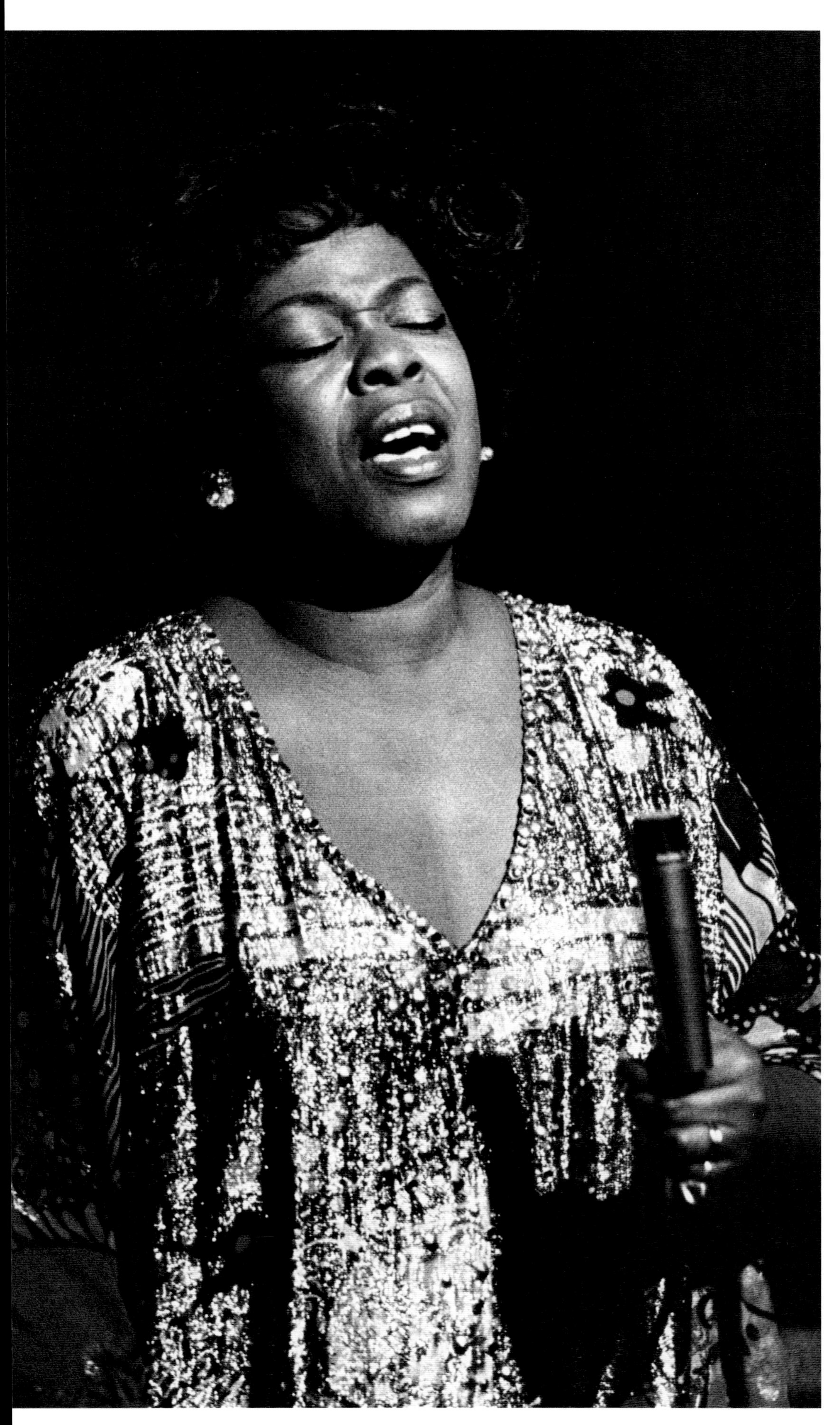

SARAH VAUGHAN

SOMETIME IN THE LATE 1960s, Sarah Vaughan was appearing at the Copacabana, the old landmark New York night club. I was supposed to photograph her during the performance. When she saw me, she wanted to make sure that I didn't take any pictures of her with her eyes closed. But during the entire performance she never had her eyes open, so in every picture I took she had her eyes closed. Sorry, Sarah, I really tried.

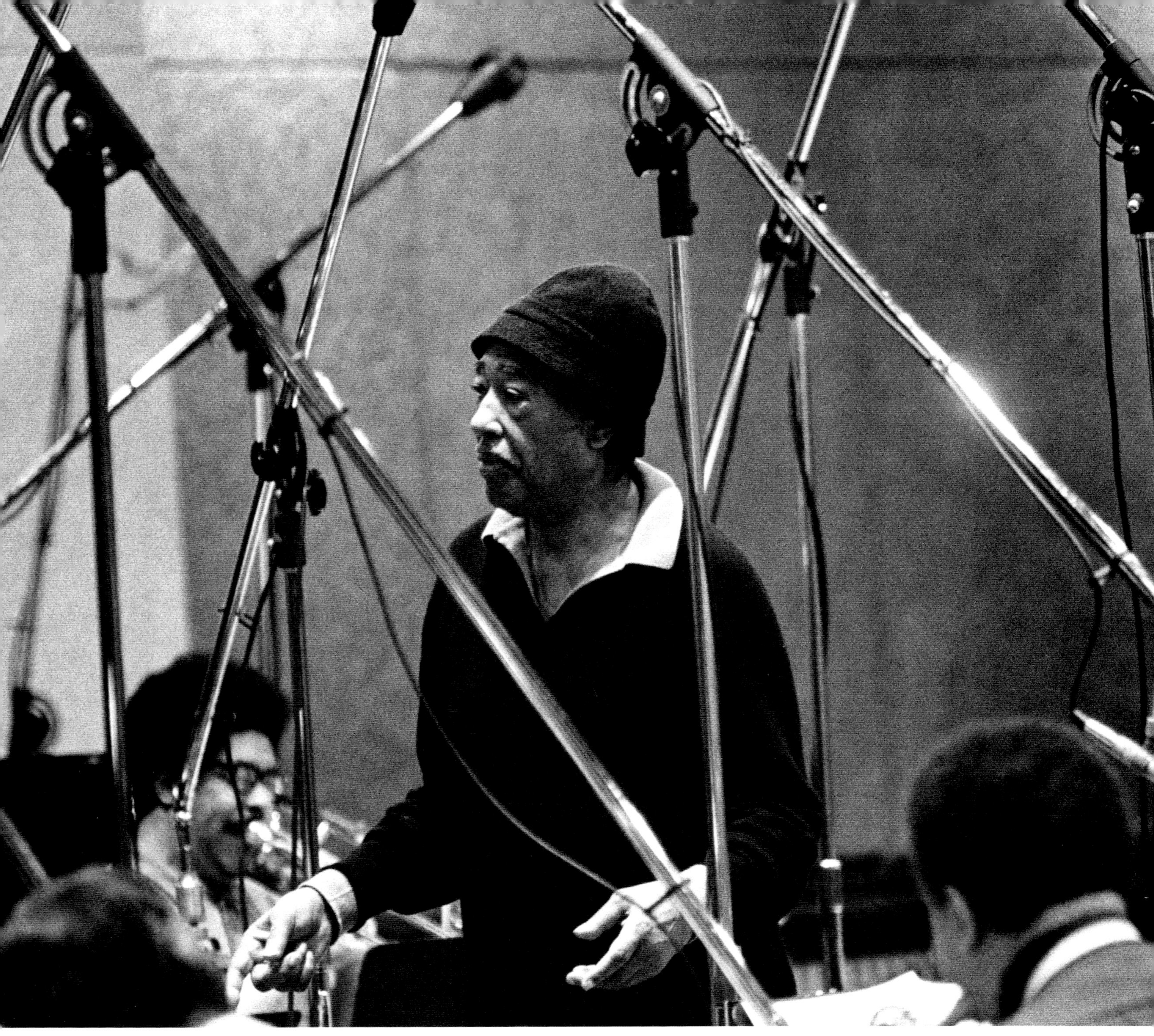

DUKE ELLINGTON

THE STUDIO in which Duke Ellington was rehearsing with his band was noisy and cluttered with all kinds of instruments and microphones. He was busy moving around, adjusting equipment, and talking to the musicians. He was dressed casually, but what concerned me especially was his denim hat, which cast a shadow across his forehead. I wasn't allowed to use any strobe lights, only available light, and that wasn't very bright. I finally cornered him, and asked if he would remove his hat.

He looked at me with astonishment and said, "I don't take off a hat for anybody, not even for the Queen of England."

"I thought I would try, Mr. Ellington."

"You certainly did," he said. Some hours later, after the recording session was over and I was getting ready to leave, I saw the Duke remove his hat.

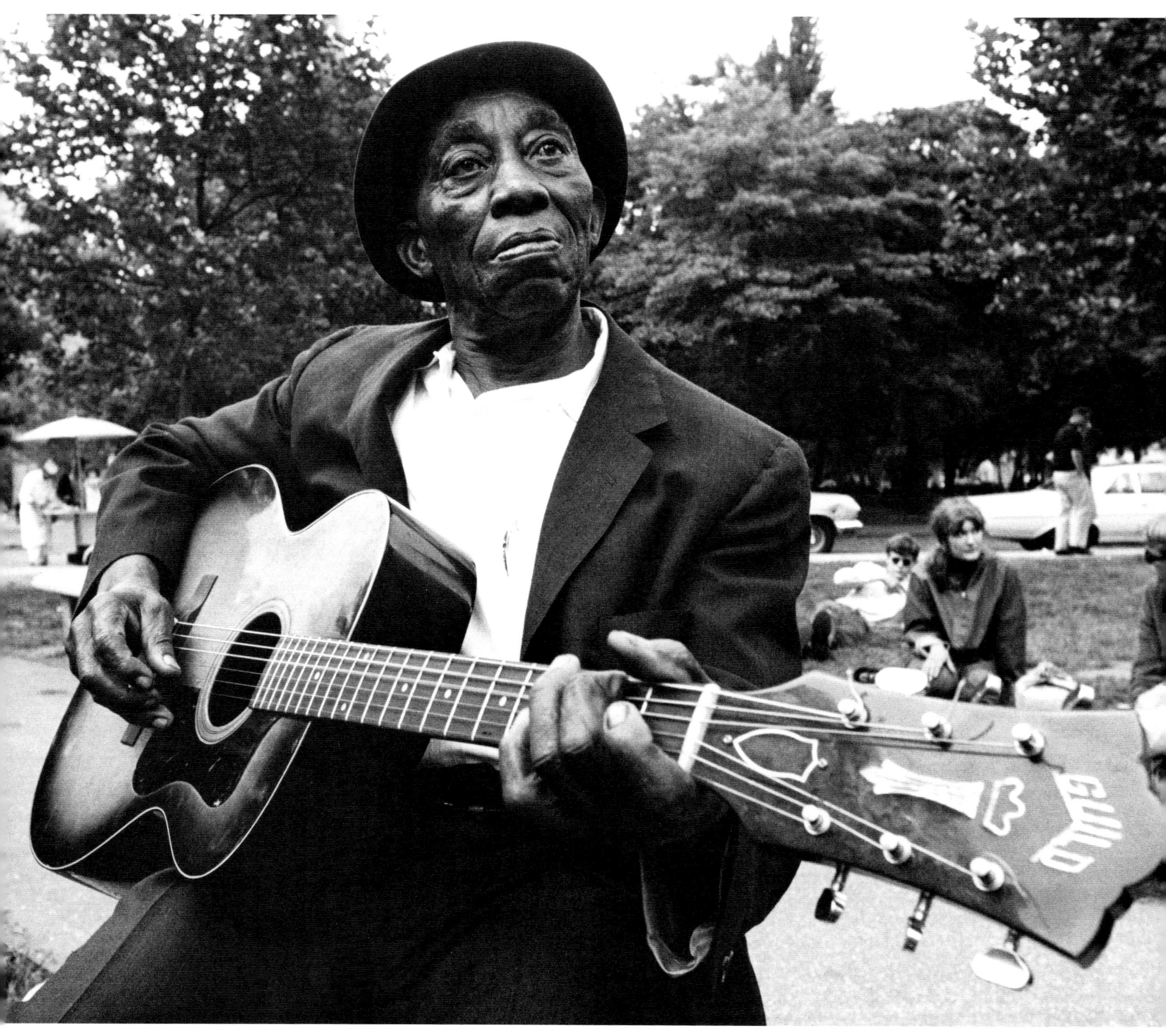

MISSISSIPPI JOHN HURT

MANY YEARS AGO, Mississippi John Hurt was performing in the Jazz Festival at Carnegie Hall. After the concert, the reporter I was with invited him to a nearby restaurant for an interview. John Hurt was a gentle man with a deep, scratchy voice, and an appetite for bourbon. When I suggested that he order some food as well, he said, "I only eat in the morning, and after that I get mighty thirsty." He couldn't understand how anyone could drink coffee. "Doesn't it make you sick?" he said, when I ordered a cup. He certainly managed to get a few under his belt by the time the interview was over.

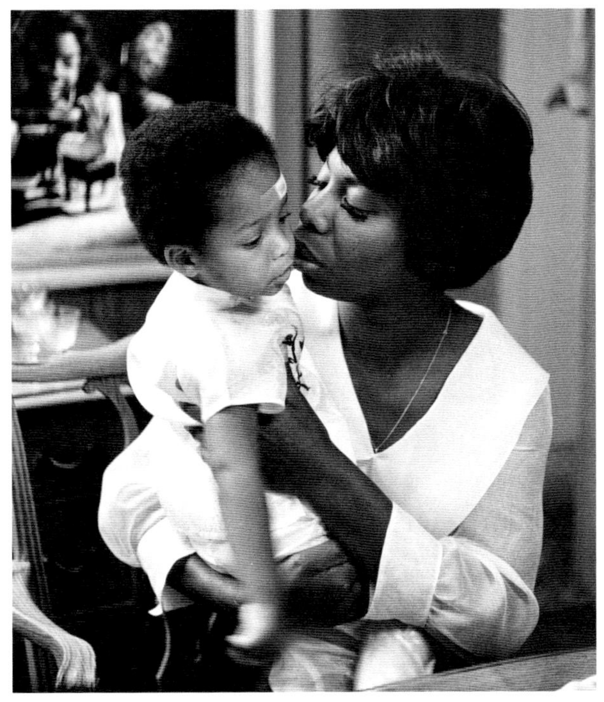

NINA SIMONE

I WAS MESMERIZED by Nina Simone's artistry. Her trembling, suffering voice left a deep, unforgettable impression. I photographed Nina and her family on many occasions, and after several photo sessions we became friends. My favorite picture of Nina is when she's holding her one-year-old daughter Lisa at her first birthday party. Very often I play Nina's old records so as not to forget her.

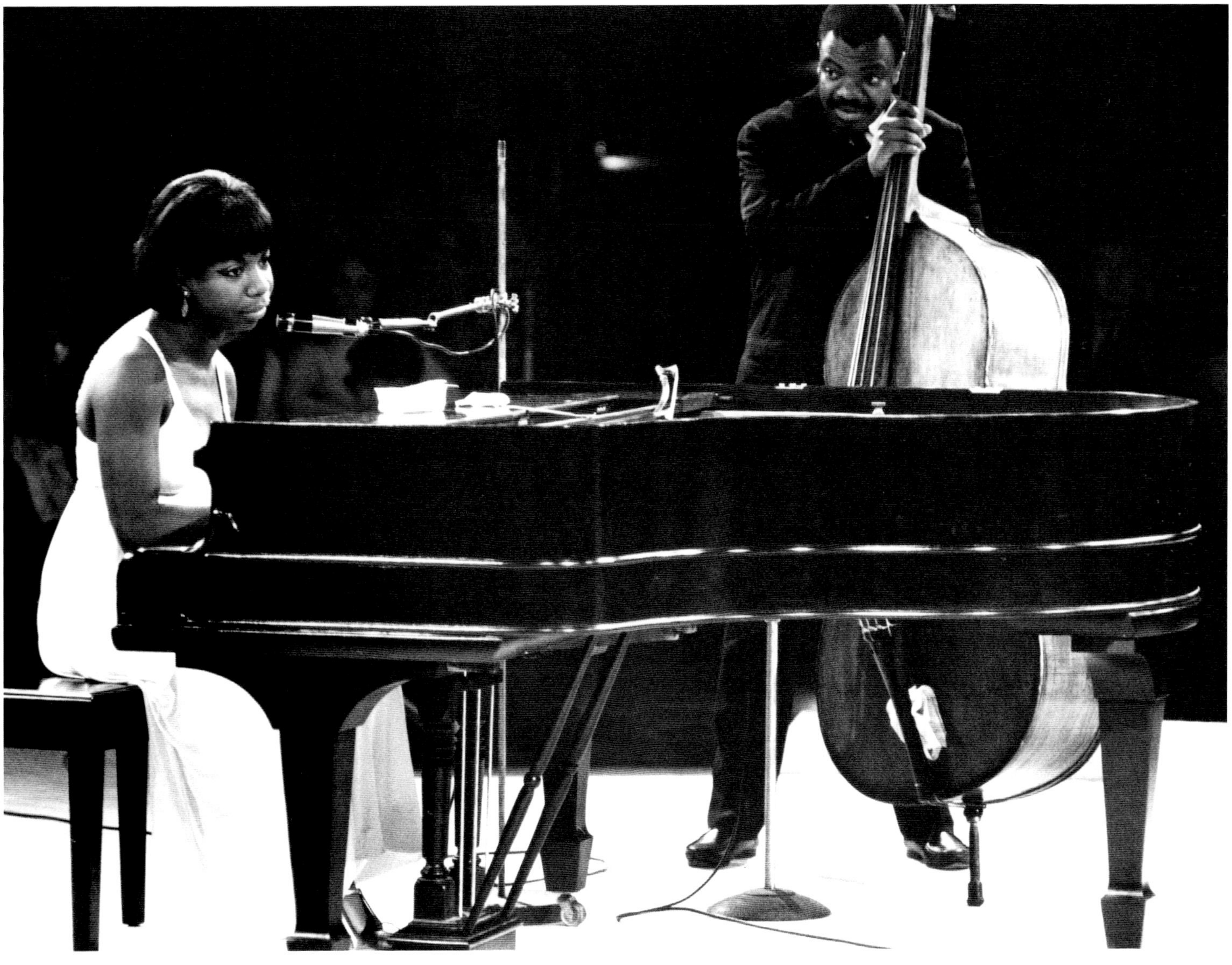

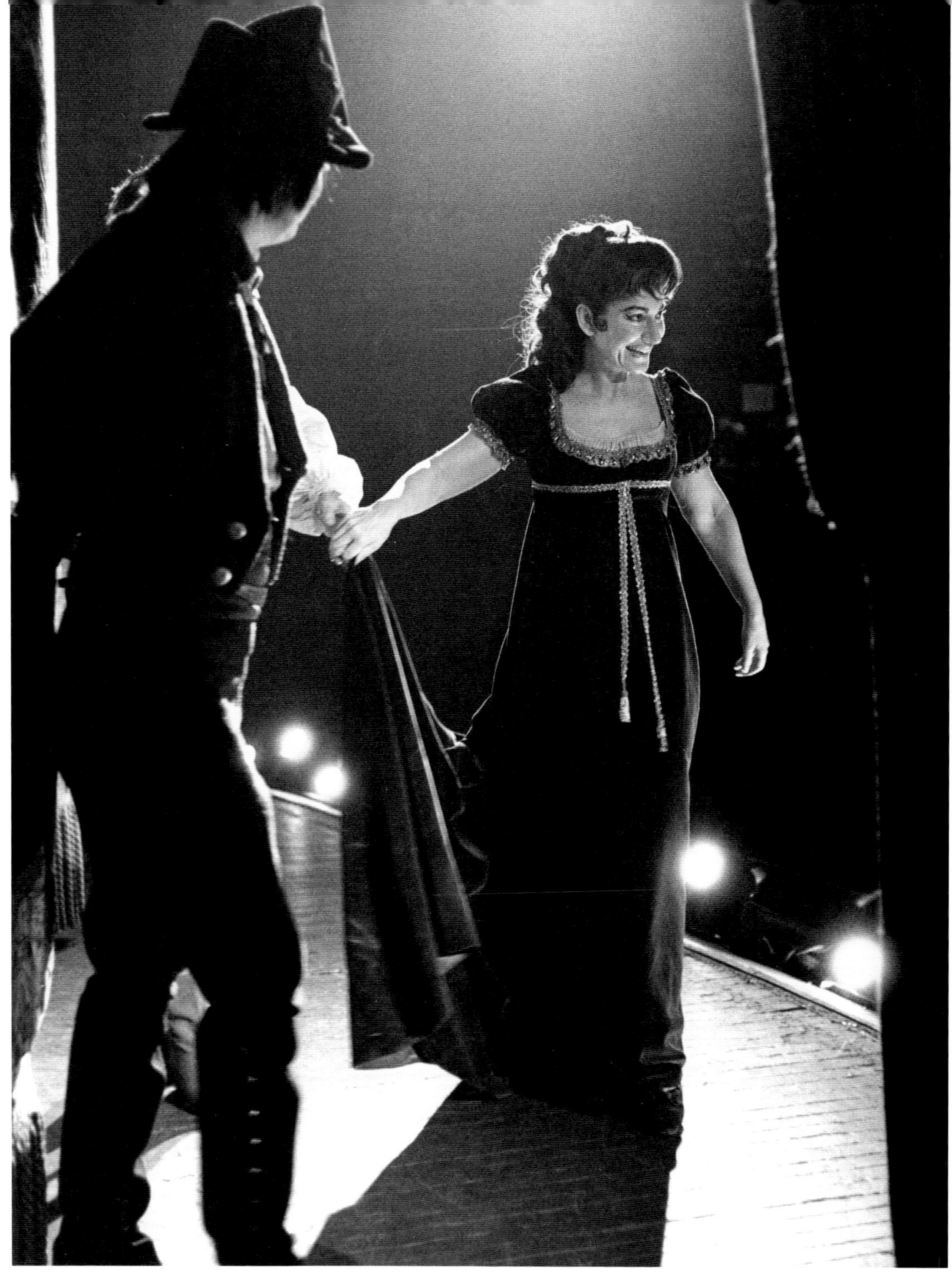

MARIA CALLAS

MARIA CALLAS was appearing in *Carmen* on opening night at the Metropolitan Opera. She was electrifying. At the end of the performance, I was allowed to go backstage. As she stood there waiting for the curtain calls, I took a picture with available light and no flash.

She must have heard the click of the shutter, because she turned quickly and said, "Why are you so impatient? Can't you wait another second?"

"Miss Callas," I said, "that was the moment."

I wasn't sure if she heard me. She waved her arm, as if to say, who cares? what moment? At least, that's what I thought she meant. When it was over, I was told that she was too tired to be photographed in her dressing room.

When I saw her again one year later, she remembered me. She said, "When I saw the picture I knew what you meant by the moment. Thank you very much."

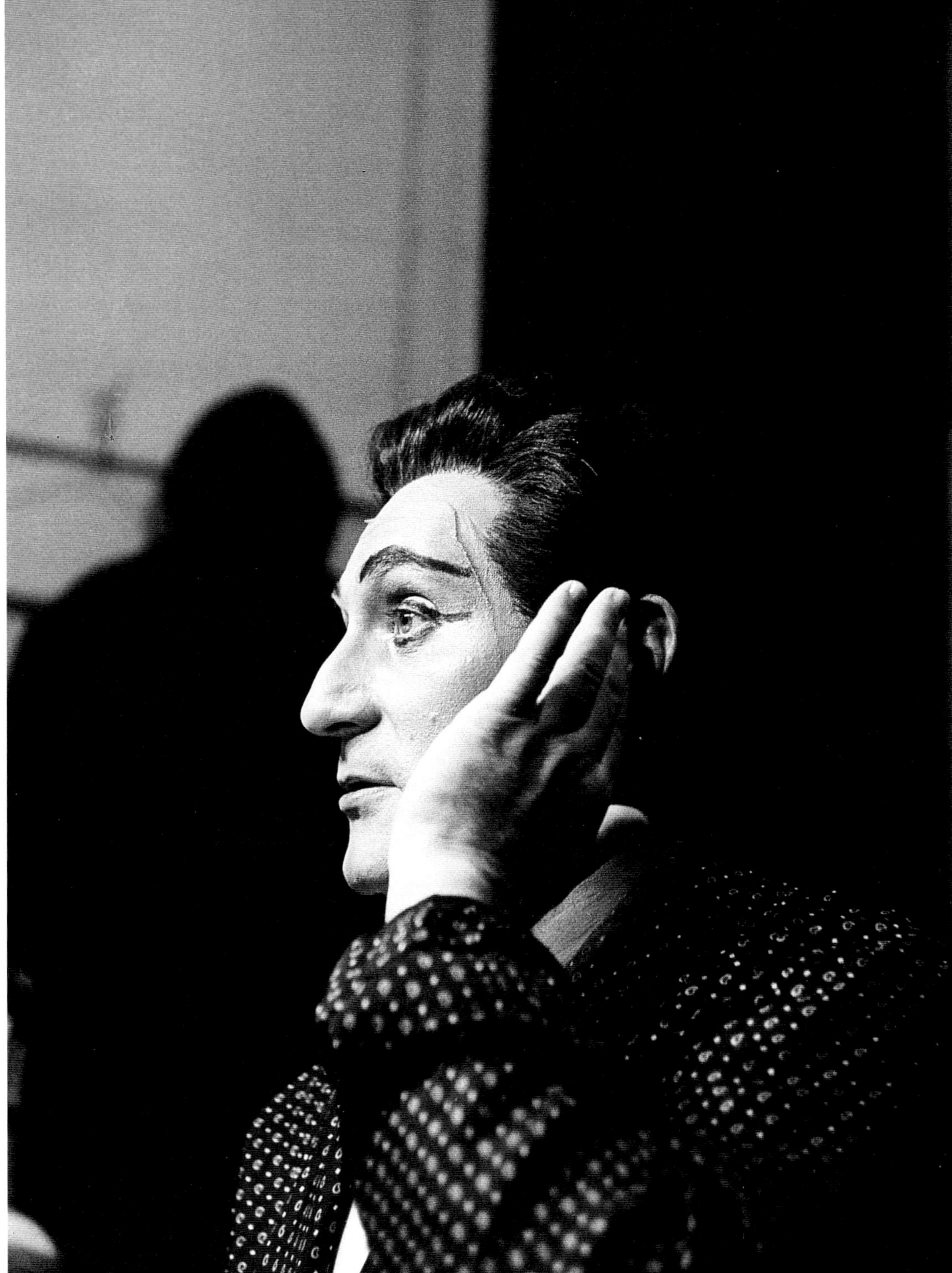

RICHARD TUCKER

AFTER A DRESS REHEARSAL, there was to be a photo shoot of Richard Tucker alone, at the studio of the old Metropolitan Opera House. He came out dressed in costume, with a drawn sword in his hand. This was the pose he insisted on. When I asked for a different pose, he said: "Who is the boss here, you or me? And you don't have to answer." Eventually, he changed his mind, but then the lights went out and we were left in complete darkness.

Somebody went to look for a flashlight. "Nobody move," Tucker yelled out, "the sword is out of the scabbard." By the time someone came with the flashlight, the lights went on again, but Tucker was called to the phone and the session was over. I couldn't wait any longer and had to rush to my next assignment. But at least I had a picture of him with the drawn sword.

When I photographed him again some months later, he said, "I look in this picture like a Cossack who had his horse shot out from under him. I know I should have listened to you. Well, from now on you'll be the boss, I promise."

But he didn't keep his word. At the next session he got his way, just like before.

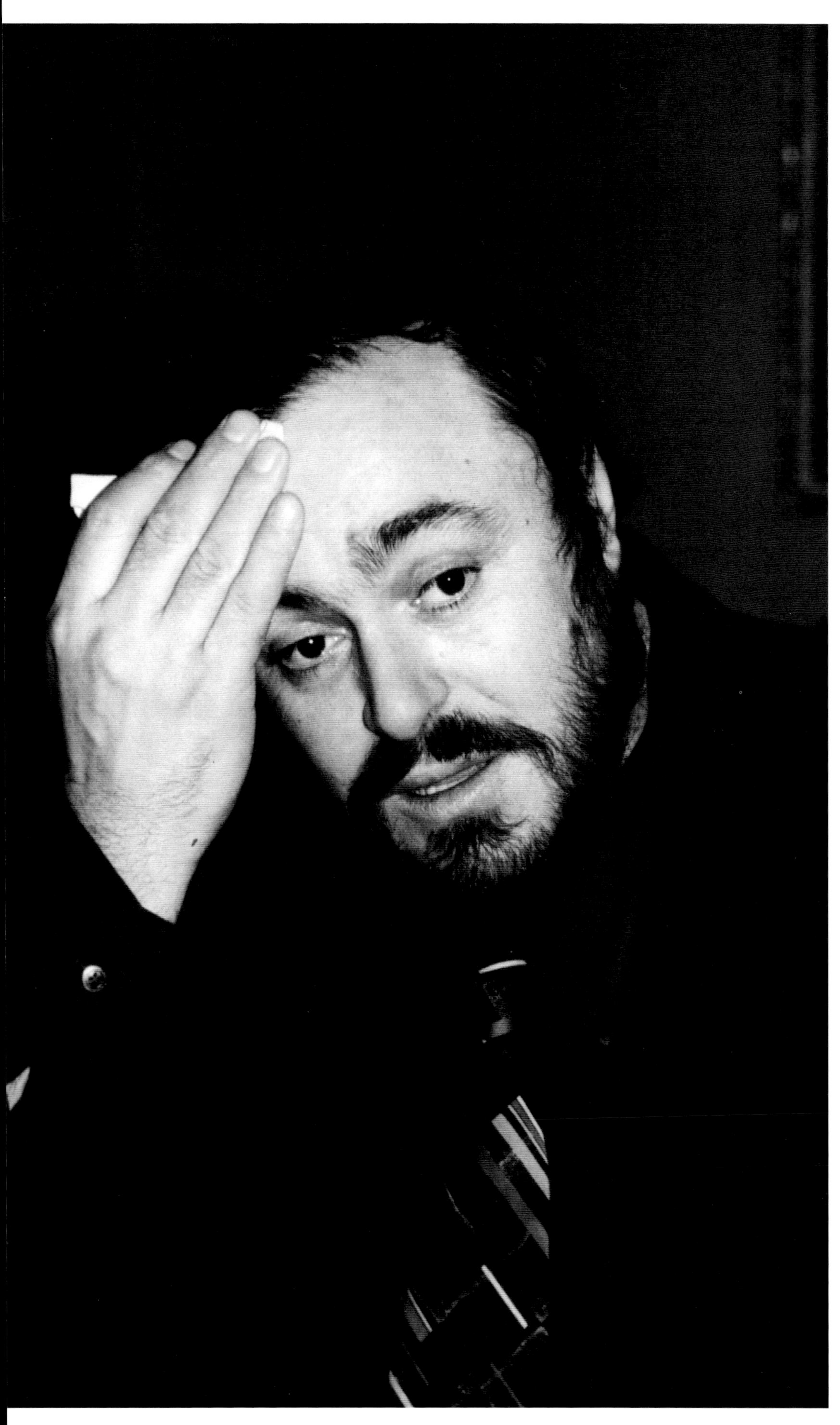

LUCIANO PAVAROTTI

WHEN LUCIANO PAVAROTTI first came to New York in 1973, I was assigned to photograph him at a party at La Scala restaurant after the performance. I arrived late, having been detained at an earlier photo session, and Pavarotti was already gone.

On my way home, driving by Carnegie Hall, I noticed a group of young people talking animatedly to someone who I thought looked like Pavarotti. I only knew him from pictures. Convinced that it was him, I went over and asked him if he was Pavarotti and if I could take some pictures of him. He obliged and never questioned why I needed his picture.

"Don't I look like him?" he asked, laughing. His friends stood nearby, watching us.

When the film was processed the following day and the proof sheets were made, it turned out that it wasn't Pavarotti at all, but only someone who resembled him. I was very embarrassed.

When I finally met the real Pavarotti and told him about his look-alike, he asked if I could arrange a meeting. "I would love to meet him," he said, "maybe he's my lost, rich American uncle."

Of course, the meeting never took place.

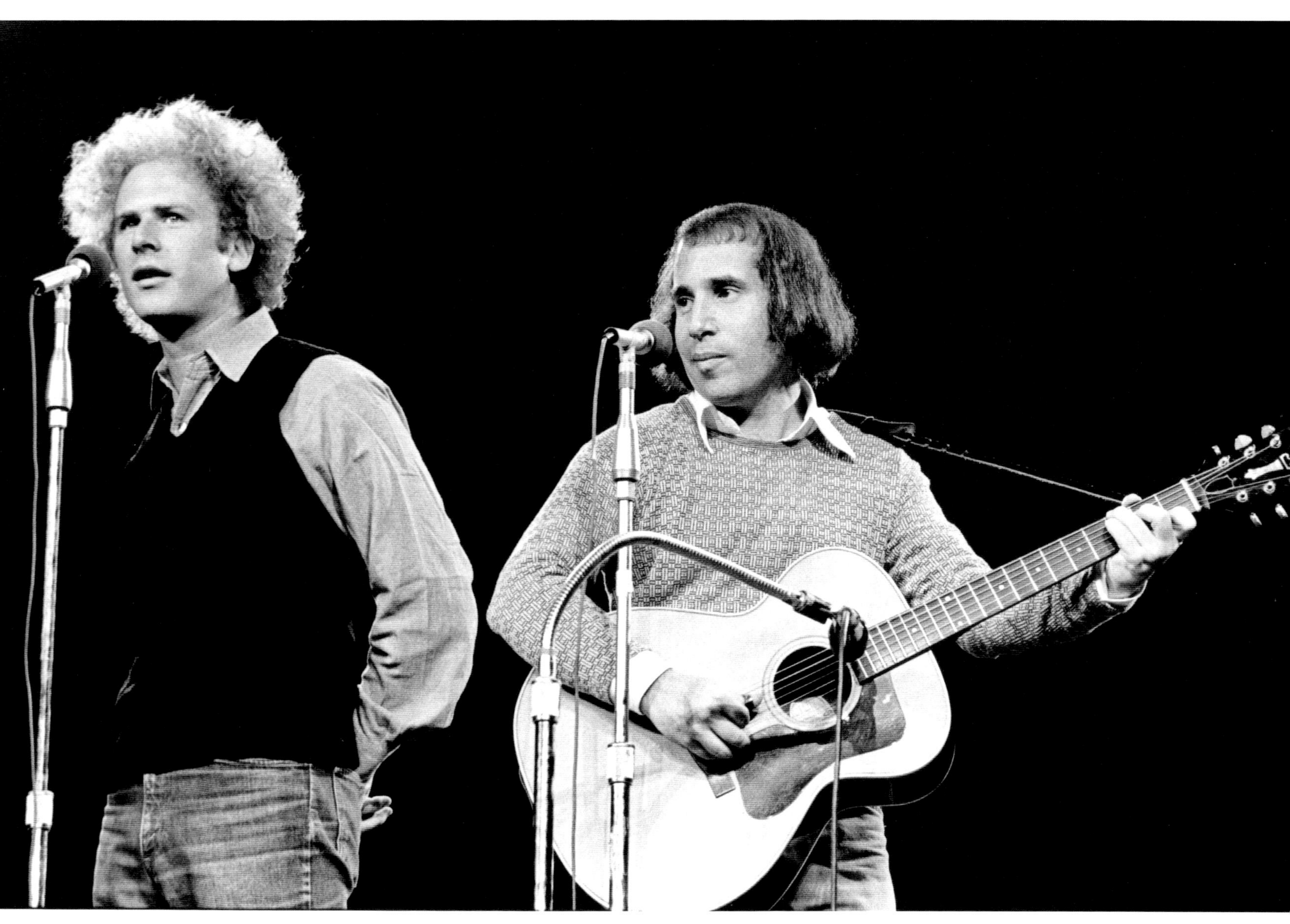

SIMON AND GARFUNKEL

ONE NIGHT, Simon and Garfunkel were part of a benefit concert at Madison Square Garden. I had never heard them before, and actually didn't know which was which. As I took the photos, I asked a young man in the audience which was Simon and which was Garfunkel. He must have thought I was joking. Pointing at them, he said, "The tall one is Simon and the shorter one is his partner." And, laughing at me, he shouted, "Are you kidding me?"

Some years later, after the two broke up, I was assigned to photograph Paul Simon. When I arrived at his home and he opened the door, I was about to ask if Mr. Simon was at home, but I didn't think he would find it amusing. That is how I finally learned which one was Simon.

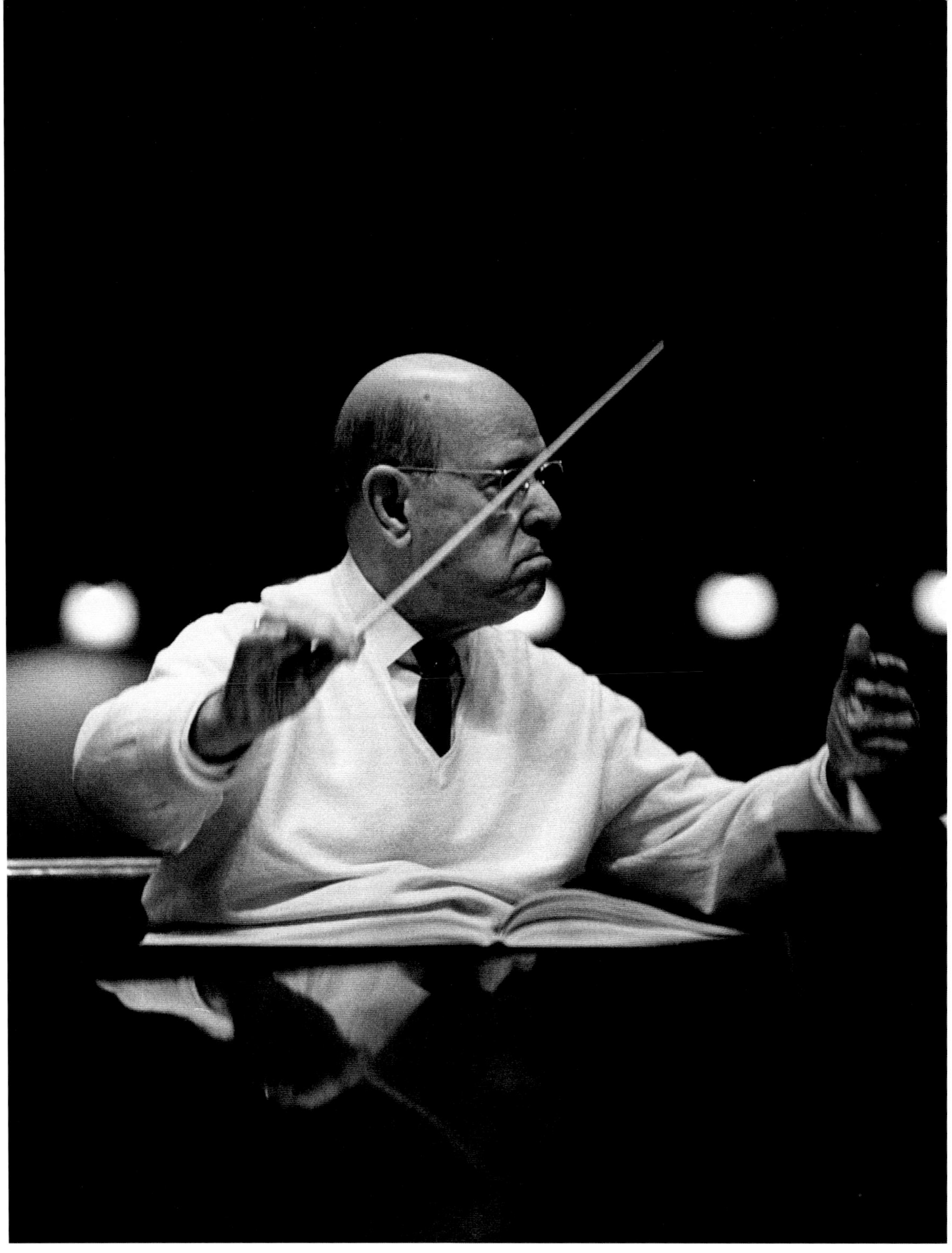

PABLO CASALS

I'VE PHOTOGRAPHED many musicians, ballet dancers, and almost every type of entertainer during my career. They were highly skilled artists each, and one could learn a great deal just watching them work. One of these was Pablo Casals, the famous cellist and conductor.

I was assigned to photograph the rehearsal for a concert that he was to conduct with the New York Philharmonic at Carnegie Hall in celebration of Isaac Stern's sixtieth birthday. I was told not to use any flash, because it would blind him and prevent him from reading the score. But there was very little available light in the hall, and when I asked permission to use the flash for just a few exposures, his assistant told me that Casals had said, "If I can conduct in the dark, I don't understand why he can't take pictures in the dark."

So I did the best I could.

LEOPOLD STOKOWSKI

TO PHOTOGRAPH LEOPOLD STOKOWSKI during a rehearsal of the New York Philharmonic was no simple matter. The stage manager told me to use a telephoto lens and to stay out of his sight. I was also told that he didn't like to be photographed at all anyway. So it was decided that I would kneel behind the kettle drums and hold the camera in my hands without a tripod. For ten minutes everything went fine, except for the soreness in my knees. As I tried to make myself more comfortable, I lost my balance and fell against the drums, knocking them over. Everything stopped. Stokowski was furious. The stage manager ran over, helped me up, and told me to leave the stage.

"Are you drunk?" he asked.

"Of course not," I said. "I'm sorry, but I lost my balance."

"This is the wrong time to lose your balance," he said. "I suggest you leave before the maestro gets cardiac arrest." Stokowski waited patiently, baton at the ready, until I could gather my equipment. As I walked off stage, my head hanging low, the entire orchestra burst out laughing. I felt awful. That must have been one of the most embarrassing moments of my entire career. I never photographed Stokowski again.

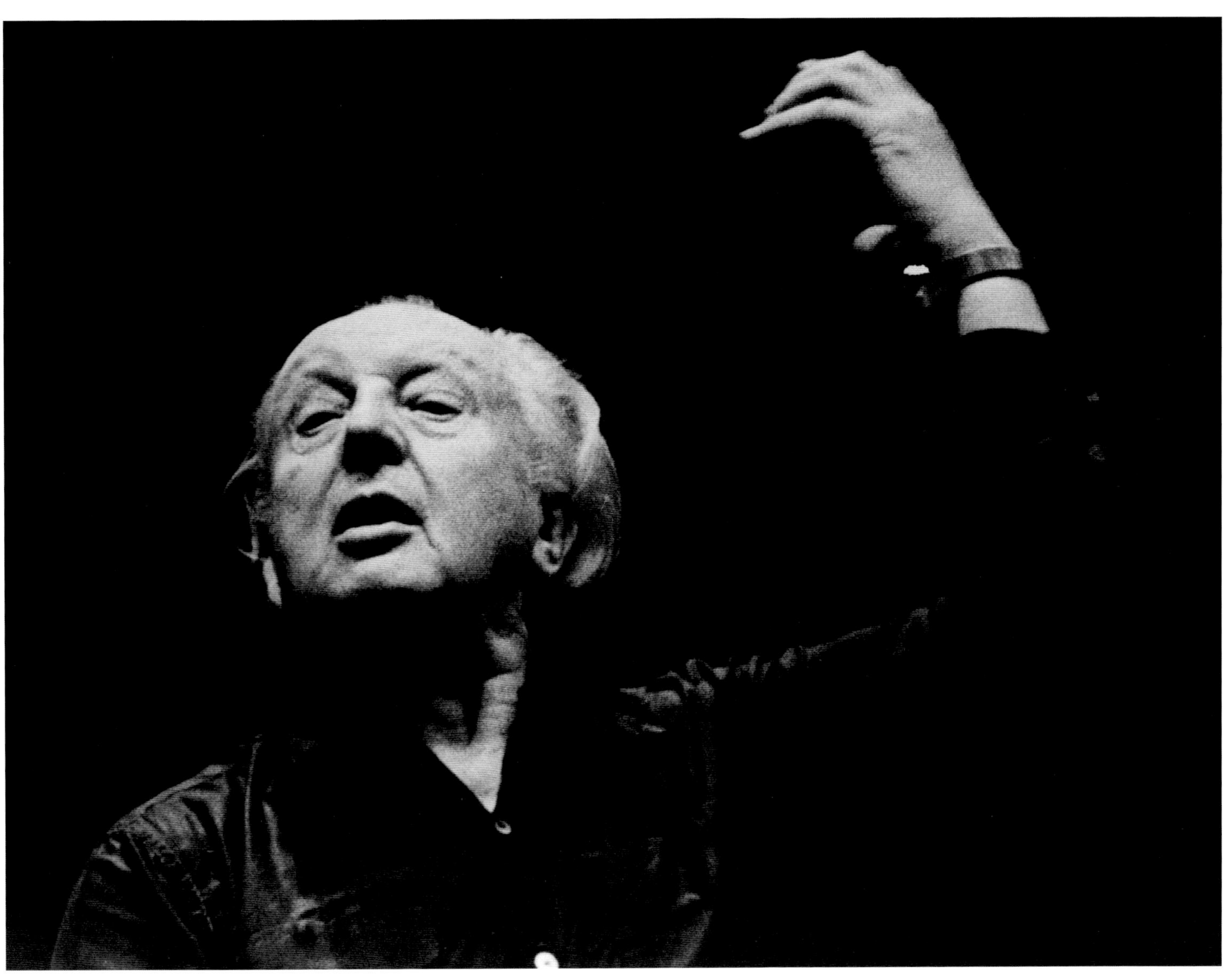

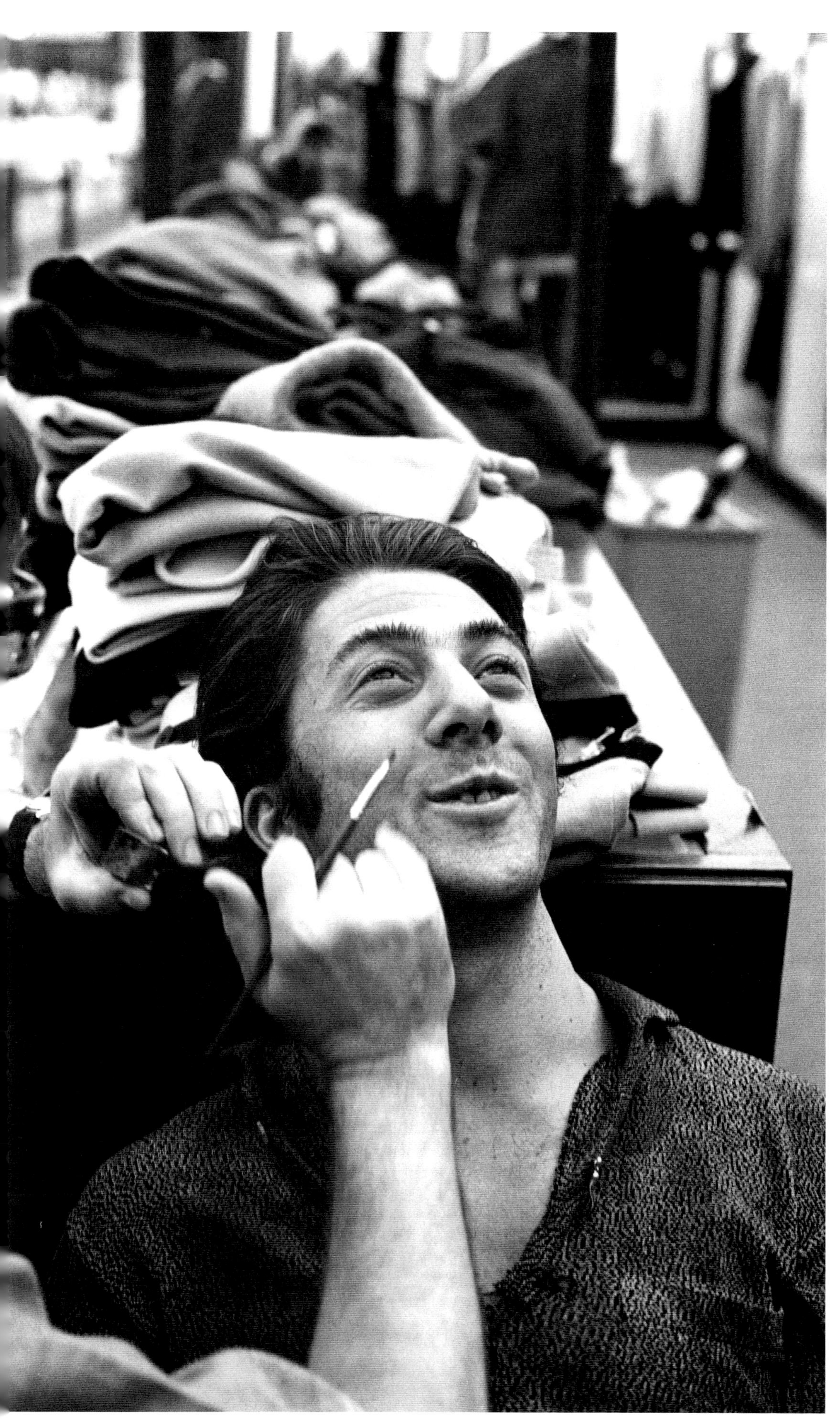

DUSTIN HOFFMAN

DUSTIN HOFFMAN was being made up for the film *Midnight Cowboy* on the main floor of Saks after the store had closed. Make-up people, assistants, and electricians were running in and out looking for each other. There was lots of commotion and confusion. I finally got to photograph him, and when he was ready to leave, I heard him say, "Can I have six of each?"

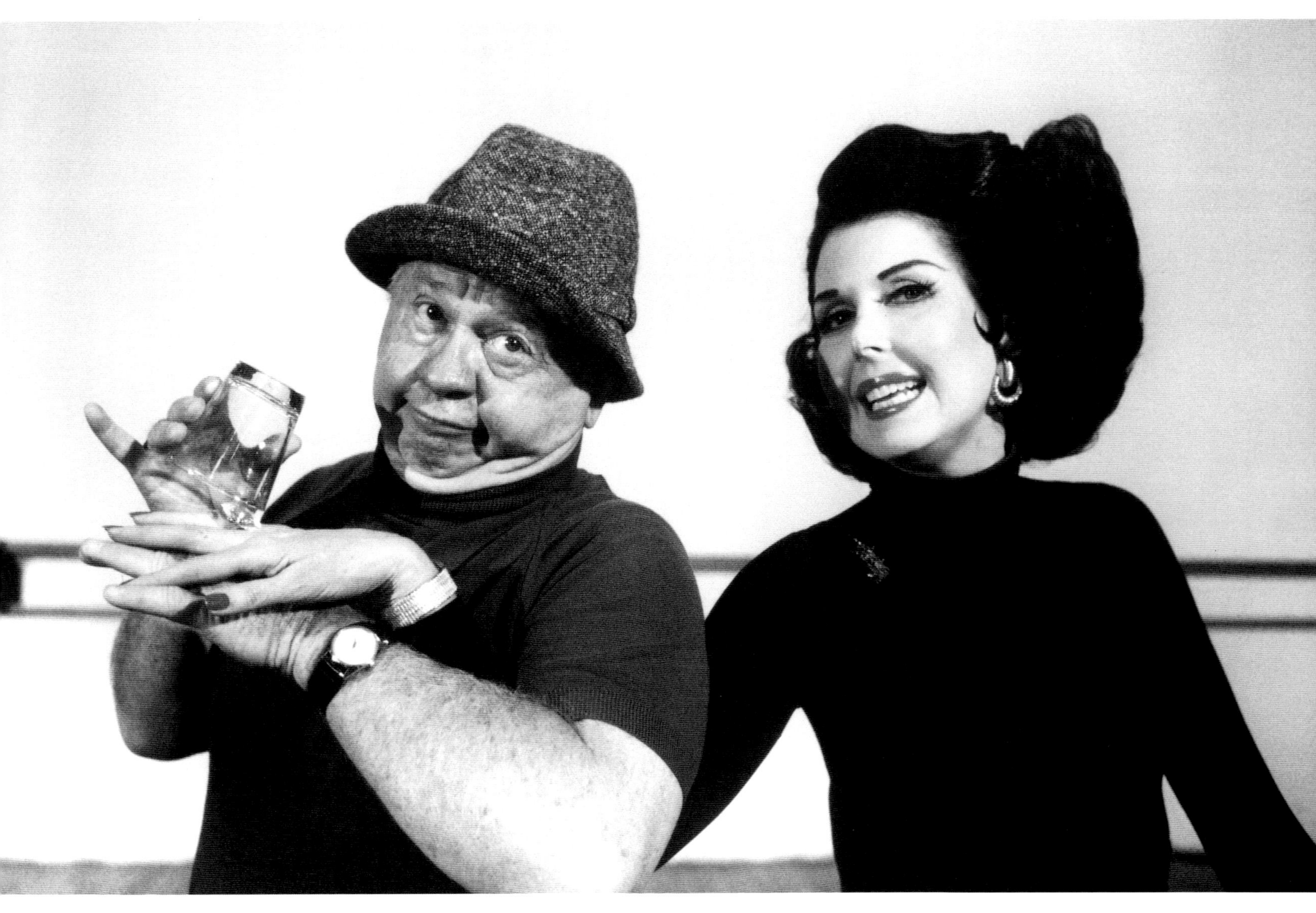

MICKEY ROONEY & ANN MILLER

IT WAS REAL FUN photographing Mickey Rooney and Ann Miller rehearsing *Sugar Babies*. It was hard to believe that this was the same Mickey Rooney I used to see in the movies when I was a youngster. He was full of energy, always entertaining, and great with women.

When he noticed me with the camera, he covered his face and said, "Do you have the right lens to fix my mug." When I assured him that I did, he started clowning around, making everyone laugh. "I once knew a photographer," he said, in a serious tone of voice, "who never had any film in the camera, but took great pictures. It wasn't you by any chance, was it?"

"It certainly was me," I said, kidding, at the same time checking my camera to make sure that it had film. In a way, it was strange the way I reacted. Whenever I load film into the camera, I think of Mickey Rooney and his power of suggestion.

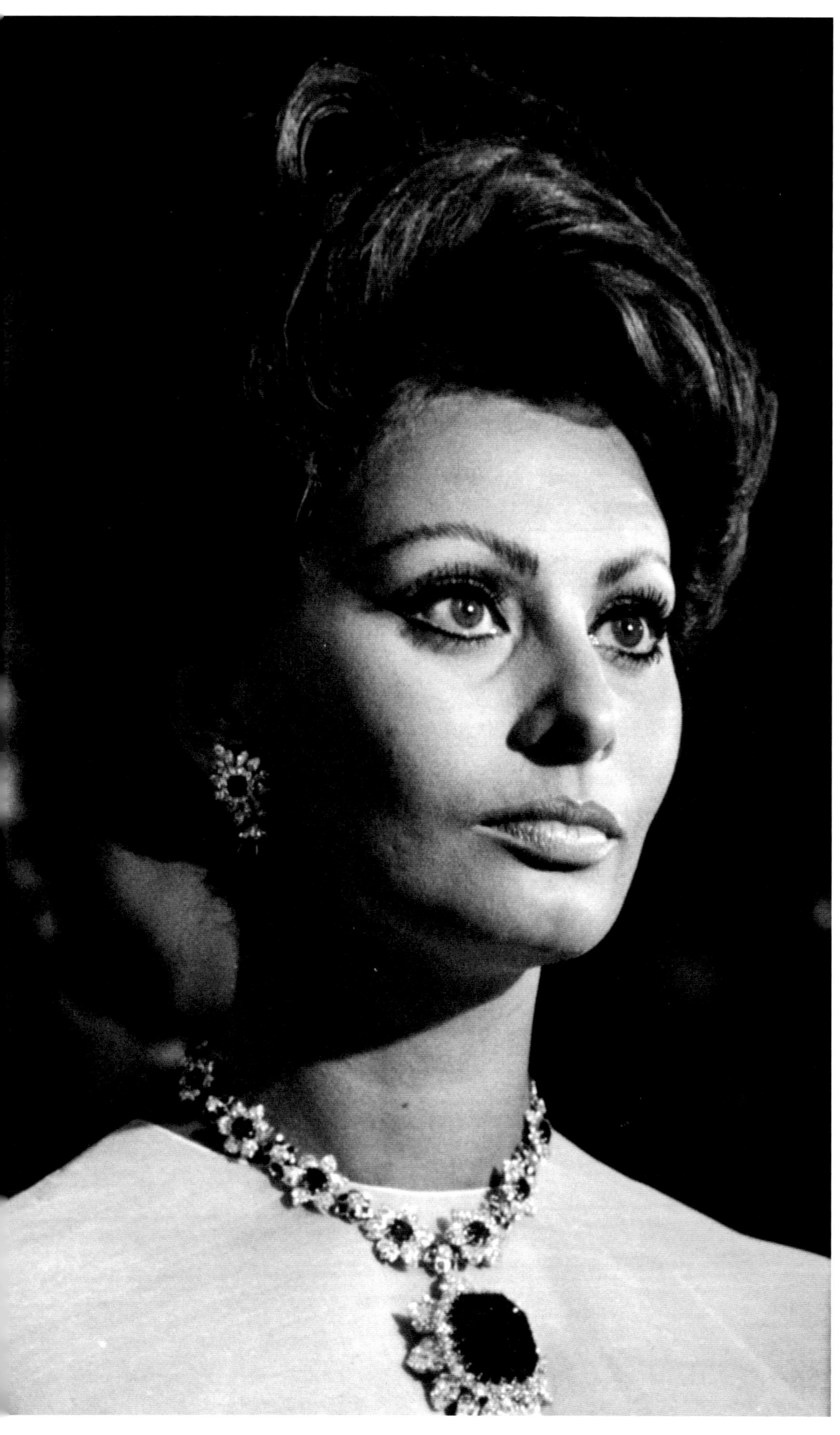

SOPHIA LOREN

MANY YEARS AGO, the Museum of Modern Art had a Sophia Loren film festival. A mob of invited guests and photographers assembled in a basement where she was going to give a press conference. It was pure bedlam. I had never seen so many papparazzi in one place. Everybody was blocking everybody else, and there was no way to find an opening for my camera. After a five-minute session, we were all asked to leave. Being the last one out, I took my time and managed to get several more exposures. She was very gracious. When I thanked her, she said, "I hope you got what you wanted."

"One never does," I said.

"That's very true," she said, smiling.

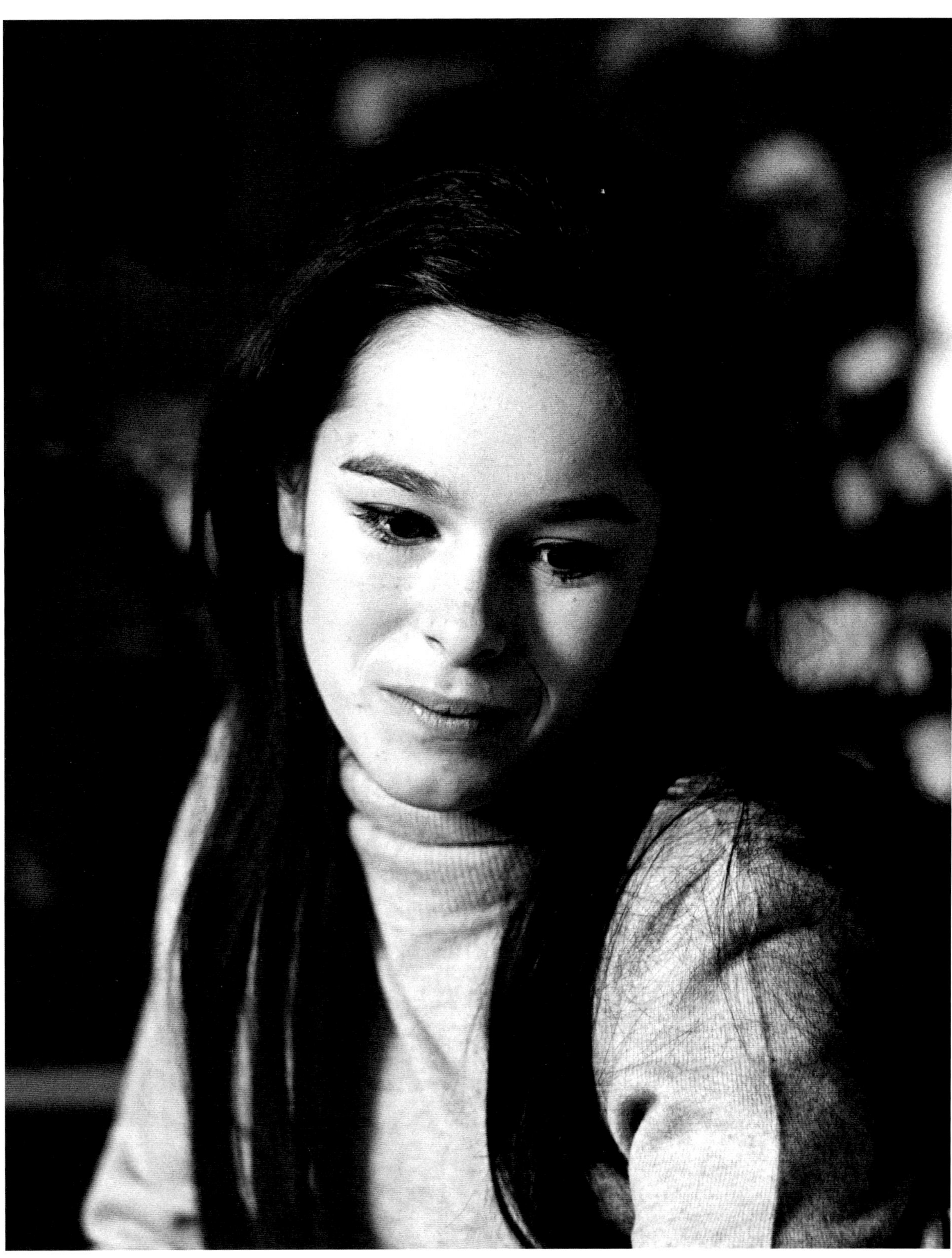

GERALDINE CHAPLIN

GERALDINE CHAPLIN strongly resembled her mother, Oona O'Neill Chaplin. Many years ago, during a photo session, I commented on this resemblance. She smiled and told me how, one day, a gentleman had approached her at a restaurant and asked how it felt to be married to Charlie Chaplin.

"I told him to ask my mother," she said.

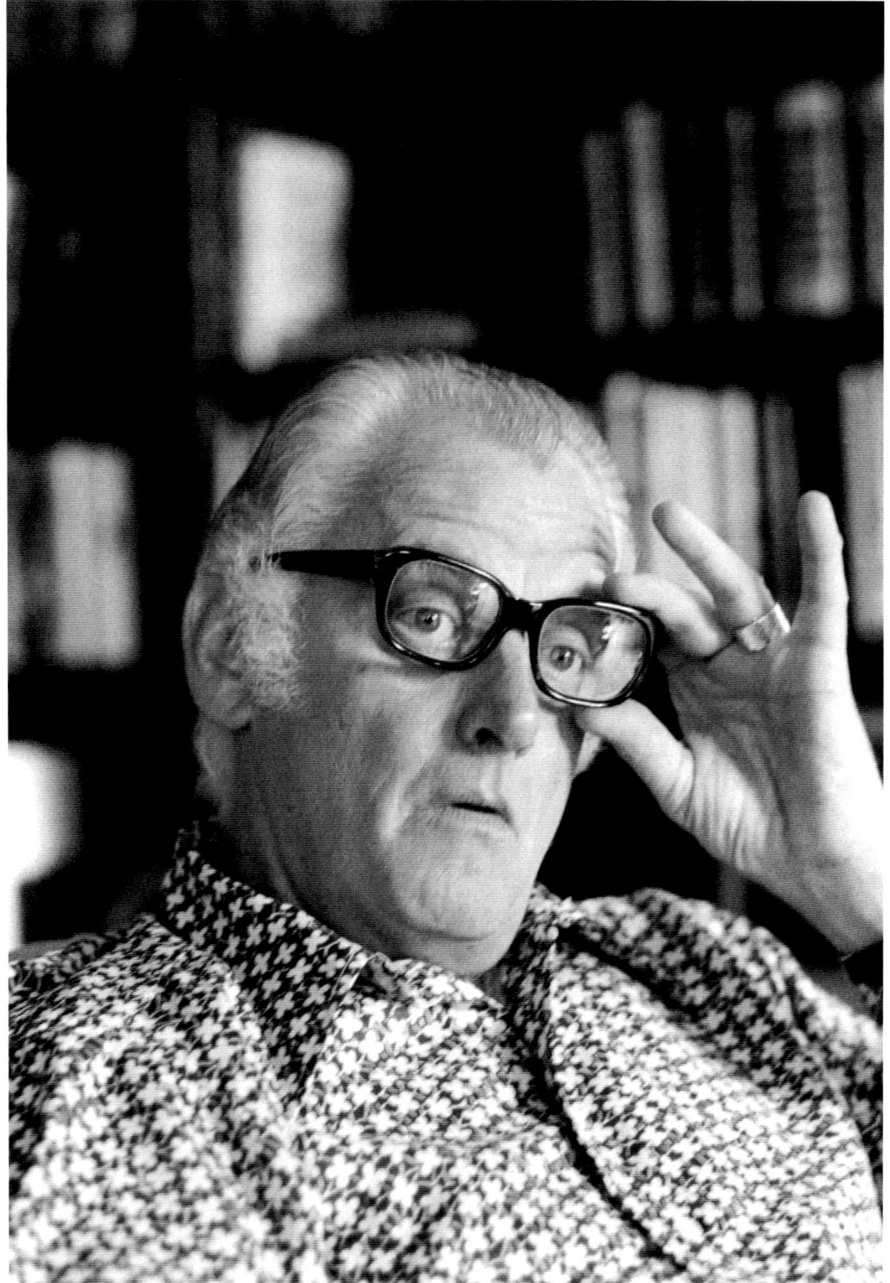

ART CARNEY

ART CARNEY, ONE OF MY FAVORITE COMEDIANS, sat in an easy chair reminiscing about his career. As I watched him from close up and listened to him talk, it was obvious to me that he missed being in the limelight. I realized that as funny as he was on stage, he must have had some sad moments in real life. After the interview was over, I told him how much my family used to enjoy him in *The Honeymooners.*

"That is awfully kind of you to say," he said, looking at me sadly, "but you know, the honeymoon is over."

LIV ULLMANN

LIV ULLMANN WAS EXHAUSTED when she finished rehearsals for Ibsen's *A Doll's House* at Lincoln Center. However, she was willing to let me photograph her in her dressing room if we kept it a brief session. What a friendly, warm person she turned out to be. There were scenic posters of Norway on one wall of her dressing room. She asked me if I could take a picture of her with a poster.

"This one is for my mother," she said. I promised to send her a print.

"I saw you in *Scenes From a Marriage,*" I said. "You were magnificent." I wasn't trying to flatter her; I really meant it.

"Are you still married?" she asked. "I certainly am," I said, and we had a good laugh.

"Is the film supposed to be the catalyst for breaking up marriages?" I asked.

"Well," she said, "in some cases it could." This made me think and wonder if it ever affected her own marriage, but I didn't have the courage to ask.

When I was leaving, she walked me to the door, embraced me, and said, "I get such good *veebrations* from you."

I was speechless. For the rest of the day, I walked on a cloud, and ever since, I think of her as the loveliest human being I've ever photographed. ▶

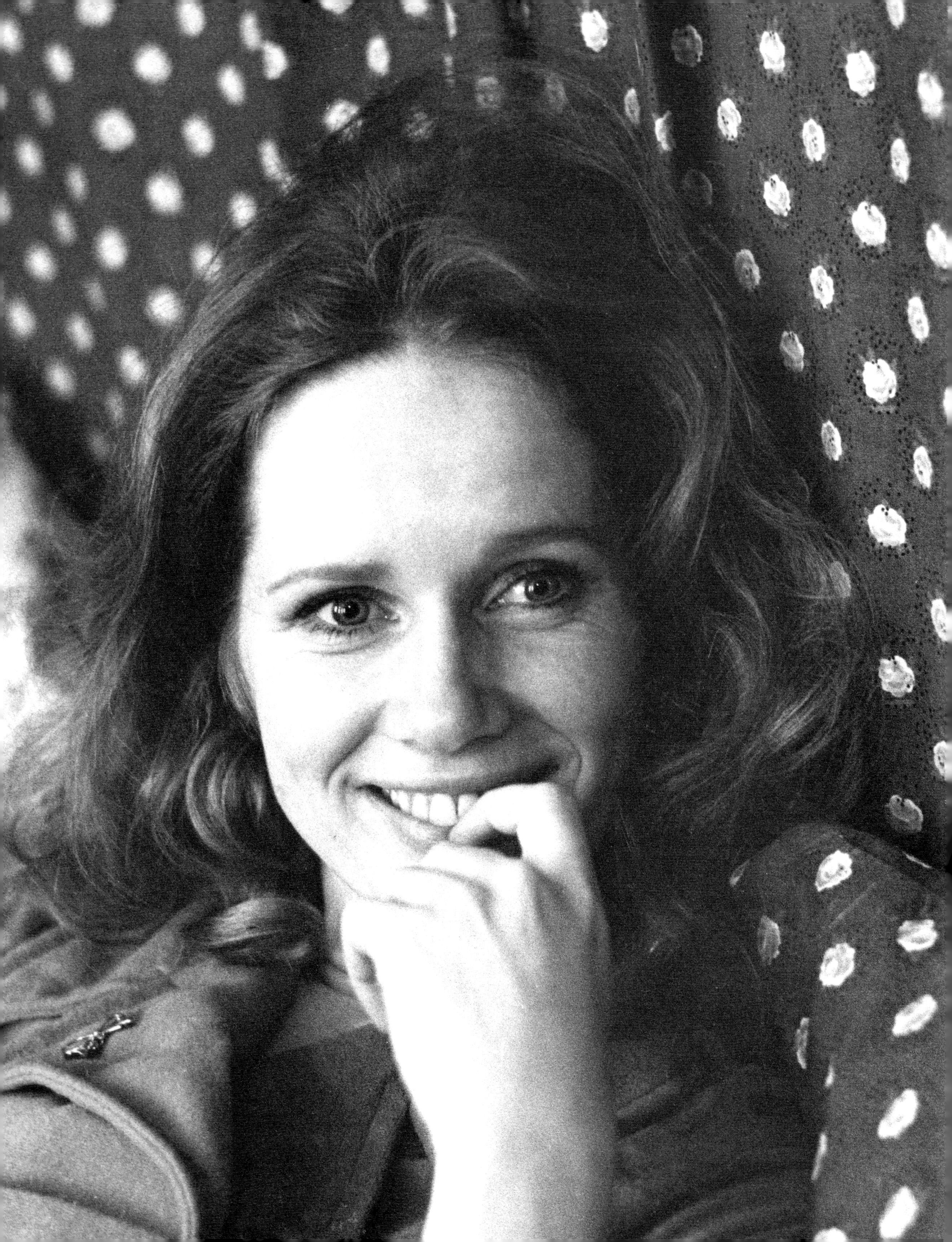

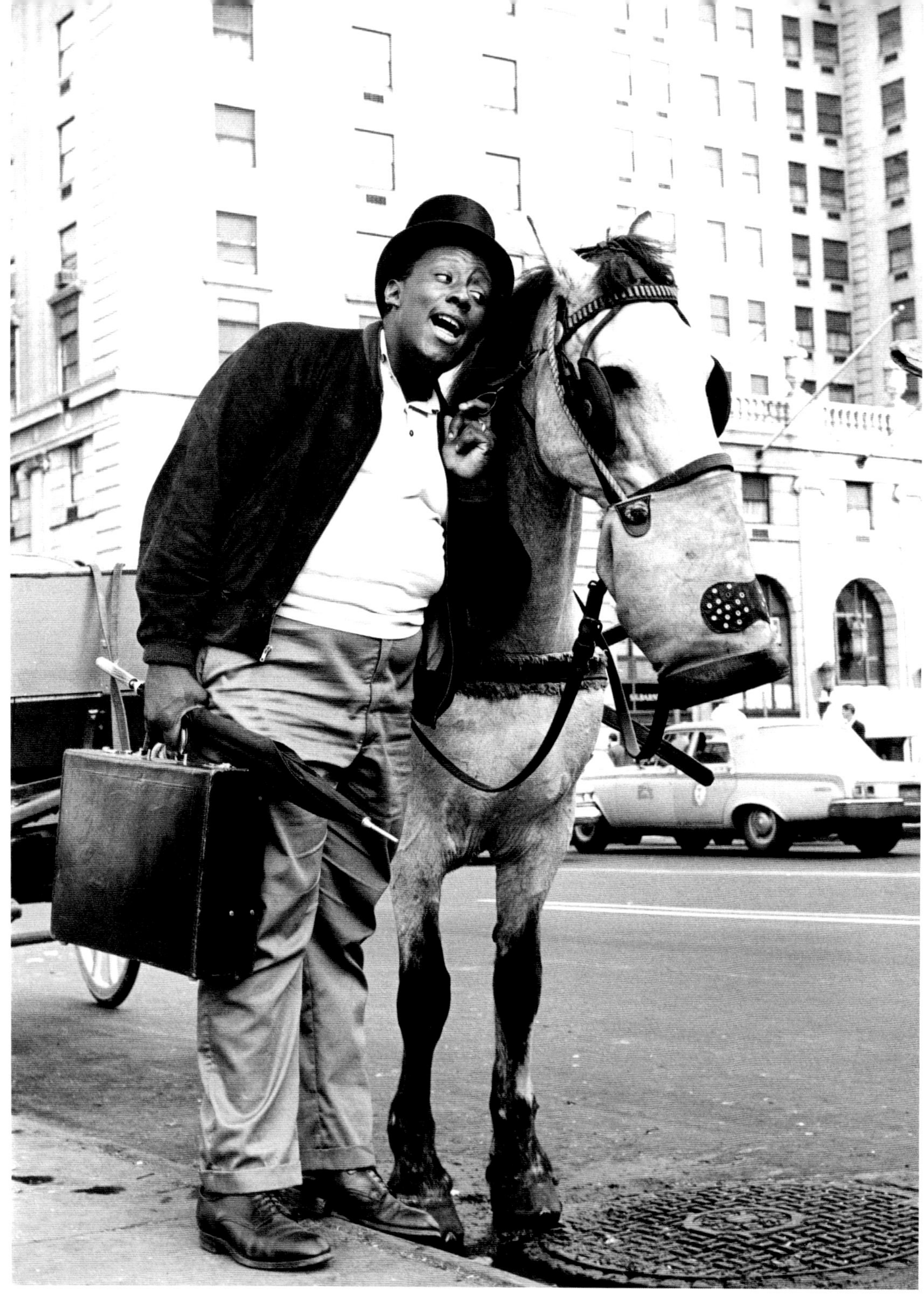

GODFREY CAMBRIDGE

I FIRST MET GODFREY CAMBRIDGE in the early 1960s when he was in Jean Genet's play *The Blacks*. I was on assignment for the *Herald Tribune* and had to show how cab drivers in New York City would ignore African-Americans and not stop to pick them up.

Godfrey volunteered to be the model. He stood on a busy street waving a ten dollar bill. Several empty cabs went by without stopping. When one cab finally stopped, Godfrey told him that it was a photo shoot and that he didn't really need a ride. The cabbie was annoyed. "Do I get paid for stopping?" he asked. "Of course," said Godfrey, in a serious tone of voice. "Send me a bill." The cabbie became angry and took off. Shortly after, Godfrey ripped the rear door off a cab that refused to take him where he was going.

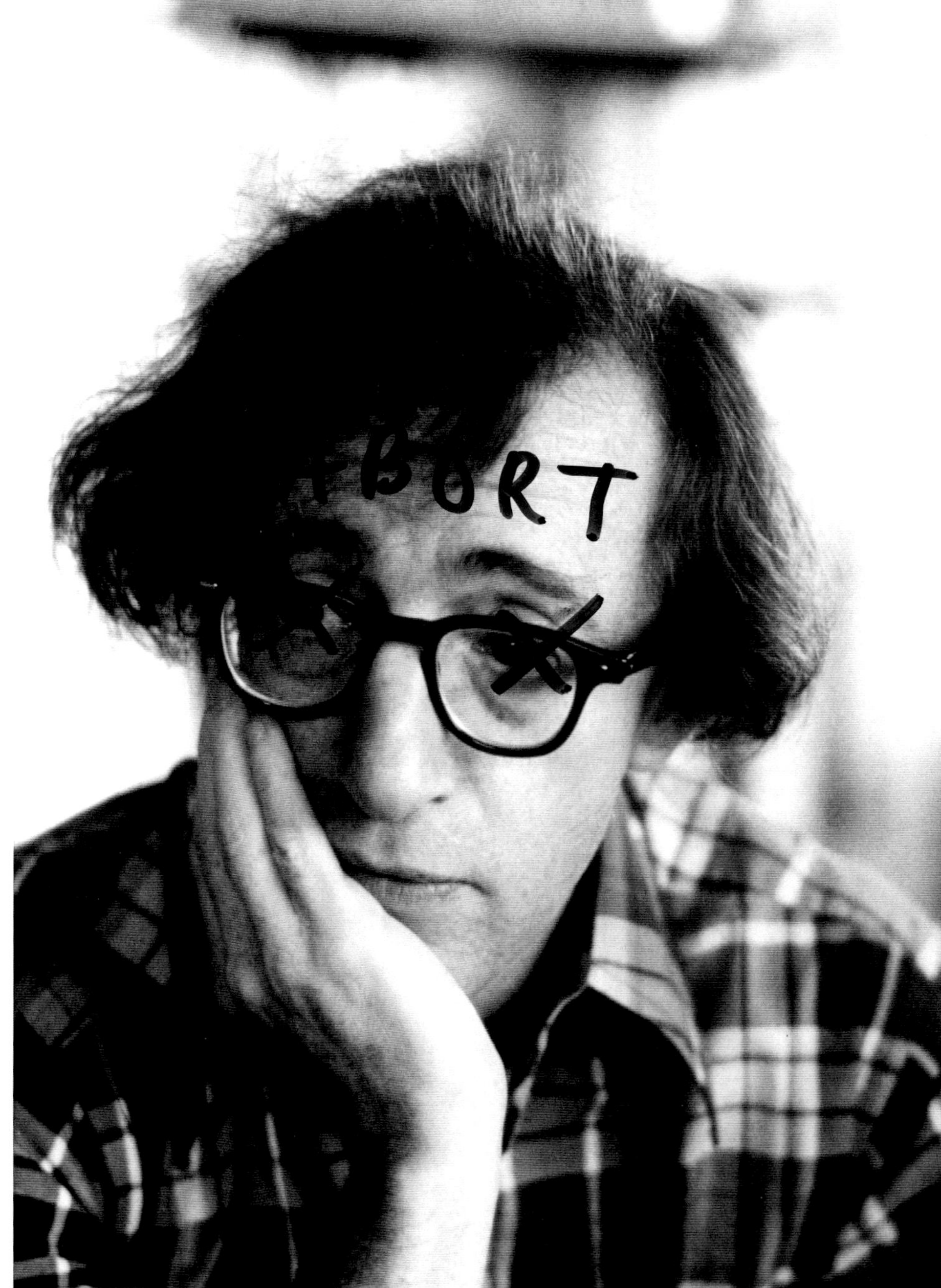

~~WOODY ALLEN~~

BEING AN ADMIRER OF WOODY ALLEN, I was very excited when I was assigned to photograph him. It was a Saturday morning when I rang his door bell. He opened the door and motioned me to come inside. When I greeted him, he told me almost in a whisper that he had a bad case of laryngitis.

"I'm sorry," I said, thinking of the interviewer. How was he going to do an interview if he couldn't talk?

He showed me into the living room and left me there alone. I could hear him puttering around in the kitchen. While setting up my equipment, I had a magnificent view of Central Park through the picture window. I stood there watching, and was totally mesmerized. Suddenly, I heard the door bell, and Allen ran to open the door.

"Hello, Jack. Come inside. Let me have your coat," I heard him say, quite loud, without a trace of hoarseness.

Soon, the interview was in progress, and Woody Allen was talking normally, elaborating about some of his film techniques. After photographing him for more than two hours, I decided that I had enough pictures and started to pack.

As I bid him good-bye, I couldn't resist asking: "Mr. Allen, could you tell me what you used for your laryngitis?" He looked at me quite puzzled, as if he had entirely forgotten what he told me when I first arrived.

BING CROSBY

THE FIRST TIME I saw Bing Crosby in person was at an awards presentation in New York City. He stood alone at one side of the stage, arms crossed over his chest, looking straight ahead. I came closer, hoping to get a picture of him.

"Hello, Mr. Crosby. How are you?"

"Not too bad," he said, extending his hand. Suddenly, he must have noticed someone he knew, some distance away, because, like a semaphore, his arm went all the way up. Quickly, without even enough time to focus, I took a picture. When he realized what had happened, he turned and said, "I sure would like to see that picture."

"Maybe you shall," I said, "but I can't promise." Several months went by before I could mail a print to him. But one day later, I read his obituary in the newspaper. ▶

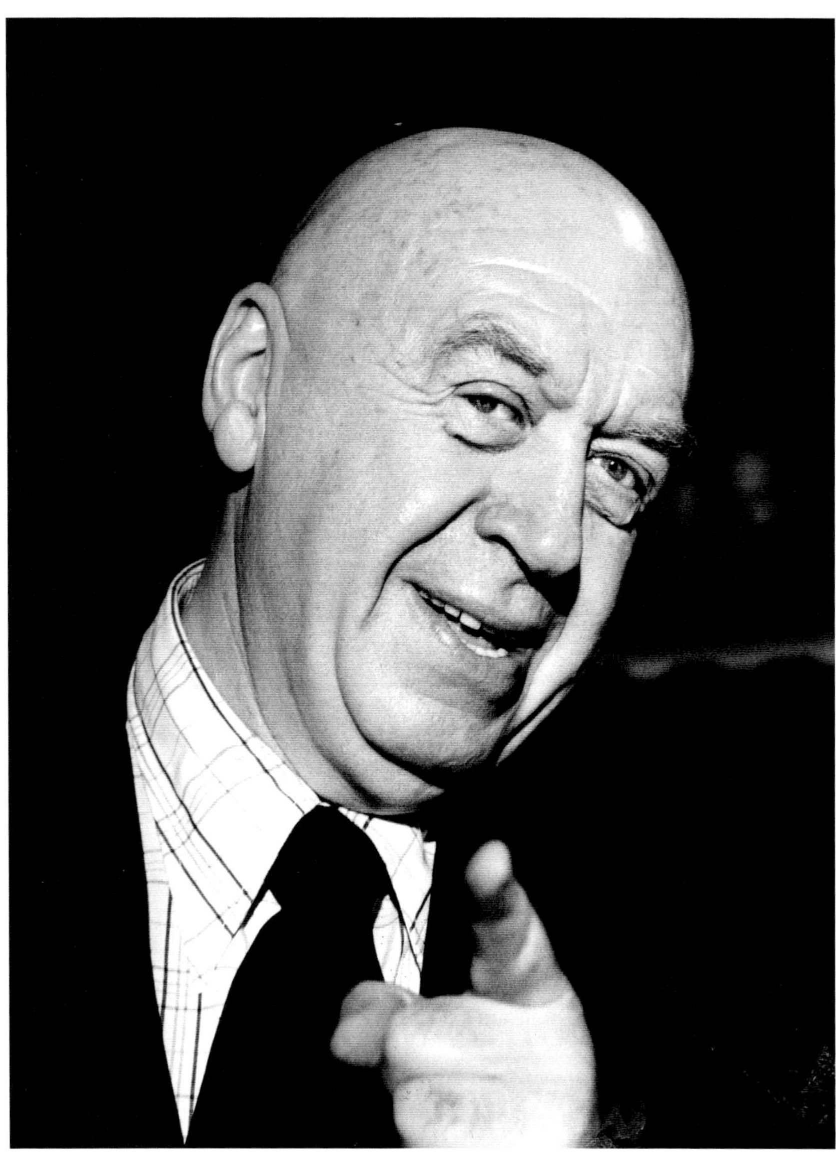

OTTO PREMINGER

OTTO PREMINGER, the film producer and director, was having a reading at a Broadway theater. As soon as I came in, he greeted me and said, "As soon as I appear in New York, you seem to follow me around. Do you by any chance work for J. Edgar Hoover?"

"Do I look like I do?"

"One never knows," he said, and started laughing.

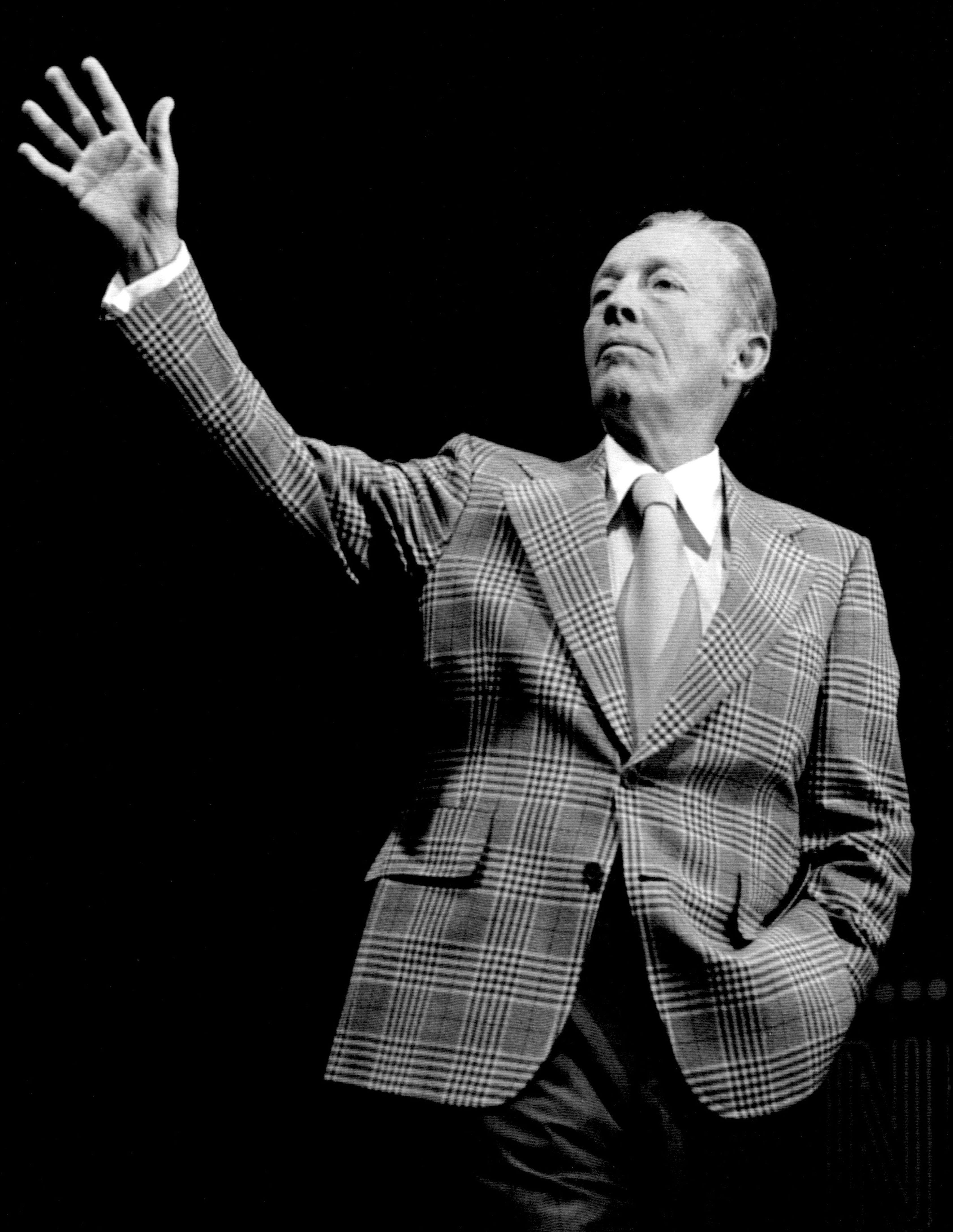

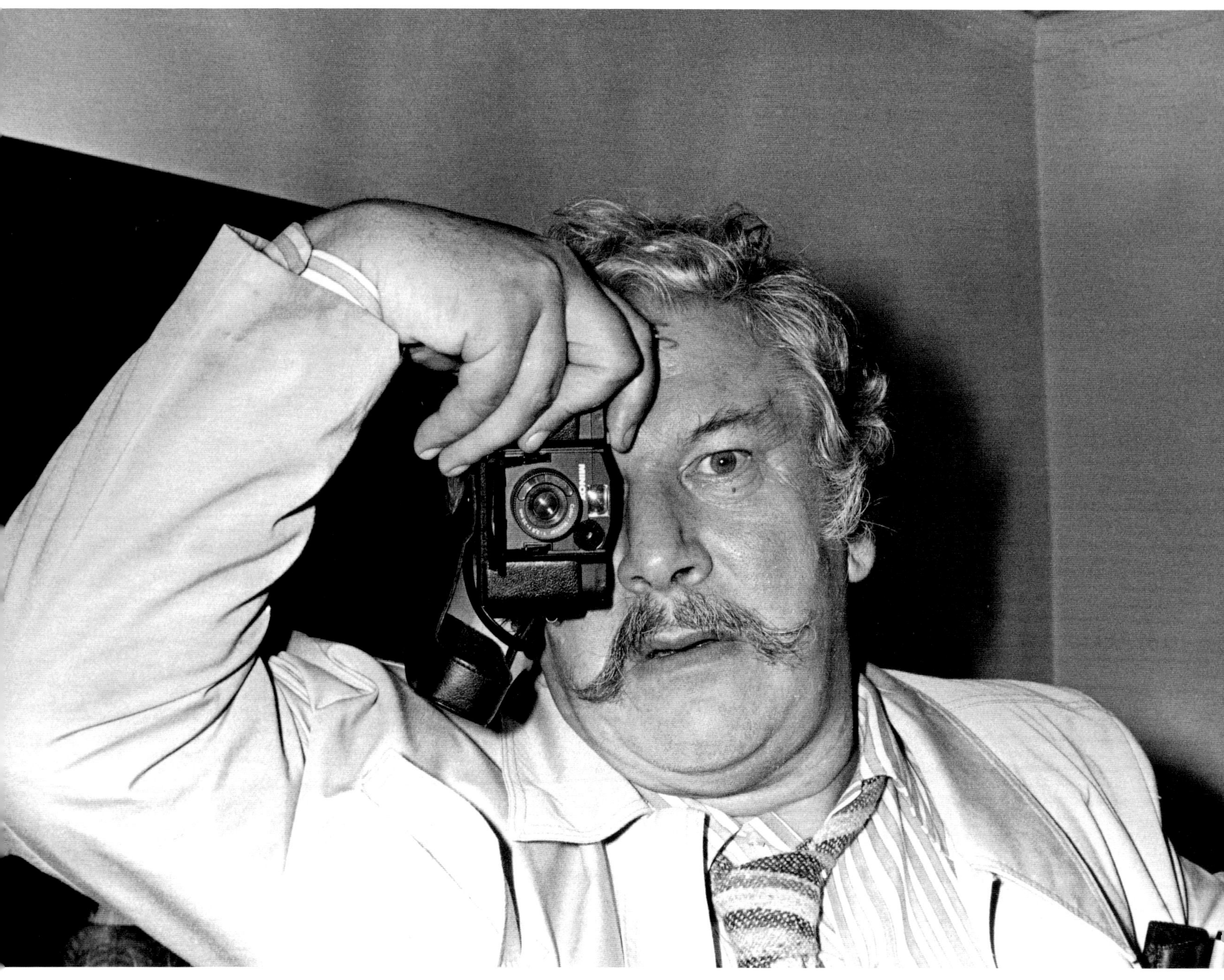

PETER USTINOV

WHEN I ARRIVED at the hotel to photograph Peter Ustinov, the popular British actor, the first thing he said was that I was fifteen minutes late, which was true. I told him that I couldn't get a cab, and that in New York very few people are ever on time.

When I took out my camera, he went over to his suitcase, took out a pocket-sized Minox camera, pointed it at me, and took a picture. I thought I heard the buzz of a shutter. "You don't mind," he asked, "to be photographed by Ustinov?"

We agreed to exchange photos, provided we each liked them. Many years went by and I didn't hear from him. Nor did I see the picture. I guess he didn't like what he did, or maybe he lost my address. I still like the pictures I took of him.

Politicians & Public Figures

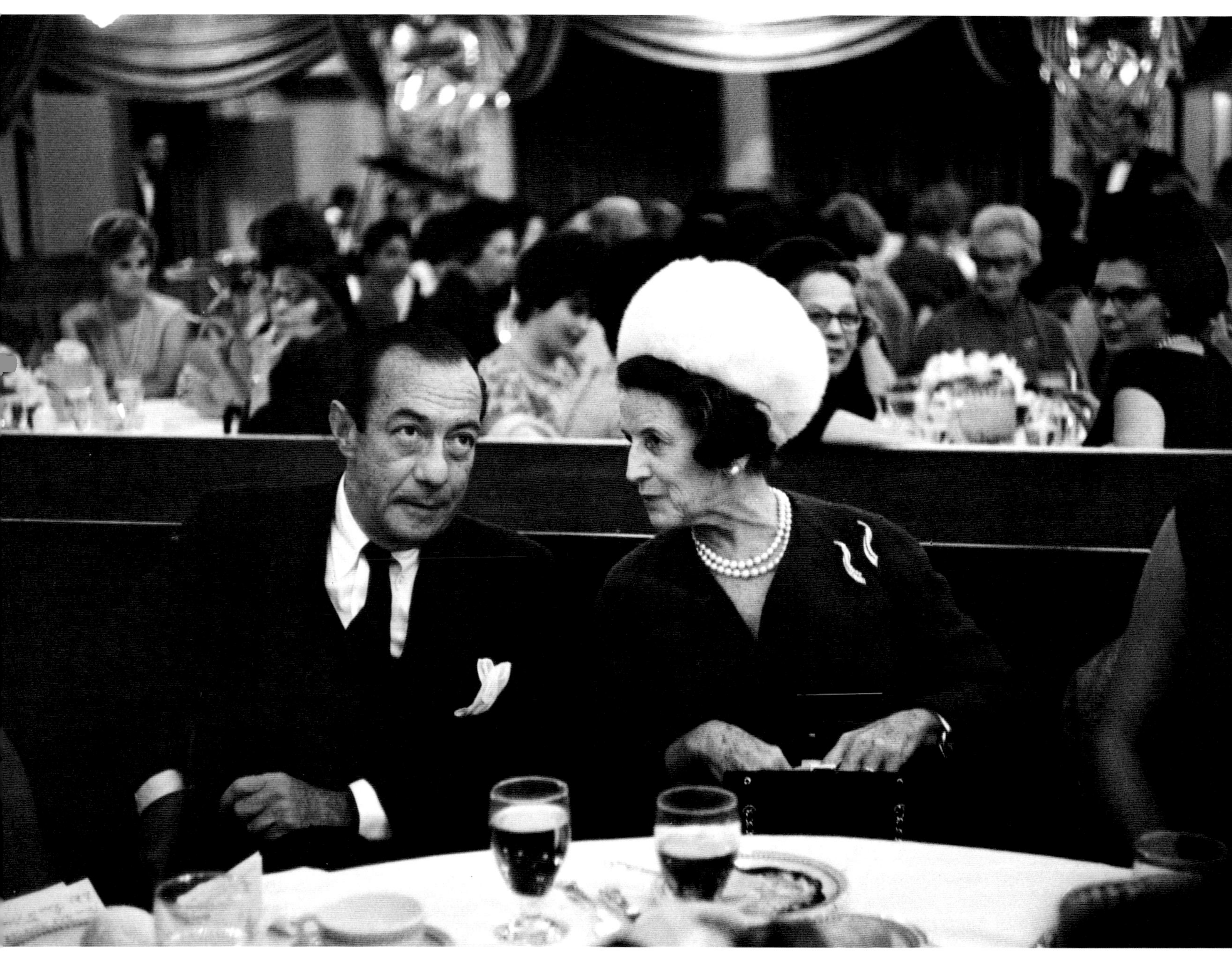

ROSE KENNEDY & ROBERT F. WAGNER

SOMETIME IN THE 1960s I photographed a luncheon at the Hotel Astor in New York City that was to raise funds for the benefit of mental health programs. I saw Rose Kennedy with Mayor Robert Wagner at one of the tables, and thought it would be nice to have a picture of the two of them together, a rare opportunity.

After I took the picture, Rose Kennedy thanked me for not using any flash. "It always blinds me," she said.

The mayor nodded in agreement.

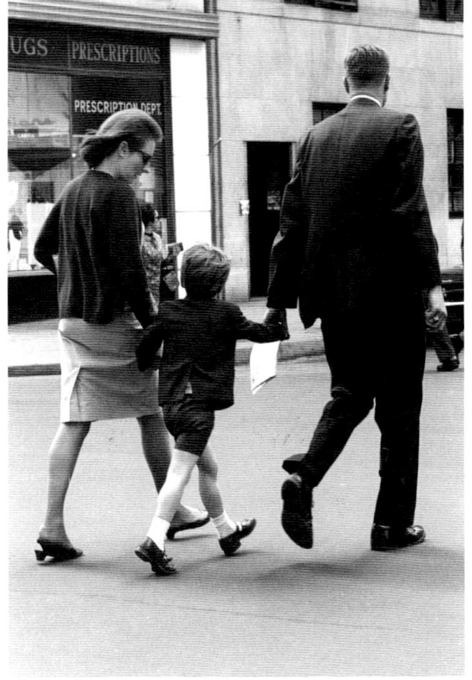

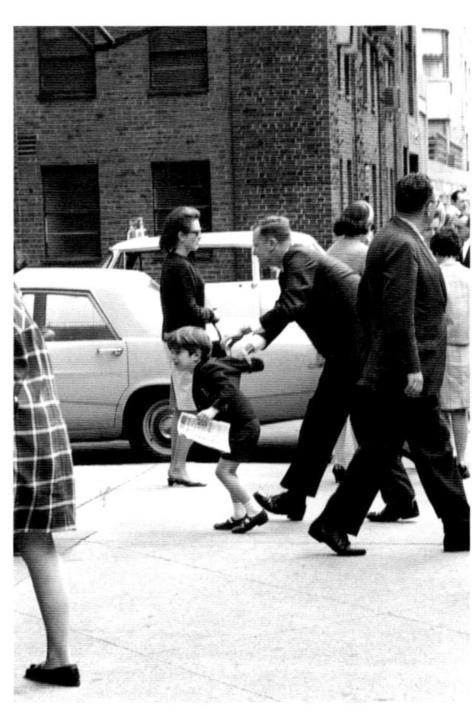

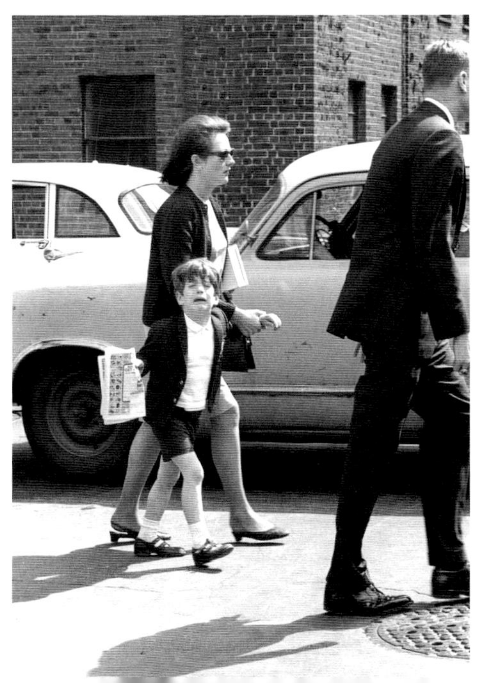

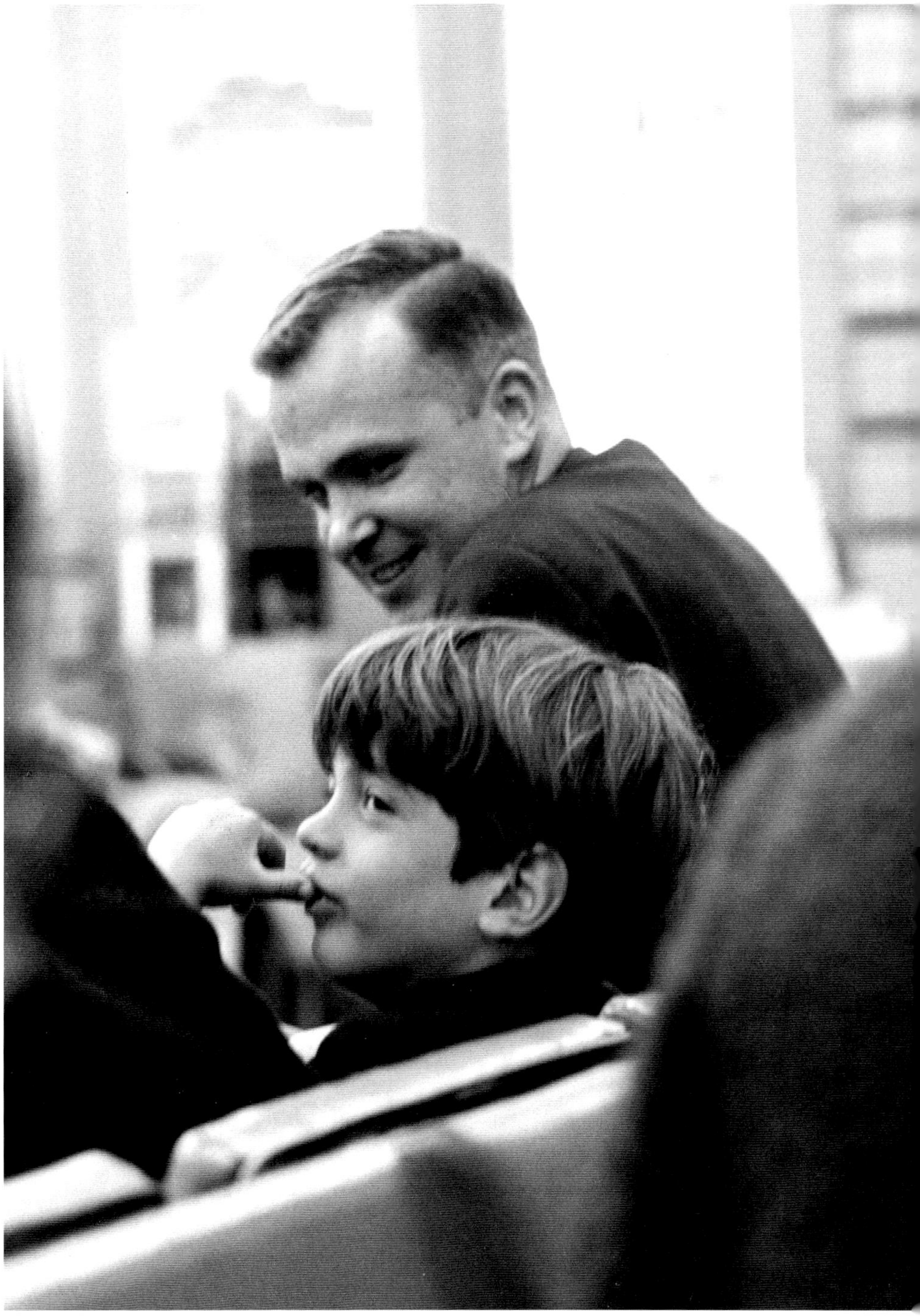

JOHN F. KENNEDY JR.

ON MY WAY BACK from an assignment sometime in the 1960s, I noticed a commotion across the street. Some bystanders were watching as two men were trying to take little John F. Kennedy Jr. down the block. He did his best to free himself from them, but didn't quite succeed. I realized that they were Secret Service agents and decided to follow for a bit. I got a few shots from across the street with a telephoto lens and then they went inside a shoe store. I was curious and entered the shop after them, showing my press card and asking permission to shoot. He was already trying on some shoes, and when he saw me, he gave me a big smile. I returned the smile, thanked him for being so nice, and said goodby.

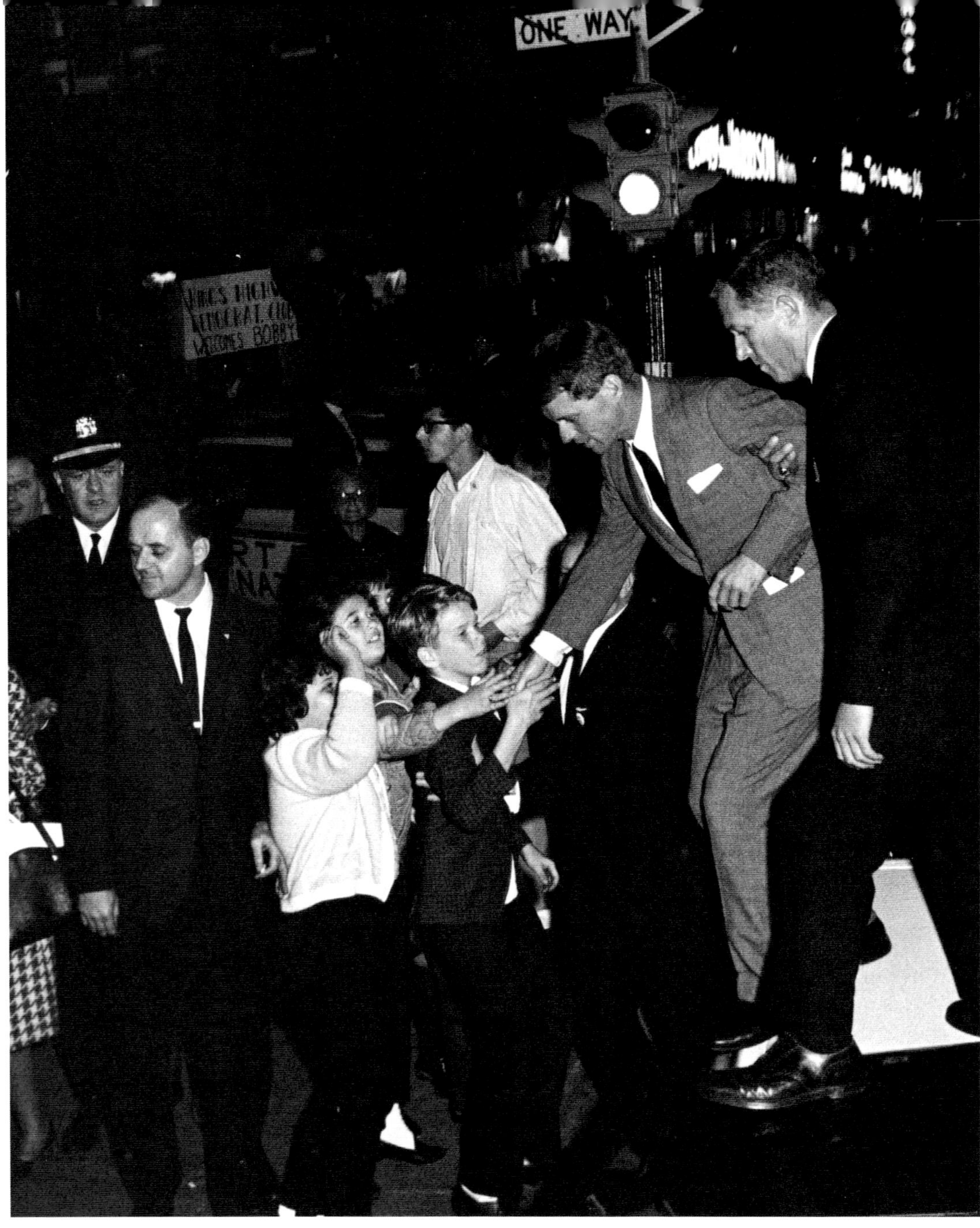

ROBERT F. KENNEDY

I WAS WITH SENATOR ROBERT KENNEDY when he campaigned in upstate New York on behalf of Frank O'Connor, who was running for governor. The chartered plane was very crowded, and the weather was bad. During the trip, reporters would ask Kennedy for his autograph, and he often obliged. I thought of my two young children who would have liked to have his autograph, but I didn't feel right asking. At some point I overcame my shyness and somewhat reluctantly asked if he wouldn't mind signing his name for my two children. He asked their names and ages. "Howard and Eva," I said, and he wrote it down. I thanked him, and he smiled. "The kids will appreciate it," I said.

One year later, on the Eastern Airlines shuttle to Washington, D.C., the Senator sat across from me on the left at the single window seat, with a briefcase in his lap, reading some documents. Suddenly, a piece of paper fell under my seat. When I picked it up and handed it to him, we exchanged greetings and he said, "How are Howard and Eva?" I was stunned. "How could anyone remember the names of two kids he never met?" I asked. "These things happen," he said, and he gave me a big smile.

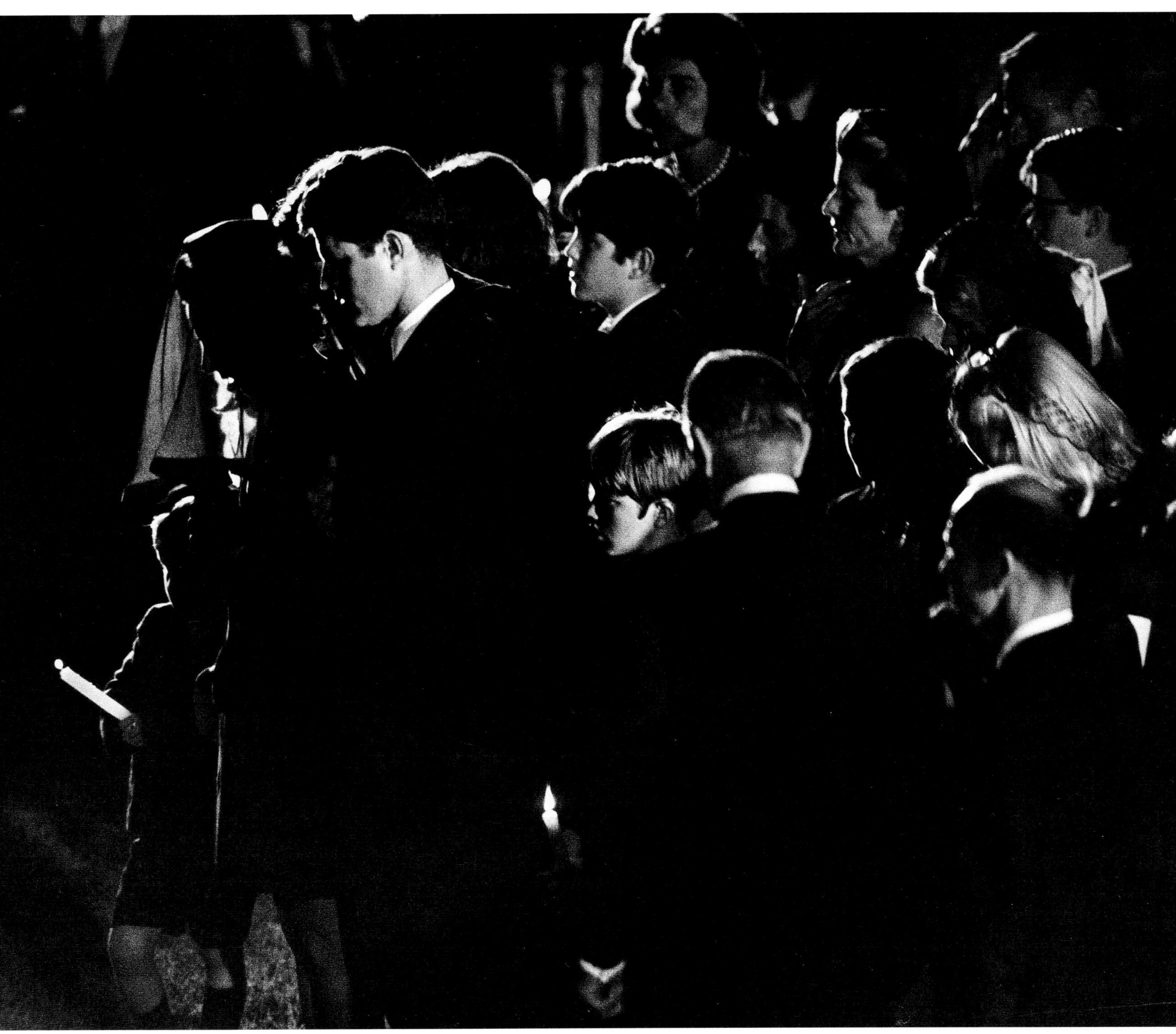

ROBERT F. KENNEDY

THE WEATHER WAS BEAUTIFUL on June 8, 1968, when I arrived at Arlington National Cemetery to photograph Robert F. Kennedy's funeral. There were several hundred journalists and diplomats from various countries. At some point it was announced that due to an accident the train carrying the coffin would be delayed. It finally arrived late at night. It was a long, sad day for everyone.

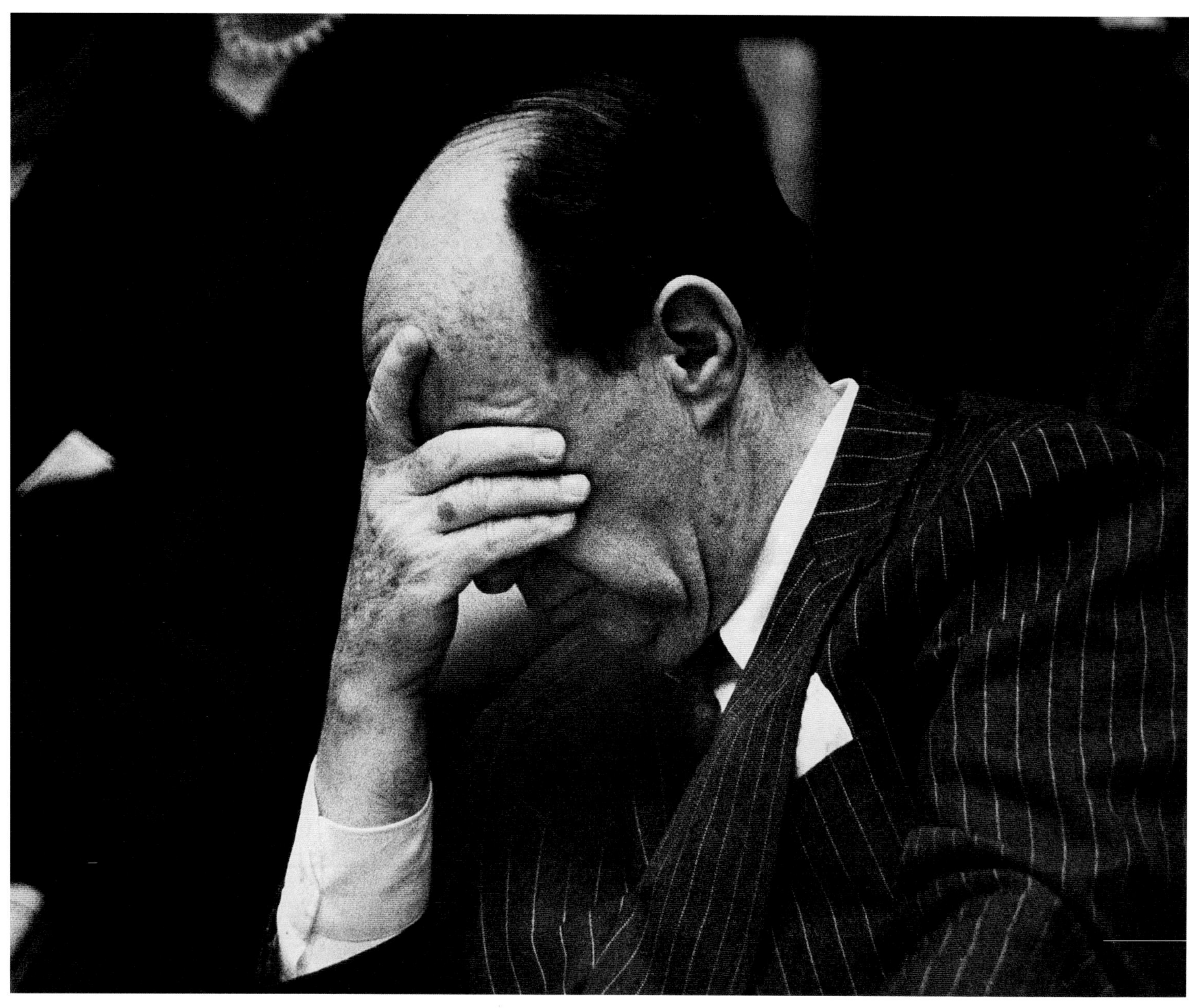

ADLAI STEVENSON

I PHOTOGRAPHED MANY DIFFERENT STATESMEN at the United Nations over a period of two decades, but I will never forget Adlai Stevenson. He was the U.S. delegate during the Cuban Missile Crisis. I saw him at his desk during a break between meetings, with his hands covering his face, resting. I had seen him on the floor before the meeting began. There was an air of resignation about him, and a tired look. He wasn't the same man I remembered from earlier years.

Some weeks before, I gave him a photo that I had taken of him at his desk. I didn't hand it to him directly, but only left it there, so as not to disturb him. Some time later, as I walked by his desk, he looked up and smiled. "Young man," he said, "thank you for the photograph. It was very kind of you." That shot was taken from a long distance, maybe 50 or 75 feet, with a telephoto lens. We had never spoken before, and I'll never know how he knew that I had taken it.

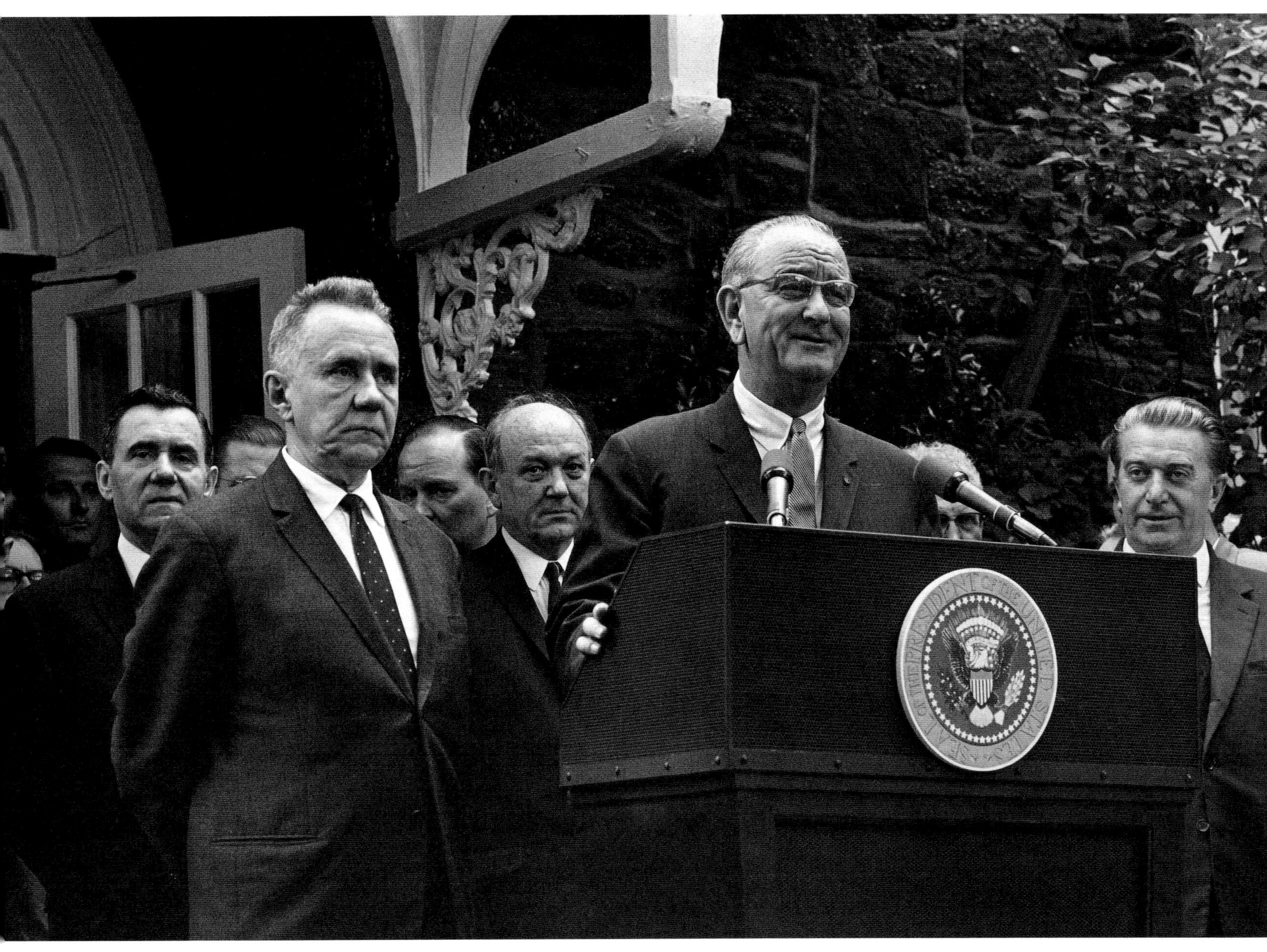

LYNDON JOHNSON & ALEXEI KOSYGIN

NOT MANY OF US REMEMBER the historic meeting of the two superpower leaders at Glassboro College in New Jersey.

After a long meeting, President Johnson and Premier Kosygin had an outdoor press conference. The security was unprecedented. Federal, state, and local police were everywhere. They looked inside camera bags and inside ladies' pocketbooks, as well as any suspect parcel they could lay their hands on.

Waiting for the press conference to begin, I was pushed from behind by a mob of reporters and forced to step out of line. Suddenly, two state troopers appeared, ready to arrest me, and they might have done so if it weren't for President Johnson, who noticed the commotion and instructed one of his aides to intervene.

When the conference was over, I was surprised to hear the police chief apologize for the misunderstanding.

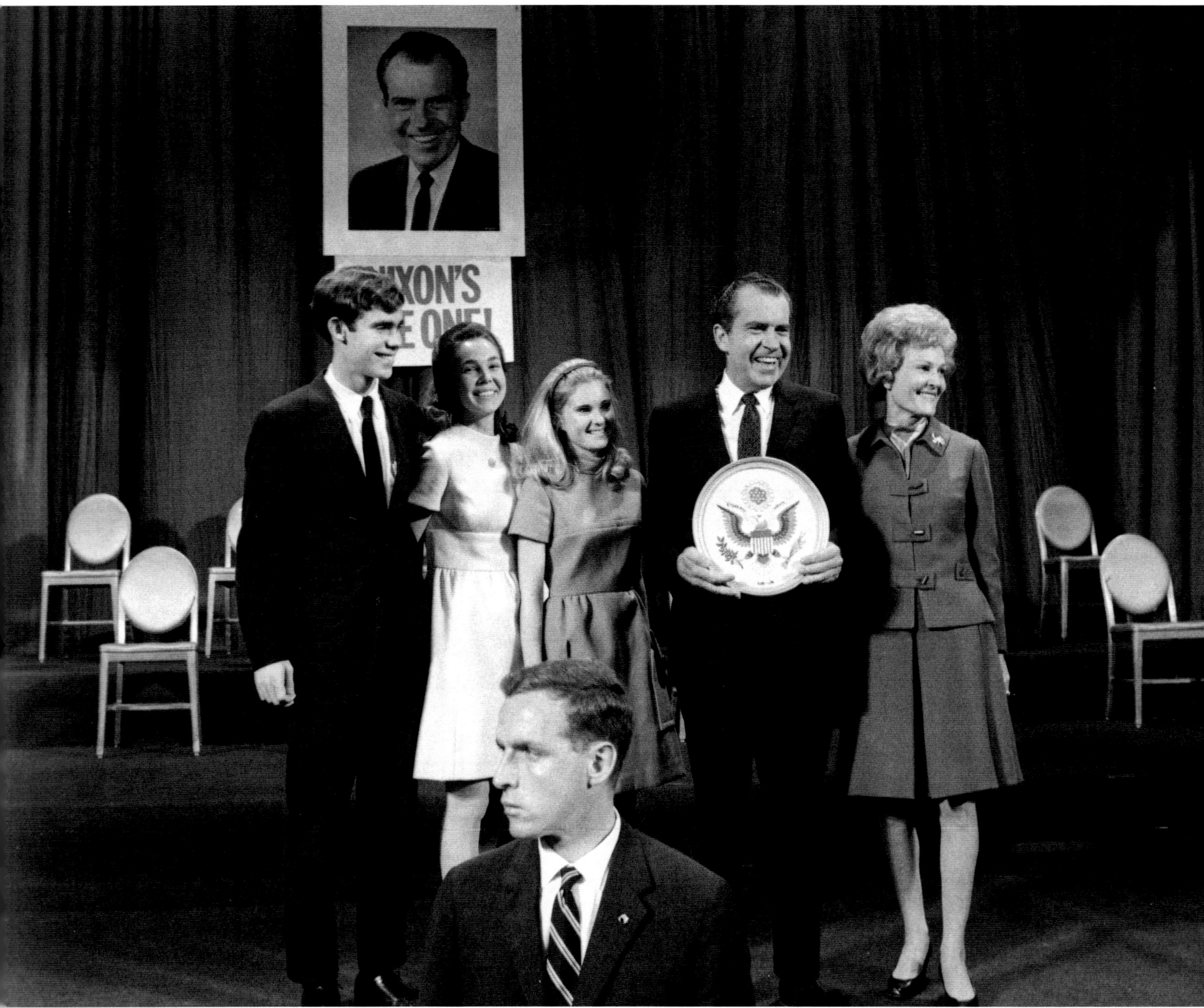

RICHARD NIXON

WHEN RICHARD NIXON WON the 1968 presidential election, he gave his acceptance speech in the ballroom of the Waldorf Astoria Hotel, which was his New York City headquarters.

It was well past midnight when he appeared onstage with his family. After the speech, he proudly displayed a needlepoint depicting an eagle made by his daughter Tricia as a surprise in case he won the election.

Suddenly, a member of the press corps asked how long it took to make, and how much wool was needed. He was told that due to protocol no questions could be asked during or after a presidential acceptance speech. After all, it wasn't a press conference! There was a lot of chuckling all around.

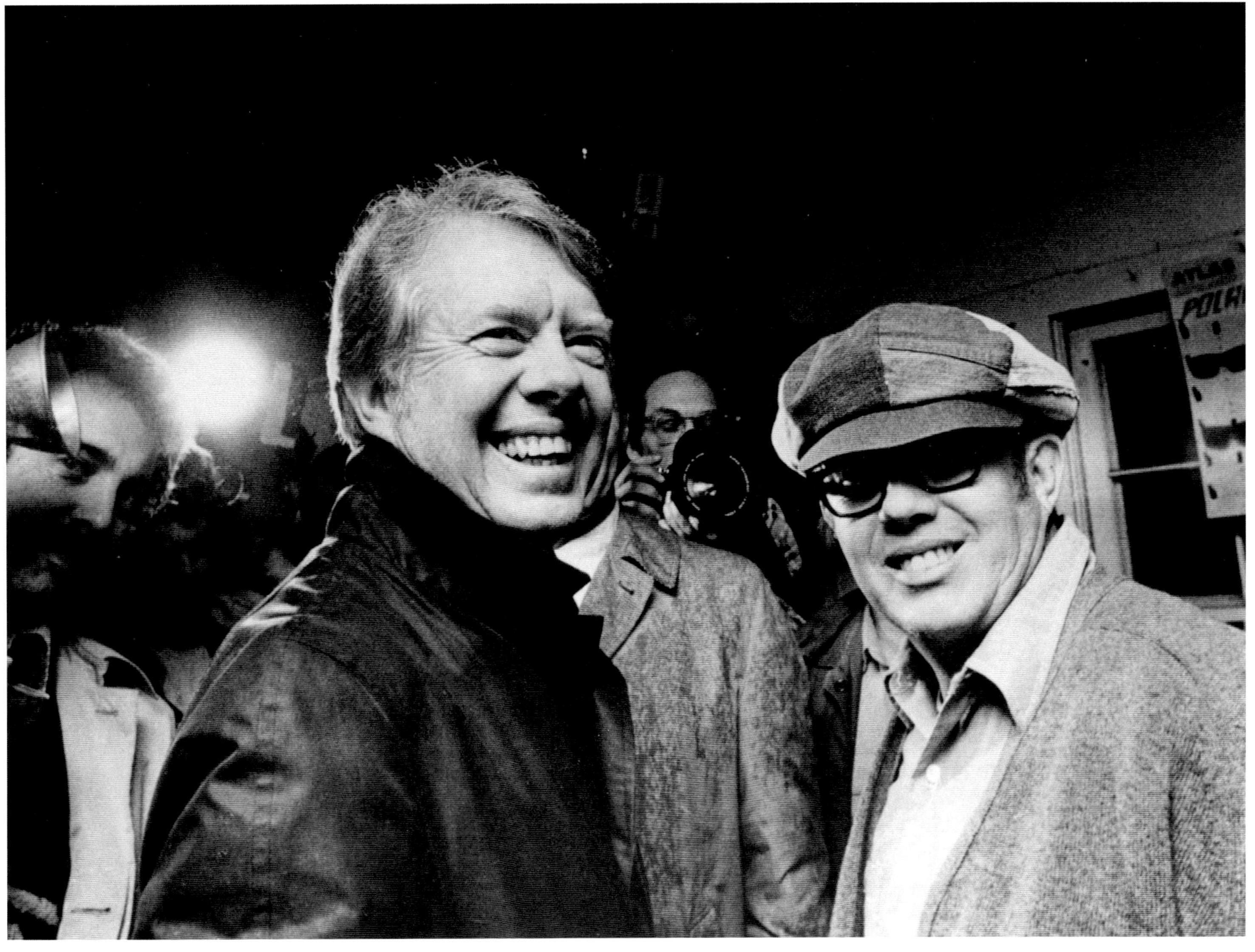

JIMMY CARTER & BILLY CARTER

SHORTLY AFTER JIMMY CARTER BECAME PRESIDENT, his brother Billy decided to run for mayor of Plains, Georgia, against the incumbent four-term mayor, who was also the local barber.

"No one in his right mind should ever run against him, not even Billy Carter," a local shopkeeper said.

Sure enough, Billy lost the election. He obtained a recount, but it didn't change anything. Nevertheless, Billy decided to celebrate. He invited all his friends, and the White House press corps, which was in town with the president, to his gas station.

Everyone was having a good time and cans of Pabst Blue Ribbon beer were plentiful. Unexpectedly, in the middle of a torrential rain, a limousine pulled up and out came President Carter, escorted by two Secret Service men. Billy came out to greet him, they embraced, and they were surrounded by a mob of reporters. My view was blocked, but I was desperate not to miss a good shot, so I yelled out, "Will the two brothers please turn around and look at the camera?" They obliged and that was the only picture I could get that evening.

When I saw Billy the next day, I asked him why he ran for mayor. "It was a lot of fun," he said.

DAVID BEN GURION

ON ONE OF HIS TRIPS TO NEW YORK, David Ben Gurion, the Israeli Prime Minister, was asked to judge a televised Bible contest. The network's stage manager told me that "There is no time for pictures." But after I pleaded with him, he let me into the studio during a five-minute break. Ben Gurion sat there like a monarch, with a serious expression on his face, looking straight ahead, snow-white hair circling his head. There was constant commotion, with technical staff hurrying in and out. I took several shots and then realized that he had not noticed me at all. As I prepared to leave, I went over to thank him for his time.

"Who are you?"

"I'm the photographer," I said, "and I would like you to know that our names begin with identical initials."

"So why aren't you the prime minister?"

"Because I'm too busy taking pictures," I answered. Ben Gurion said something in reply, but I couldn't hear it, because at that moment I was ushered out of the studio. ▶

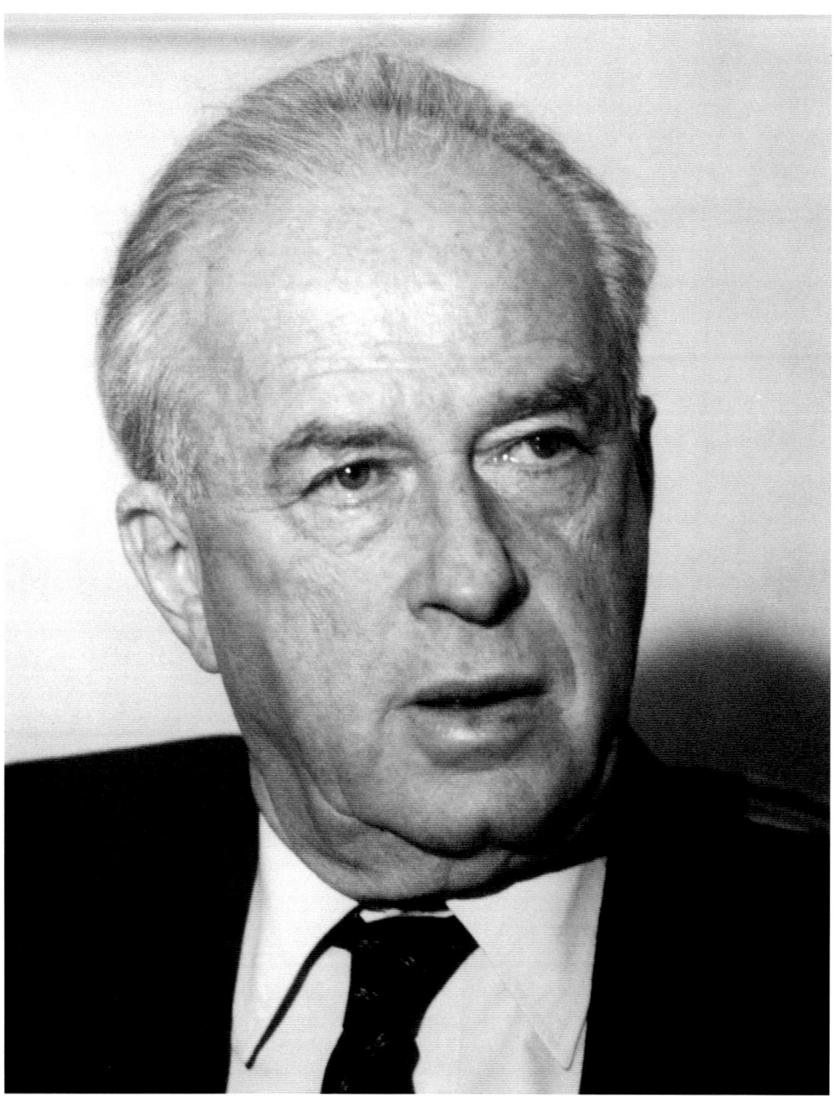

YITZHAK RABIN

YITZHAK RABIN, THE PRIME MINISTER OF ISRAEL, visited New York in 1965 and I was assigned to photograph him. He was very pressed for time, and I was told that I could have only five minutes. When the five minutes were up, I realized that I hadn't put any film in my camera. I was very embarrassed, to say the least. When I admitted my mistake, Rabin thought I was joking.

"Could I have another five minutes," I pleaded.

"Make it in two minutes and not a minute more, and this is not negotiable," he said, quite annoyed.

I had to agree. It was the shortest photo session I ever had.

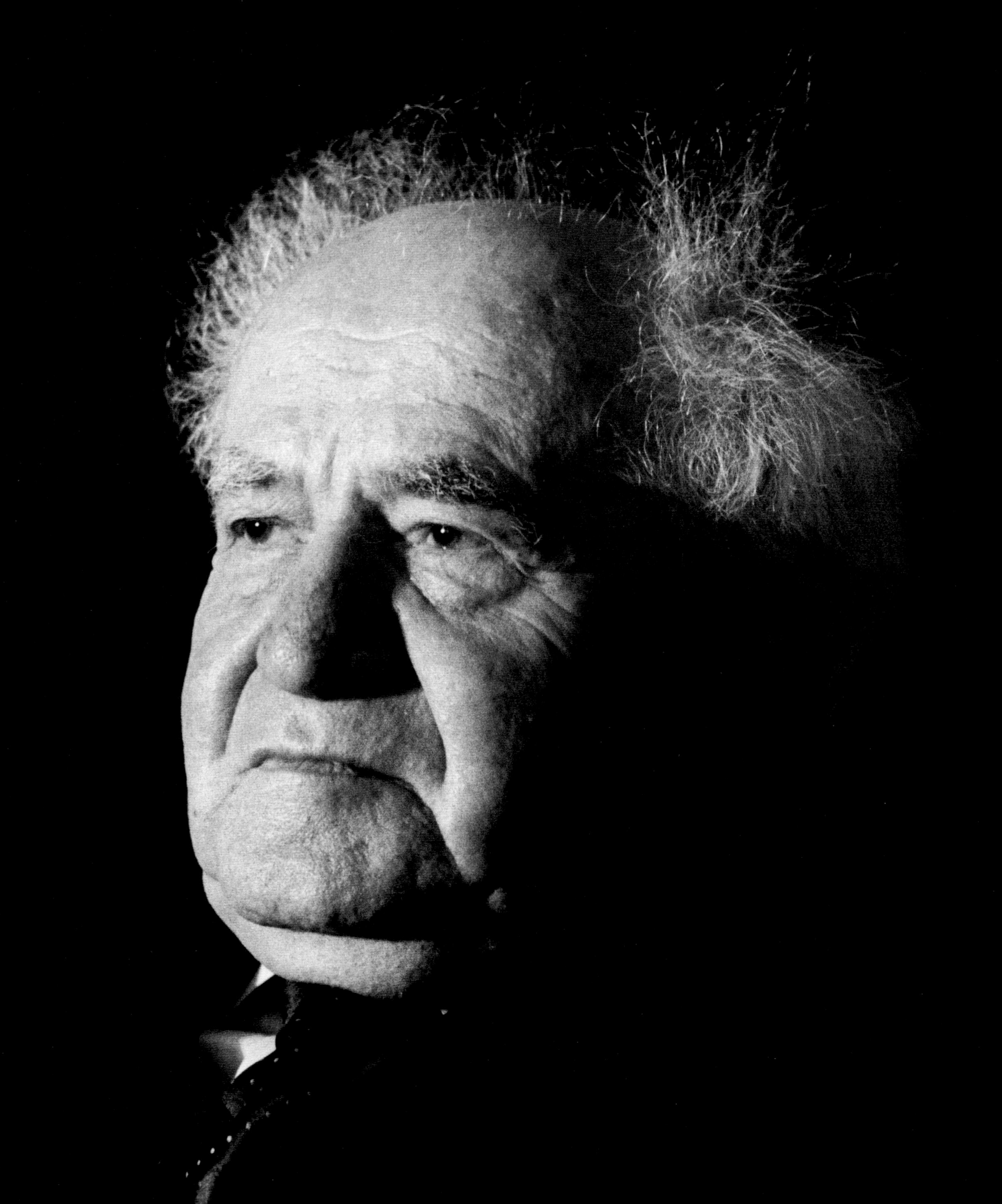

FIDEL CASTRO

THERE WAS A LOT OF EXCITEMENT when Fidel Castro came to speak at the United Nations. Every seat in the General Assembly hall was taken, and security was very tight. Members of the press were checked in, and camera bags were opened and searched. By the time he finally got to speak, I was exhausted just from waiting in the crowded photo booth. All I remember seeing was an animated bundle of energy, and a beard. But one phrase from the speech still stands out in my mind: "La bomba atomica will be doing the rumba." When he finished, there was a standing ovation. ▶

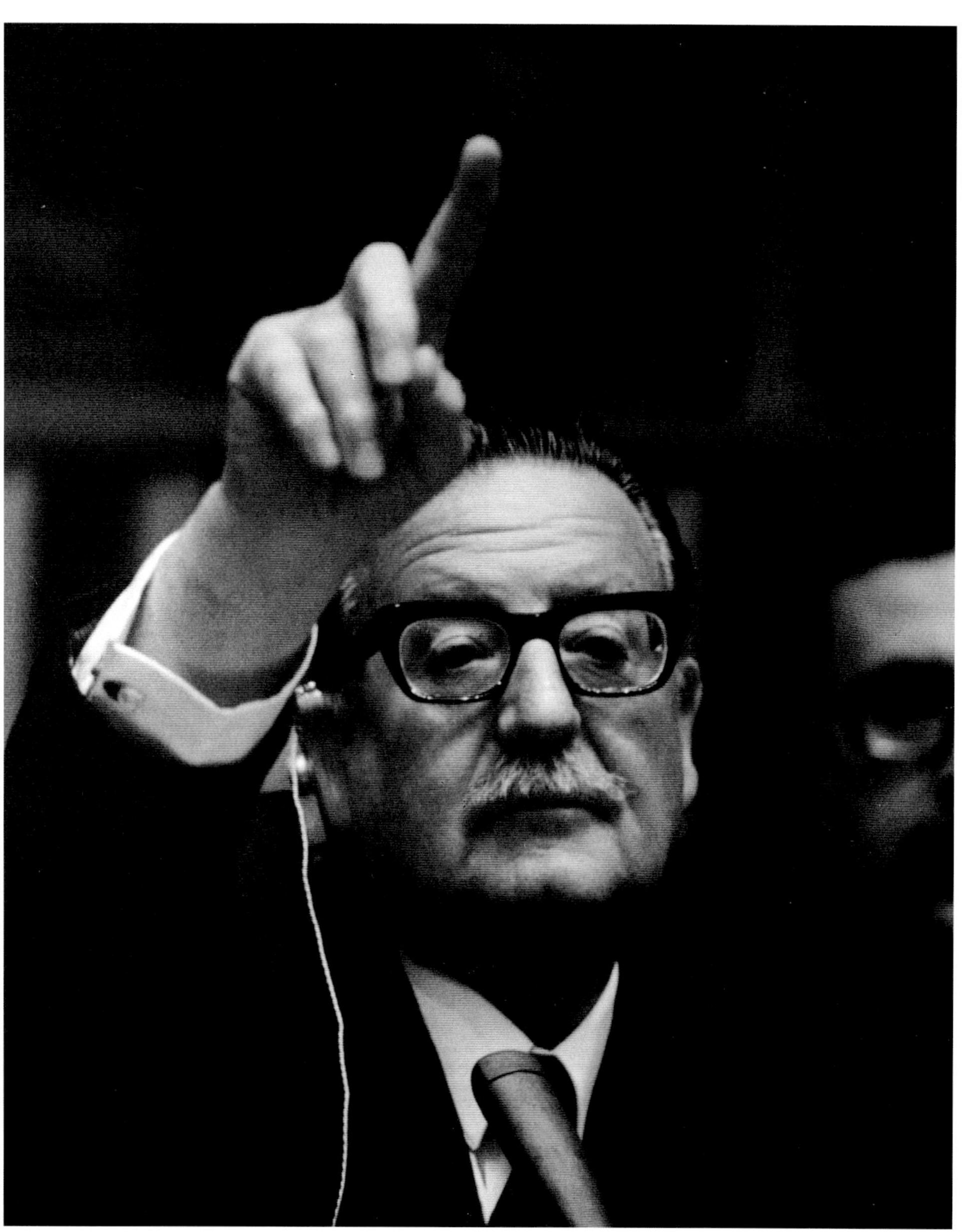

SALVADOR ALLENDE

PRESIDENT ALLENDE OF CHILE was having a press conference at the United Nations. On his way out of the conference hall, he walked by where I was standing, shook my hand, and thanked me for taking his picture. "Muchas gracias," he said twice. This was the only time I photographed him.

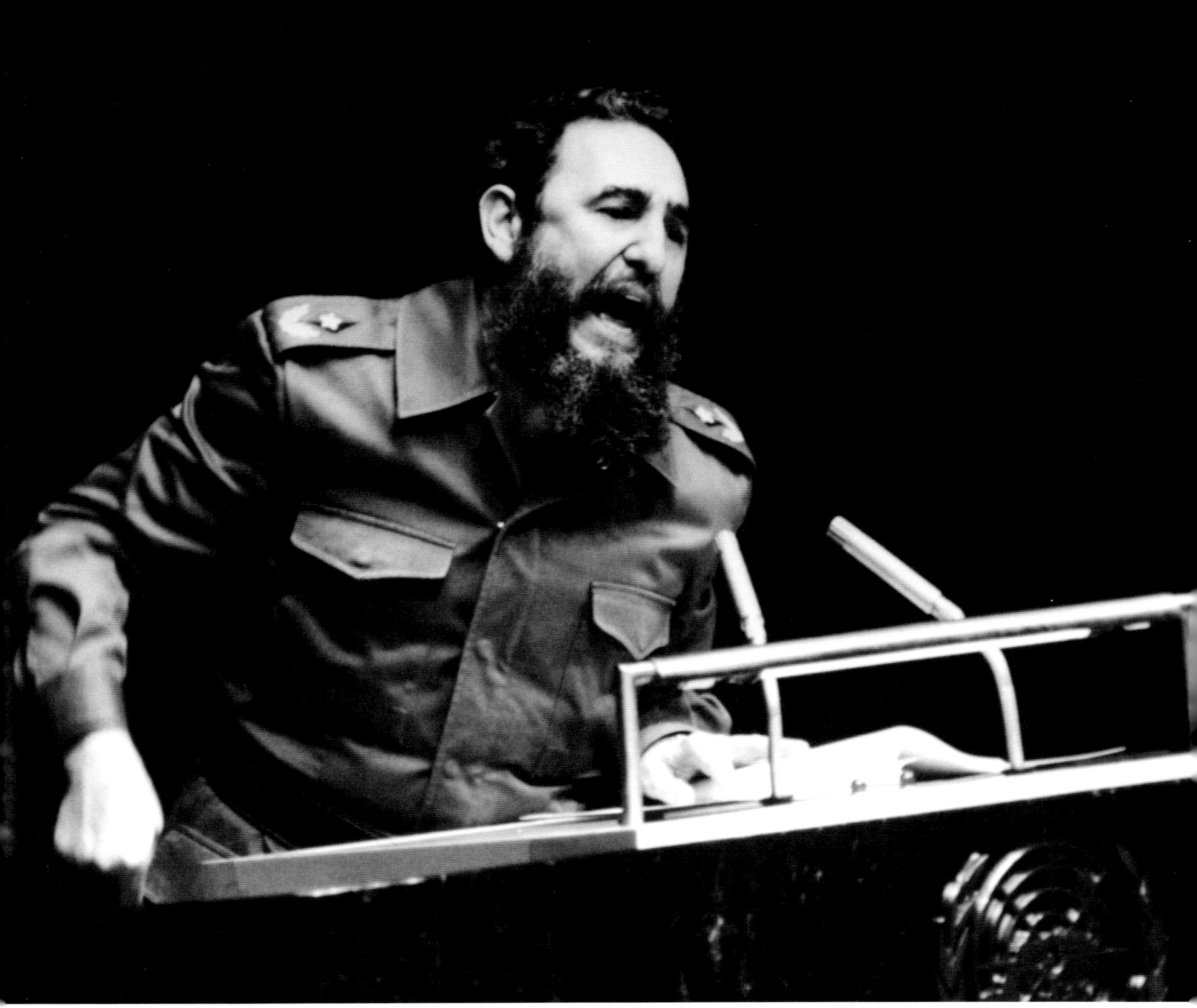

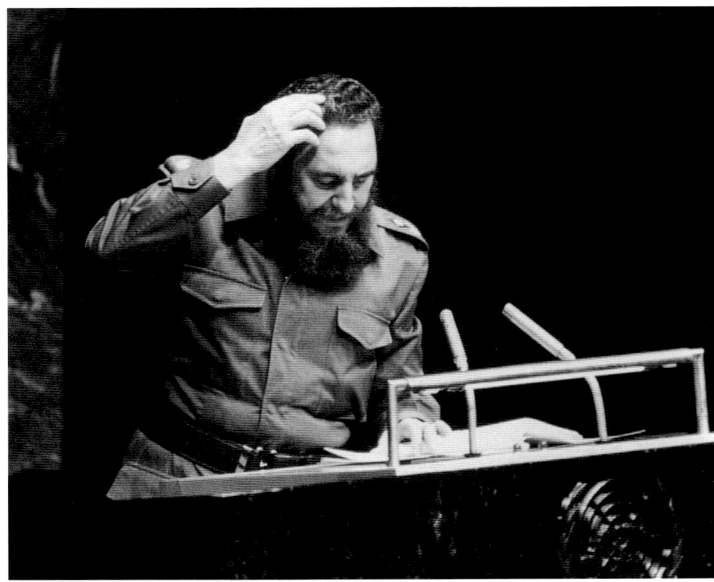

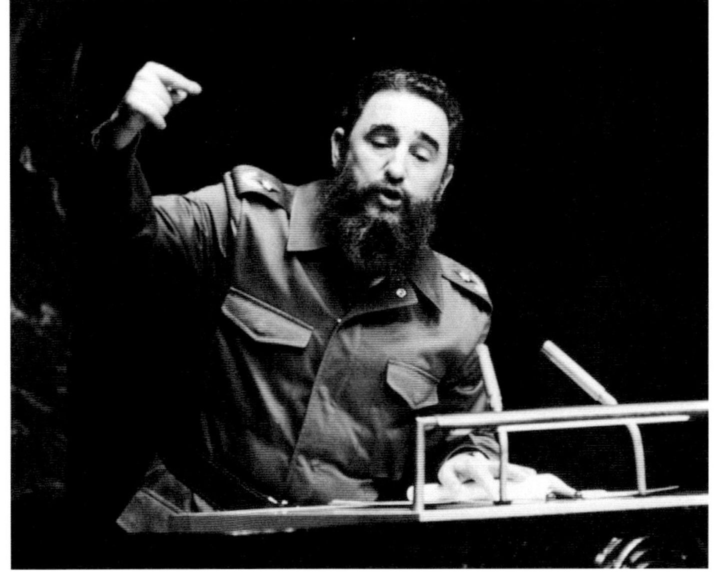

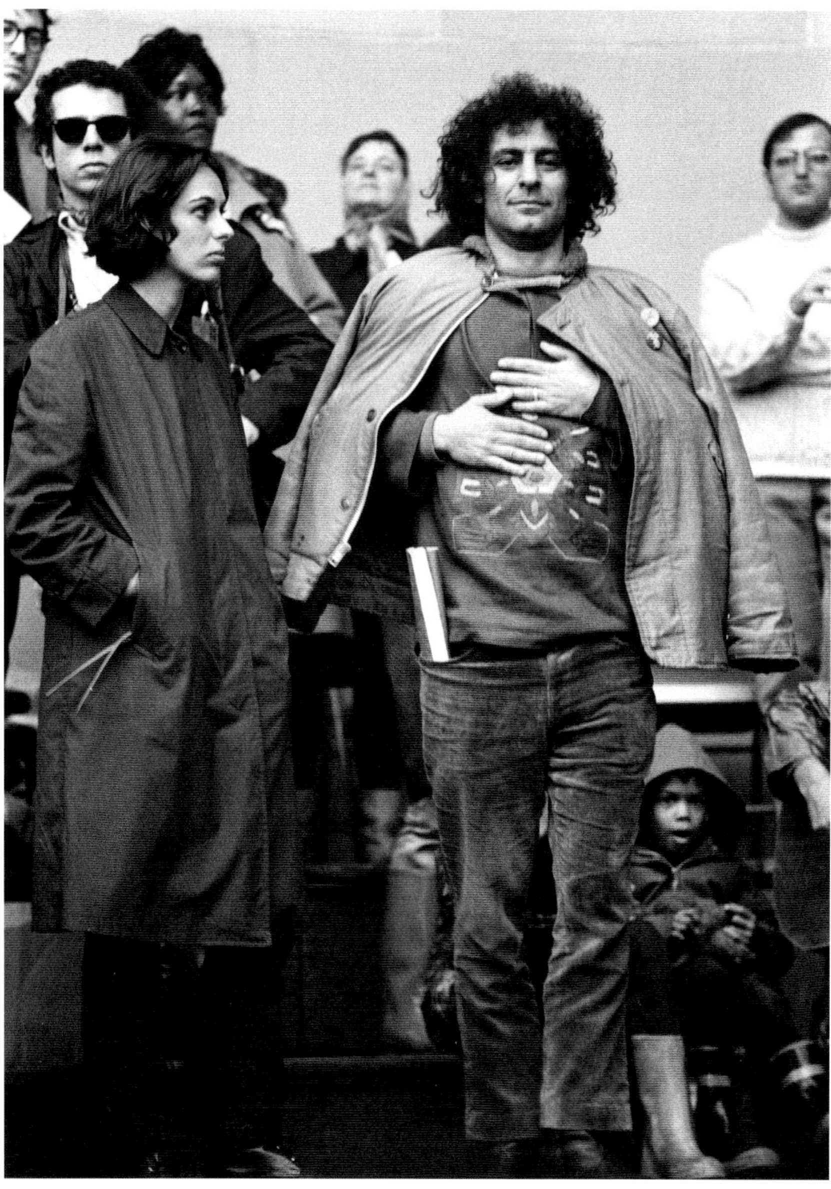

ABBIE HOFFMAN

I WAS PHOTOGRAPHING an anti-war demonstration in Central Park sometime in the 1960s when Abbie Hoffman arrived with Jerry Rubin. There was a lot of shouting of slogans and a great deal of excitement. The two of them stood side by side, as if waiting to be photographed. As soon as I came close to them, they began to pose.

"Take a good shot," Abbie yelled out. "I hope to see it in the papers."

I was too busy to engage in conversation, so I just smiled. Years later, when Abbie came out of hiding and appeared with his wife at a press conference, I was there with my camera. He came over to me at the end and said, "I remember you. I should thank you for the lousy shot you took of me and Jerry for the *New York Post* at the rally in Central Park."

"I remember you too," I said, "except that you're talking to the wrong man. I never worked for the *New York Post*, but thank you for the compliment just the same."

Quite embarrassed, he covered his eyes with his hands and walked away. I never saw him again.

BILLY GRAHAM

MANY YEARS AGO, I photographed Billy Graham at a prayer meeting in Shea Stadium. To my dismay, I realized that if I stayed in the designated press area I wouldn't be able to get any close-up shots of him, because my telephoto lens wasn't adequate. So, discreetly, under cover of darkness, I walked away and found an opening beneath a row of bleachers.

Luckily, the guards didn't notice me and for two hours I was on my knees holding my heavy camera with its motor drive in my hands. Before long, I became completely numb. If the Rev. Graham had only known that fifty feet away from him someone with his same initials was on his knees taking pictures, I thought surely he would have sent some blessings my way in order to make it easier on me.

Suddenly, I felt someone pulling at my jacket sleeve. I turned around and saw a huge uniformed guard standing over me. "What are you doing here? Aren't you in the wrong area?"

"Not at all, sir," I said. "This is where the Reverend Graham's people wanted me to stay," I lied.

"How many of you guys are working for the Reverend?" he asked.

"Quite a few."

"Okay then," he said, "but don't make all that noise."

I couldn't figure out what noise he meant. As he walked away, I heard him say to himself, "What a way to make a living!"

▶

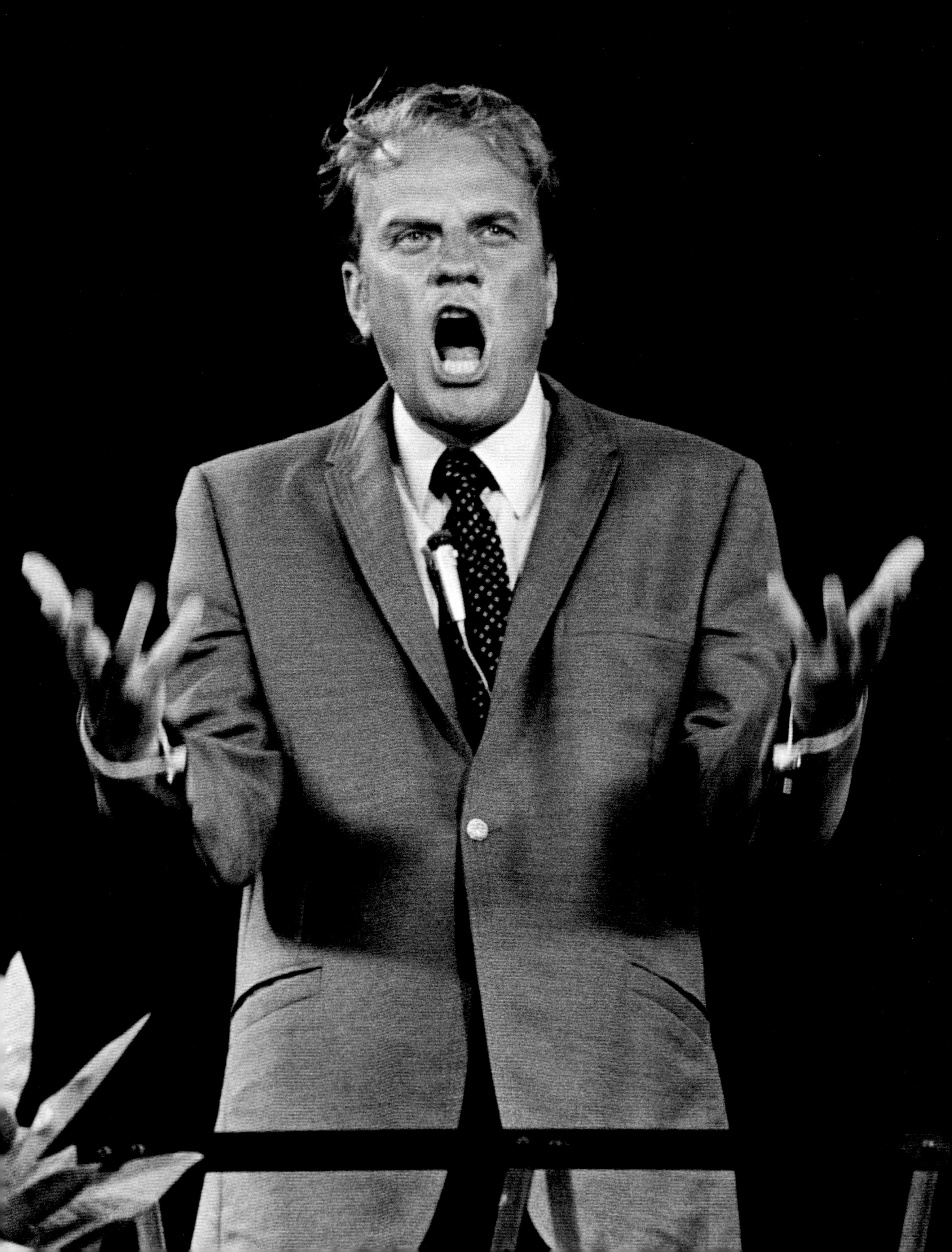

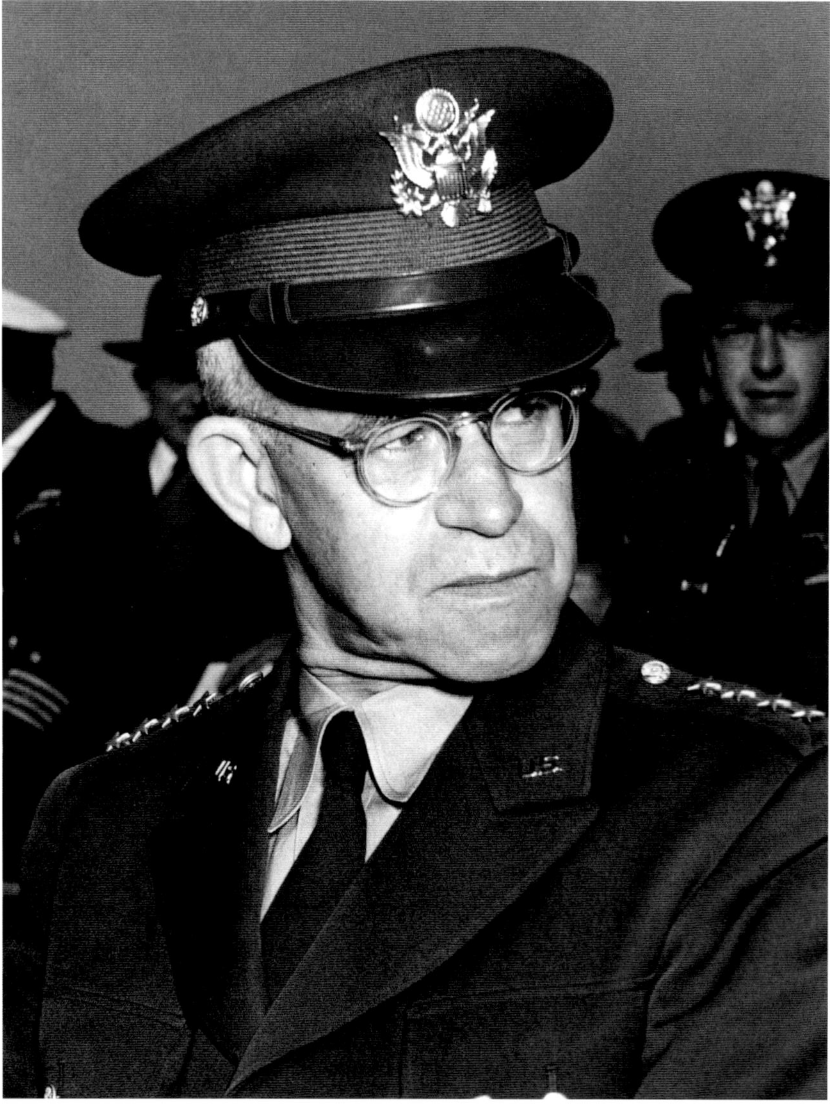

OMAR BRADLEY

WHEN I WAS STATIONED AT FORT BENNING, GEORGIA, in the Army Signal Corps in 1949, several high-ranking generals, including General Omar Bradley, came to watch army exercises involving new weapons.

During a lunch break, a man who claimed to be the Atlanta bureau chief for *Newsweek* asked me if I could take a close-up of General Bradley for an upcoming cover story. I had a hard time imagining that a private like me could point a camera at a four-star general.

It was a warm day, and I did not look presentable. My uniform was wrinkled and soaked with perspiration. But, after thinking it over, I decided to give it a try. I ran to the top of the bleachers where the general and his staff were sitting and briefly explained the situation.

"Go right ahead," the general said. I took two exposures with a 4 x 5 Speed Graphic and thanked him for being so patient.

"Will you have enough? Don't you want to take more?"

"No, sir," I said, "all they need is one cover, and I took two pictures."

"It's a good thing he doesn't work for *Life* magazine," one of the general's aides said, "or else he would be with us all afternoon." As I was leaving, I heard laughter.

WILLIAM F. BUCKLEY

THERE WAS A HUGE POLITICAL RALLY at the Manhattan Center organized by the Conservative Party for William F. Buckley when he ran for mayor against John Lindsay in 1964. The hall was filled to capacity. When Buckley came on stage, the place exploded. There were thousands of posters, placards, and signs, with shouting, applause, and the stamping of feet. In my experience, it was unprecedented pandemonium. Buckley stood behind a lectern that was decorated with flags, and the walls behind him were covered with even more flags and banners.

His very posture indicated superiority, and an aura of self-assurance seemed to emanate from him when he gave his speech. He looked as if he had already won the race. I only hoped to do justice to it with my camera. When he finished speaking, there was a deafening roar of applause. I was quite frightened and astonished by some of the threatening slogans I heard that evening. Some people even objected to my being there and threatened to have me removed.

Some months later, the photo I took was made into a poster, and Buckley asked if he could have a dozen prints. I sent them and not long after received a lovely thank you note. ▶

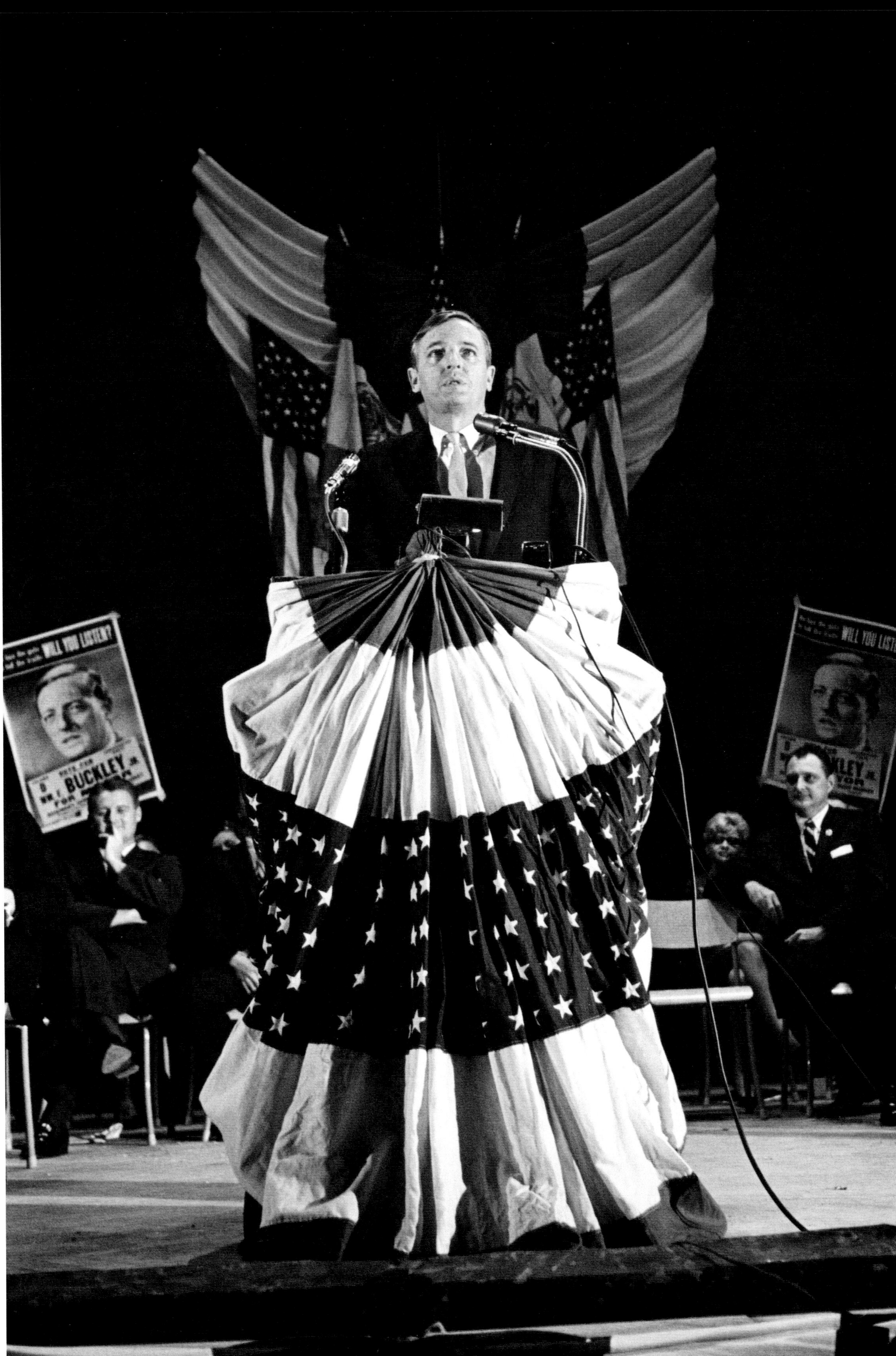
WILL YOU LISTEN?
BUCKLEY JR.

WALTER WINCHELL

THERE WAS A HIGHLY SPIRITED group at Walter Winchell's seventieth birthday party. Friends were offering toasts and there were speeches. When it came time to cut the cake, Winchell insisted that I get a double portion and loaded up my plate. Since I was still busy taking pictures, I put the plate on a table, hoping to get to it later. When I finally did get back, George Raft, the actor, was standing there, eating my cake.

"How's my cake, Mr. Raft?"

"Very good. I usually don't eat cake, but this one is rather exceptional. It isn't your cake I'm eating, is it?

"No, not at all."

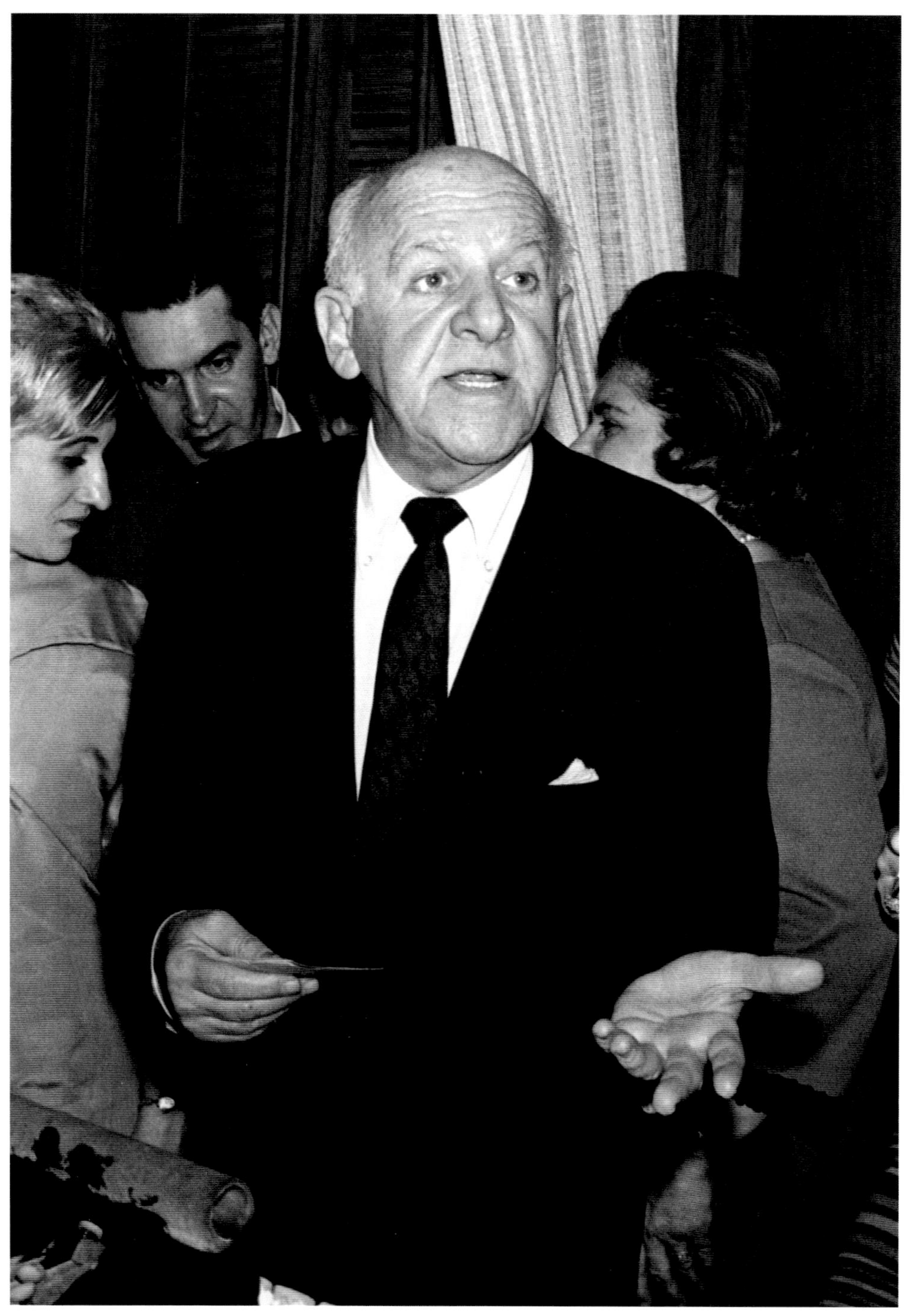

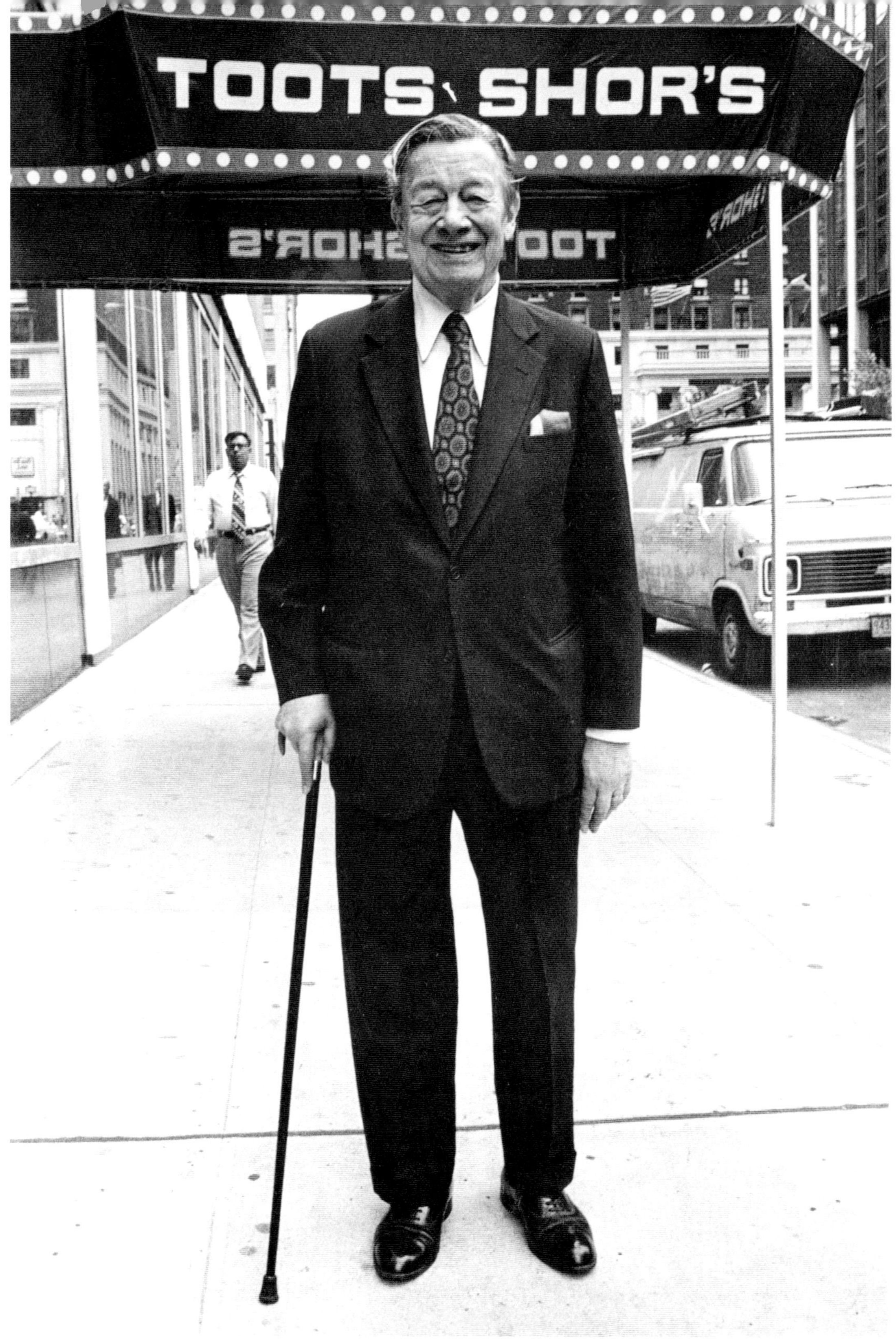

TOOTS SHOR

SHORTLY AFTER TOOTS SHOR moved his bar to the vicinity of Penn Station, I went to photograph him in his new surroundings. As soon as I walked in, he offered me a Kalhua with vodka. I said that it was too early for a cocktail, and that I had to stay in focus. He said that Kalhua with vodka was precisely what he drank when he wanted to stay in focus.

"To each his own," I said, and asked for tomato juice.

"No wonder most of the pictures I look at are out of focus," he said, "all you photographers drink tomato juice."

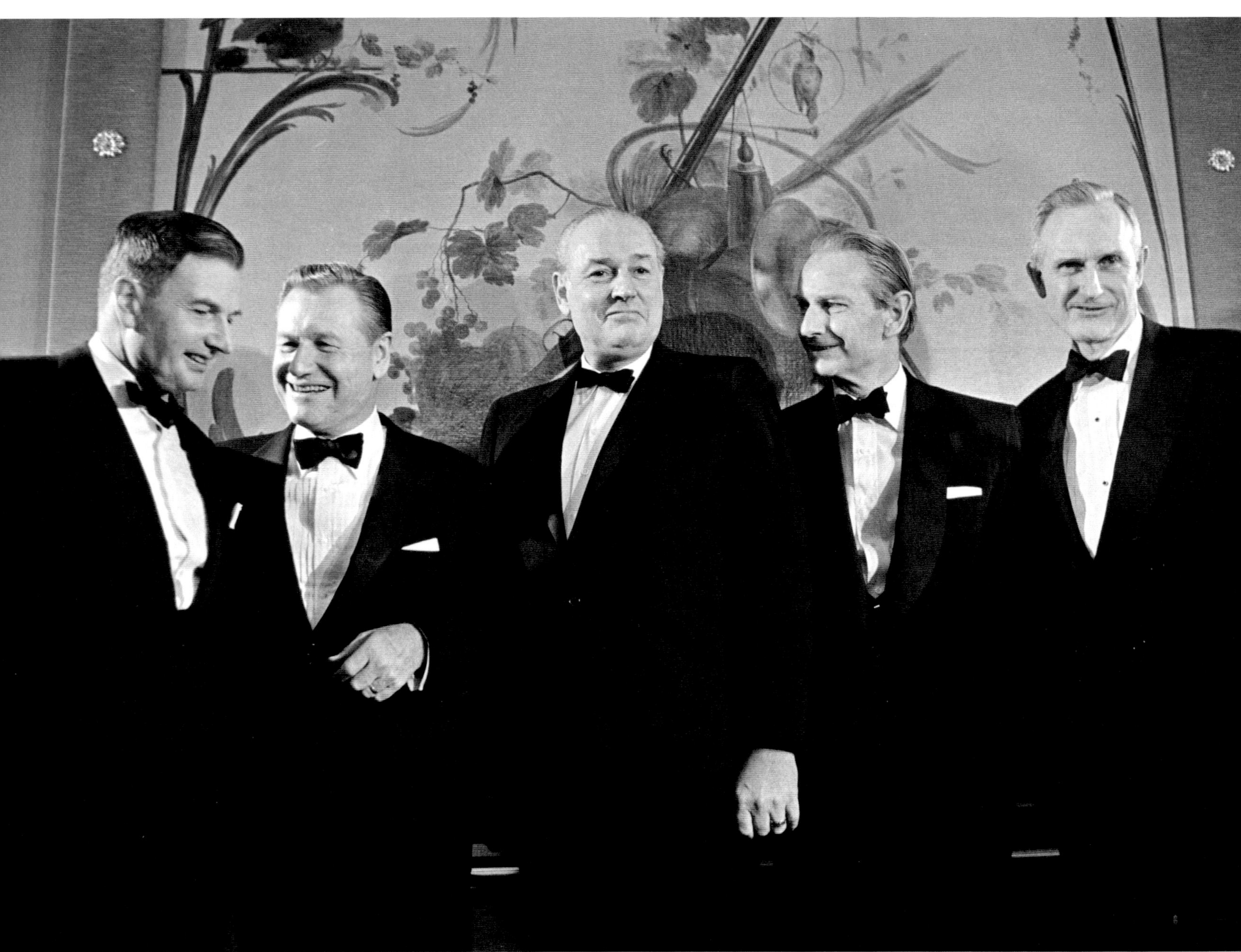

THE ROCKEFELLER BROTHERS

ONE EVENING IN THE 1970s, I was assigned to photograph the Rockefeller brothers receiving an award in recognition of their civic accomplishments. It was a big gala, with many guests from the social register and many members of the Rockefeller family. As I was about to take the picture, someone behind me said, "What a pity there aren't six of them." To which someone responded, "Five is enough." I'm not sure if any of the Rockefellers heard it.

Artists

LARRY RIVERS

I WAS ASSIGNED TO PHOTOGRAPH the painter Larry Rivers up on a scaffold at Broadway and 65th Street, working on a poster for the opening of Lincoln Center. It was a hot and muggy August day, and his head was wrapped in a white bandana. What a great idea, I thought, when I saw him on the scaffold. It reminds you of Michelangelo painting the ceiling of the Sistine Chapel. When I told Rivers, he said, "Except that Michelangelo didn't have to dodge pigeons flying overhead."

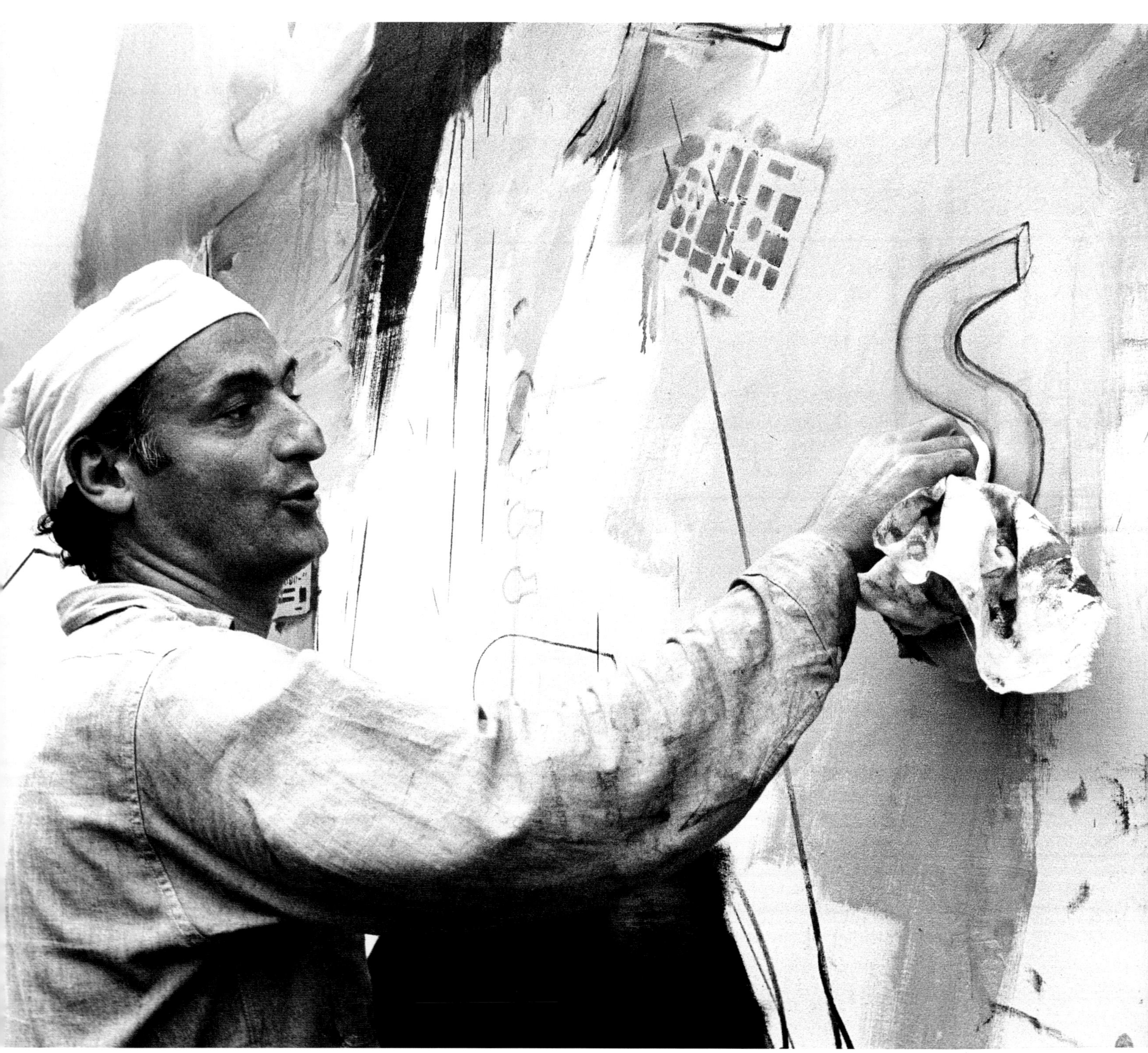

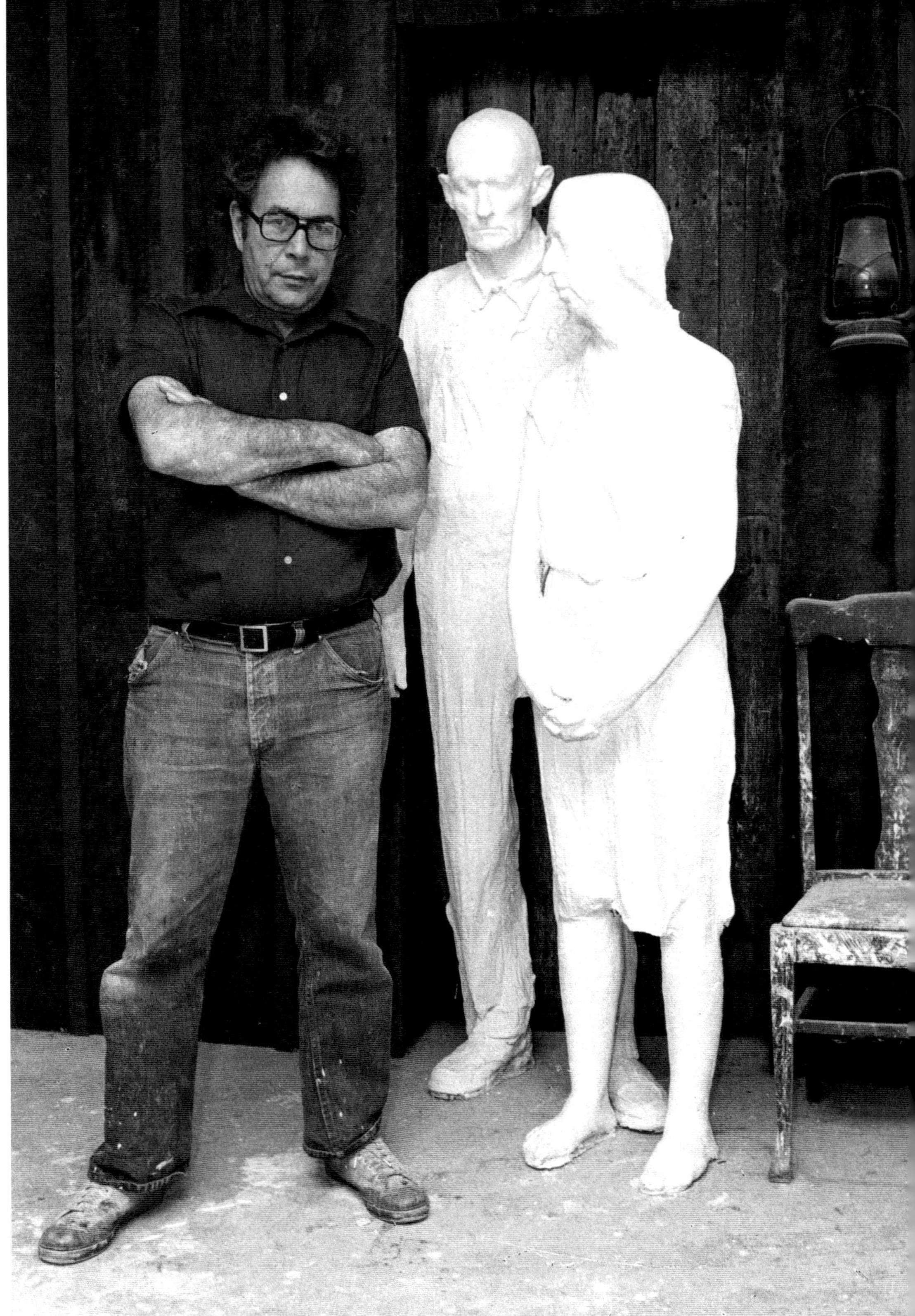

GEORGE SEGAL

I PHOTOGRAPHED GEORGE SEGAL, the sculptor, at his studio in New Jersey, which had once been his father's chicken farm. The space had been renovated, but when I arrived, nothing was there, just bare walls.

"I would like to get some shots of you working. Could you set something up?"

He immediately began pullings things together and soon a wall was covered with sculpture and there were tools and cans of paint lying around. As if by magic, the empty space became a working studio. Segal was very cooperative and very kind. He worked with me and didn't complain once.

At some point, we walked over to a couple of life-size sculptures in white plaster. "These two people are supposed to be my parents," he said.

I photographed him with them, and then, suddenly, it dawned on me how real they were. When I was leaving the studio, I thought I heard them whisper to one another.

"How incredible," I said, "your sculptures whisper."

"I know," he said very seriously, looking at me rather strangely.

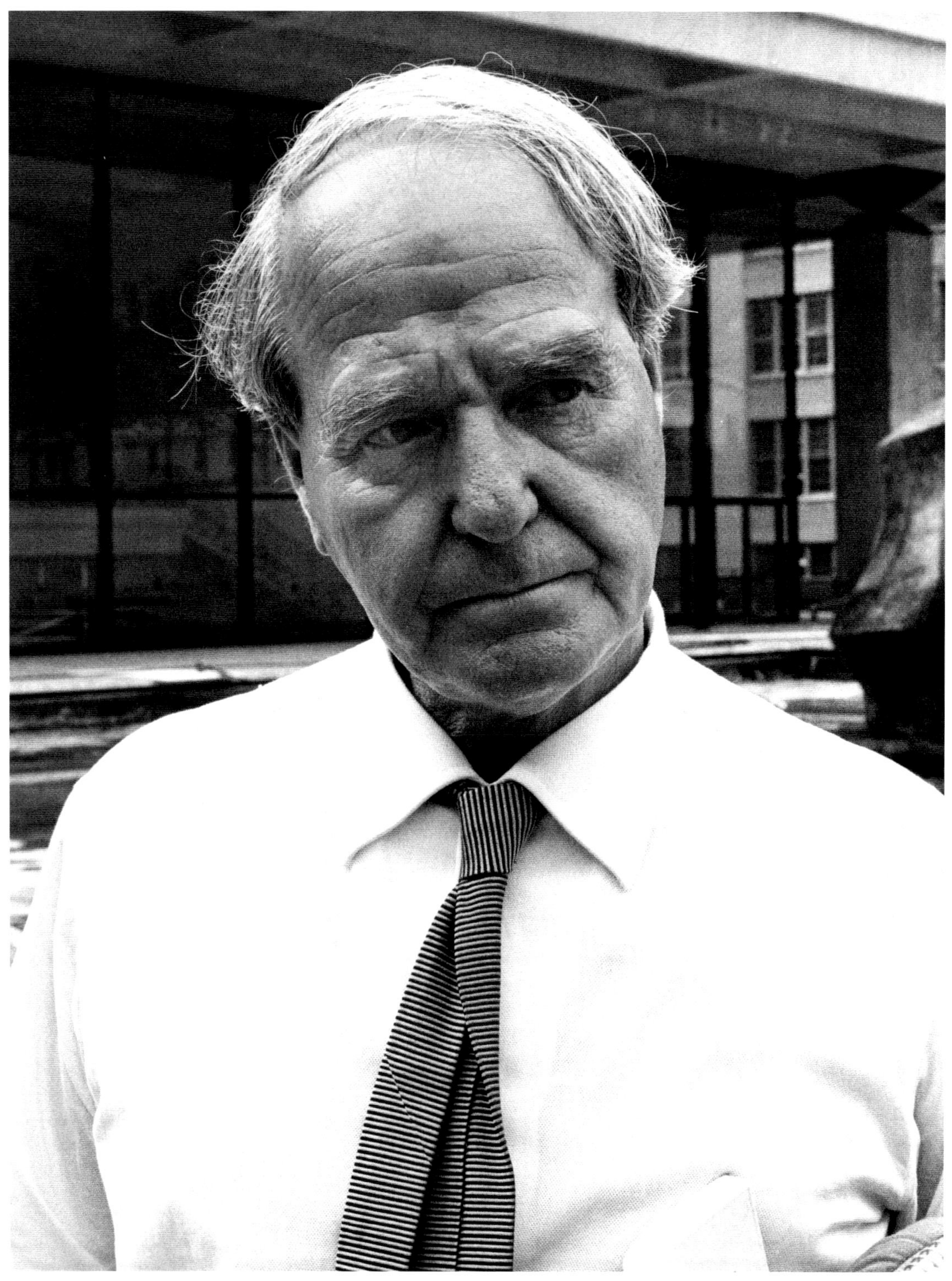

HENRY MOORE

HENRY MOORE'S SCULPTURE *Reclining Figure* was installed in front of the Vivian Beaumont Theater at Lincoln Center in 1973. He stood at some distance, watching the installation process, and would not pose with the sculpture or get too close to it.

I had no choice but to get what I could. At the end, when I went over to thank him for being patient and cooperative, he said, "Not at all, it was a pleasure. I had no idea you were taking pictures of me, but thank you just the same."

BARNETT NEWMAN

HUFFING AND PUFFING, a monocle dangling from his lapel on a long black cord, Barnett Newman arrived at the Guggenheim Museum.

"The traffic was a disaster. Sorry to be late," he said.

"Everyone I know is late, including me," I replied. To change the subject, I said, "I don't understand modern painting, but I do admire your work."

"What is there to understand? It's good enough when one can relate to it."

"And how does one paint such huge canvases?" I asked.

"The same way you paint a small canvas, except that you use a bigger brush, and you sweat a little longer," he said, laughing.

After setting up the shot, I realized there was no film in my camera. "Are you serious?" he said. "In that case, while you load the camera, I'll find a men's room."

Fifteen minutes went by, and no Newman. I went to look and then I heard him scream, "Somebody let me out, please!" The door knob had become stuck. I forced it open, and out he came, perspiring and very agitated.

"Let's get the show on the road and get out of here, shall we?" he said, quite annoyed.

When the session was over, we shared a cab downtown. "What one has to go through for one picture," Newman said, wiping his brow. "No more pictures at the Guggenheim."

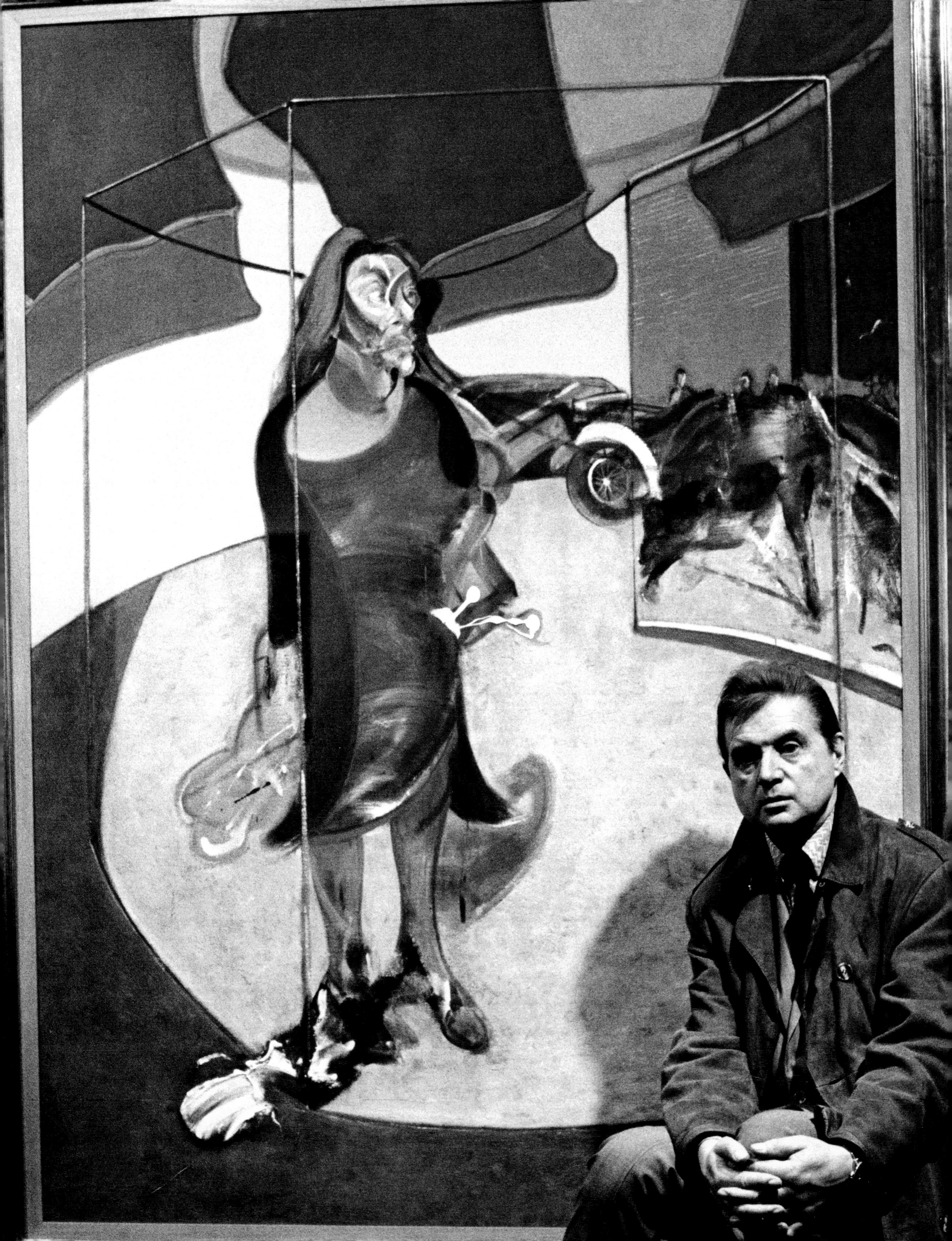

FRANCIS BACON

I WAS ASSIGNED to photograph Francis Bacon, the British painter, who was having a retrospective at the Marlborough Gallery in New York. When I saw his work, I became a bit agitated. I guess he noticed my uneasiness, because he asked me what I thought of the paintings.

"To be frank," I said, "they remind me of a slaughterhouse."

"Oh," he said, "that's very perceptive. I rather like the comparison. And now," he asked, "what would you want me to do for the photo? Hold a butcher knife, perhaps?"

"That far I wouldn't go," I said. I picked a vertical canvas and asked him to sit directly in front of it. He obliged, and we joked some more about butcher shops. ◀

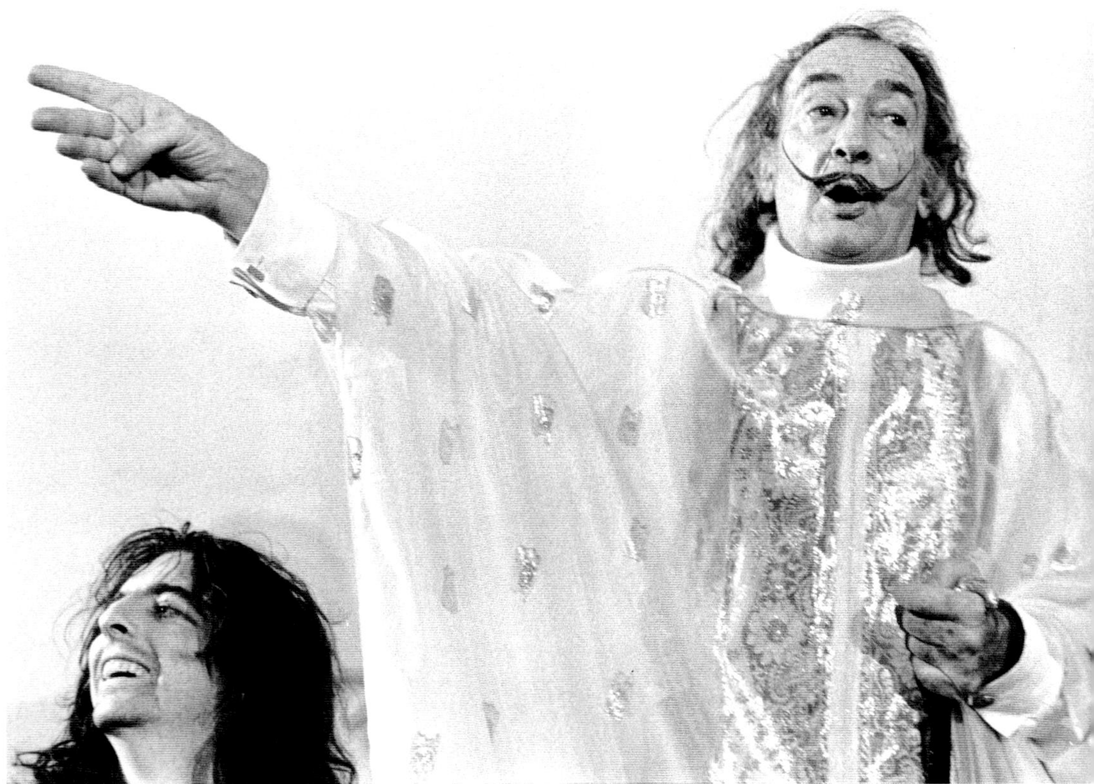

SALVADOR DALI & ALICE COOPER

I COULDN'T UNDERSTAND what Salvador Dali and Alice Cooper had in common when they appeared together at a heavily hyped "happening." They sat behind a long table, surrounded by friends. The place was filled to capacity. Dali was dressed in a flowing white silk robe, looking like a Hindu priest. His head, most of the time, was on Cooper's shoulder. When I came closer, Dali turned to me and said, "Take a sharp picture, please, and focus on my antenna."

"Of course," I said, without knowing what he meant by antenna. "What is the idea behind the show?"

"The idea is that there is no idea. Just Art and Fun. Do you see it now?"

"Thank you, Mr. Dali. Now I begin to see it." As curious as I was, I didn't dare ask him about the antenna. But someone later told me that he considered his moustache to be his antenna of life and inspiration.

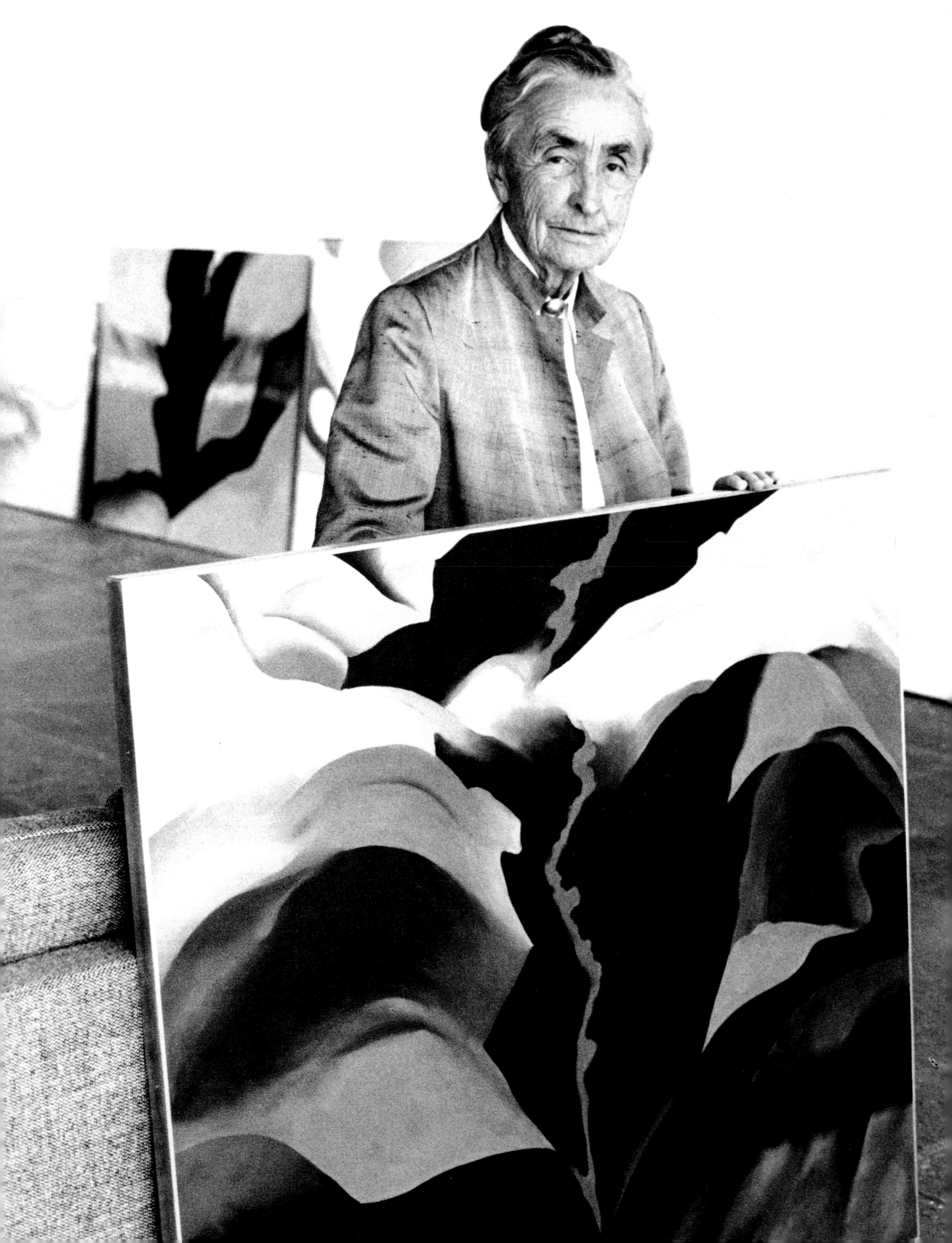

GEORGIA O'KEEFFE

JUST BEFORE THE GEORGIA O'KEEFFE retrospective opened at the Whitney Museum, I was assigned to photograph her hanging the exhibit. But I was given the wrong time, so I arrived two hours late, just when she was leaving for lunch.

"You're only two hours late," she said, a bit annoyed. I apologized and tried to explain that there was a mix-up because the person who handled assignments was out sick. But she was determined to go to lunch and I was desperate to avoid losing the session. As a last resort, I told her that if I didn't get any pictures, I would be fired.

"All I need is ten minutes," I pleaded, "not a minute more."

"All right," she said, "I don't think I could live with myself if someone got fired because of me. Go ahead. Take ten."

I never worked so fast. When I was finished, I told her how much I would like to photograph her where she lived, in New Mexico. She then gave me her phone number and said to call one week before arriving.

Some years later I had an exhibit of my work in Taos, New Mexico. I went to the opening and made a vacation of it. The first thing I did on arrival was to call Miss O'Keeffe. A man answered the phone and said that she was asleep, and that I should try again. I called every day, and always got the same response.

When I came back to New York the following week, I saw her obituary in the newspaper. ◂

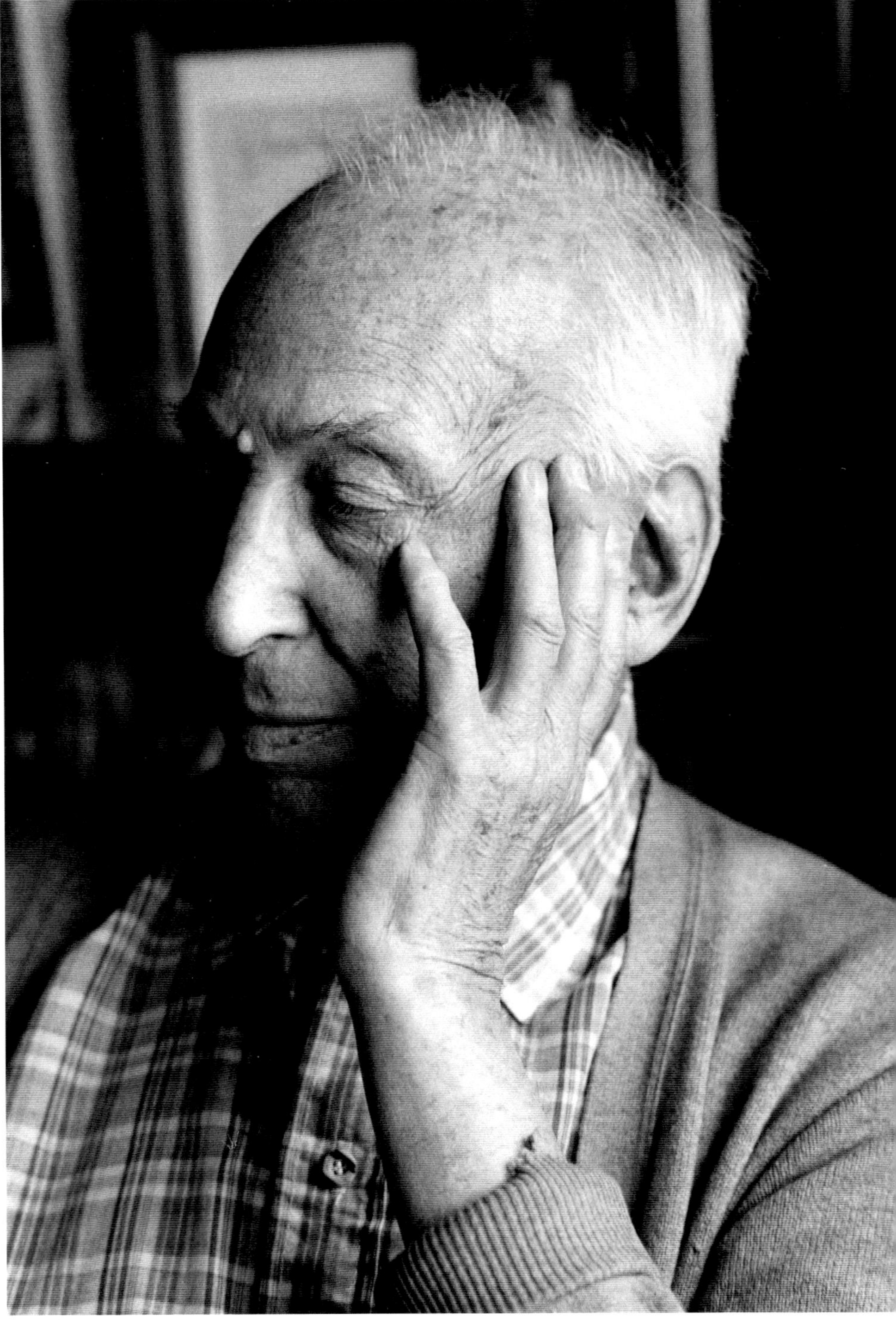

ANDRE KERTESZ

THE PHOTO SESSION WITH ANDRE KERTESZ, the noted photographer and raconteur, was very interesting. He was friendly and cooperative, and spoke at length about his career, his life in Hungary and France, his successes and his disappointments. He was nice enough to express interest in seeing some of my work, and he invited me to visit him again.

Some time later I did. He liked one of my photos, a cityscape, and asked if we could swap. I agreed, and asked for his photo of Mondrian's vestibule. He said that he would order a print, sign it, and send it. Unfortunately, he didn't, and, sadly, he is gone.

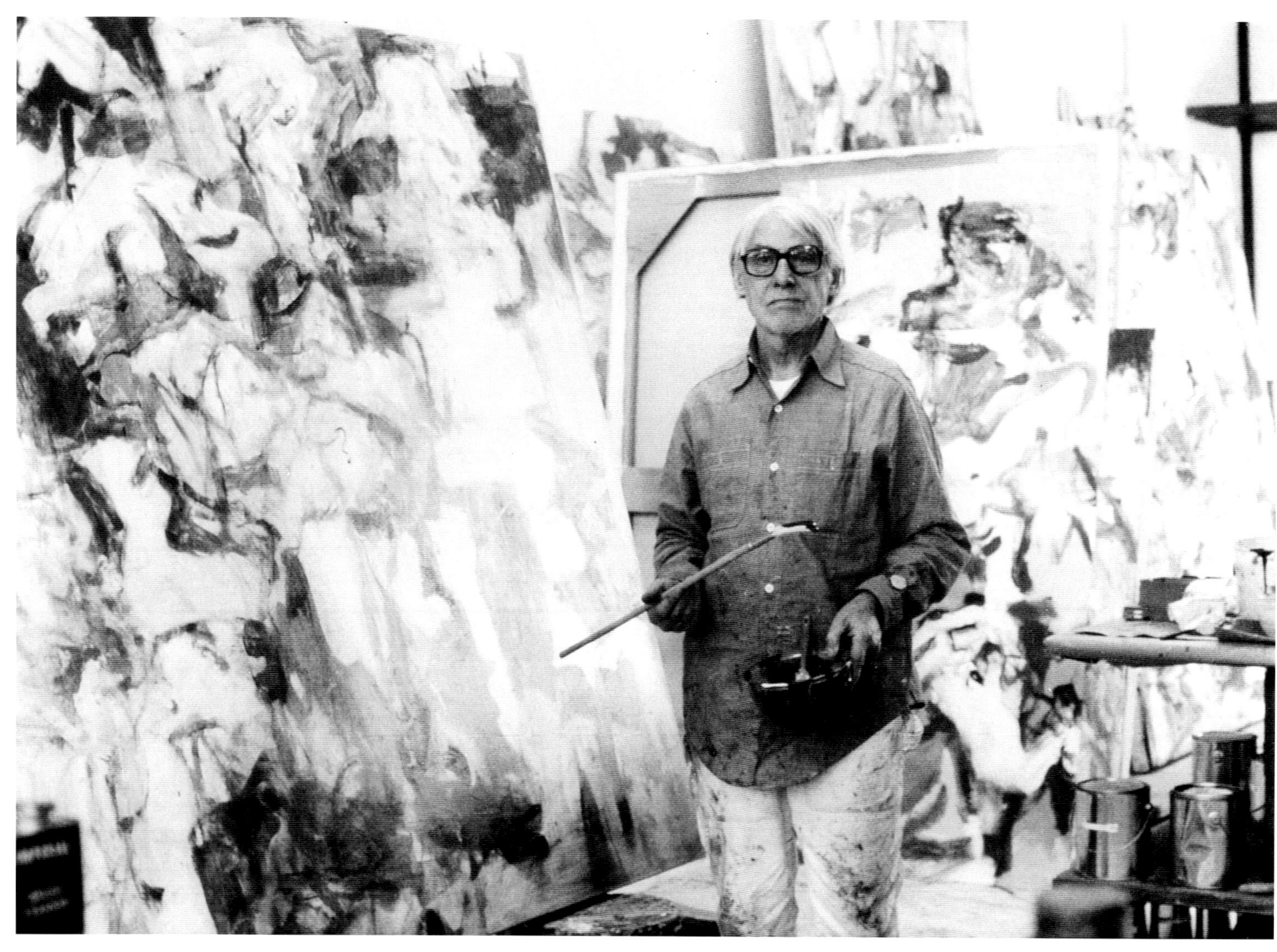

WILLEM DE KOONING

THERE WAS A LOT OF SNOW on the ground when I drove to East Hampton to photograph Willem de Kooning. Outside his studio, beneath a tree, I noticed a dead squirrel covered by a sheet of ice. I rang the bell and de Kooning came to the door. With a friendly gesture he asked me inside.

"I just saw a dead squirrel outside your studio," I said.

He seemed surprised and hesitated a moment before saying, "I wonder why it died."

"It probably froze to death, or perhaps it was sick."

"I never heard of squirrels getting sick, or freezing to death," he said. "They have fur coats. How could they freeze?"

"Unless it starved to death," I said, hoping to get off the subject. But most of the afternoon he kept wondering aloud about the squirrel.

When I took a break to reload film, de Kooning went to his apartment and brought back half a loaf of whole wheat bread and a handful of figs. "Have some," he said, "they are very good for you. I have some every day."

I tried to decline, but he insisted. I took one, and he said, "That's not enough, take some more."

Against my better judgment, I ate several. I shouldn't have, and had to stop more than once on the way home.

ANDY WARHOL

OVER THE YEARS I PHOTOGRAPHED Andy Warhol many times. No matter what he did, he always attracted a lot of attention. One time, during a photo session at the Factory, as his studio was known, I hung a composite of his paintings as a backdrop. But just as I was ready to shoot, he was called to the phone.

"It's very important," he was told. Fifteen minutes later, he still wasn't back. When I inquired, I was told that he had to run out to a meeting, but would be back before long. I wasn't going to leave without a picture, so I decided to wait.

Almost three hours later, Warhol walked in. He looked at the backdrop of his paintings and said, "I'm giving you fifteen minutes. Are you ready?"

"That's very generous of you," I said, and I began to shoot.

"Isn't this a crazy business we're in?" he asked.

"It certainly is," I said, "especially when you have to wait three hours for just fifteen minutes of shooting time."

"I'm sorry," he said, "but fifteen minutes is a long time."

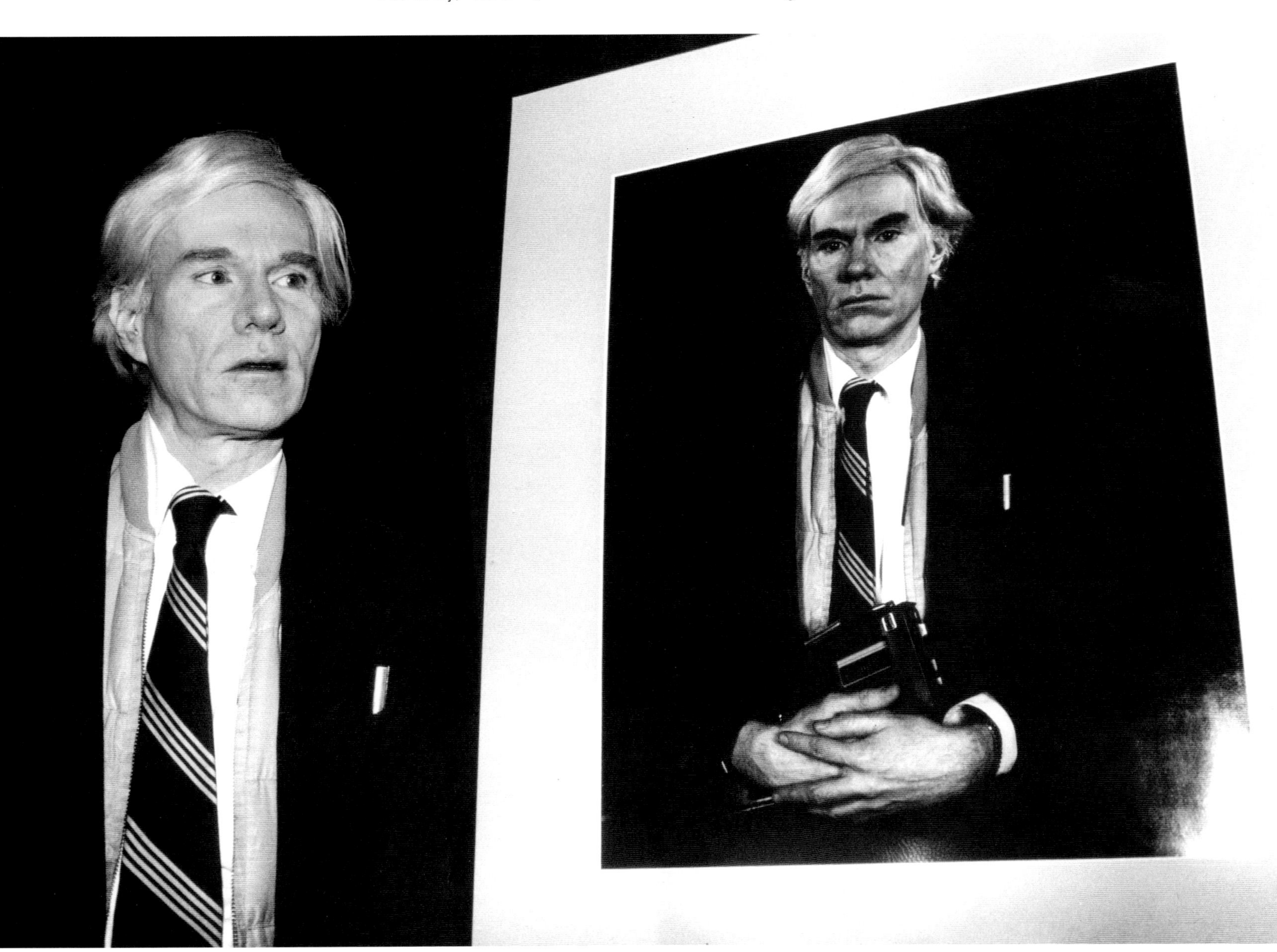

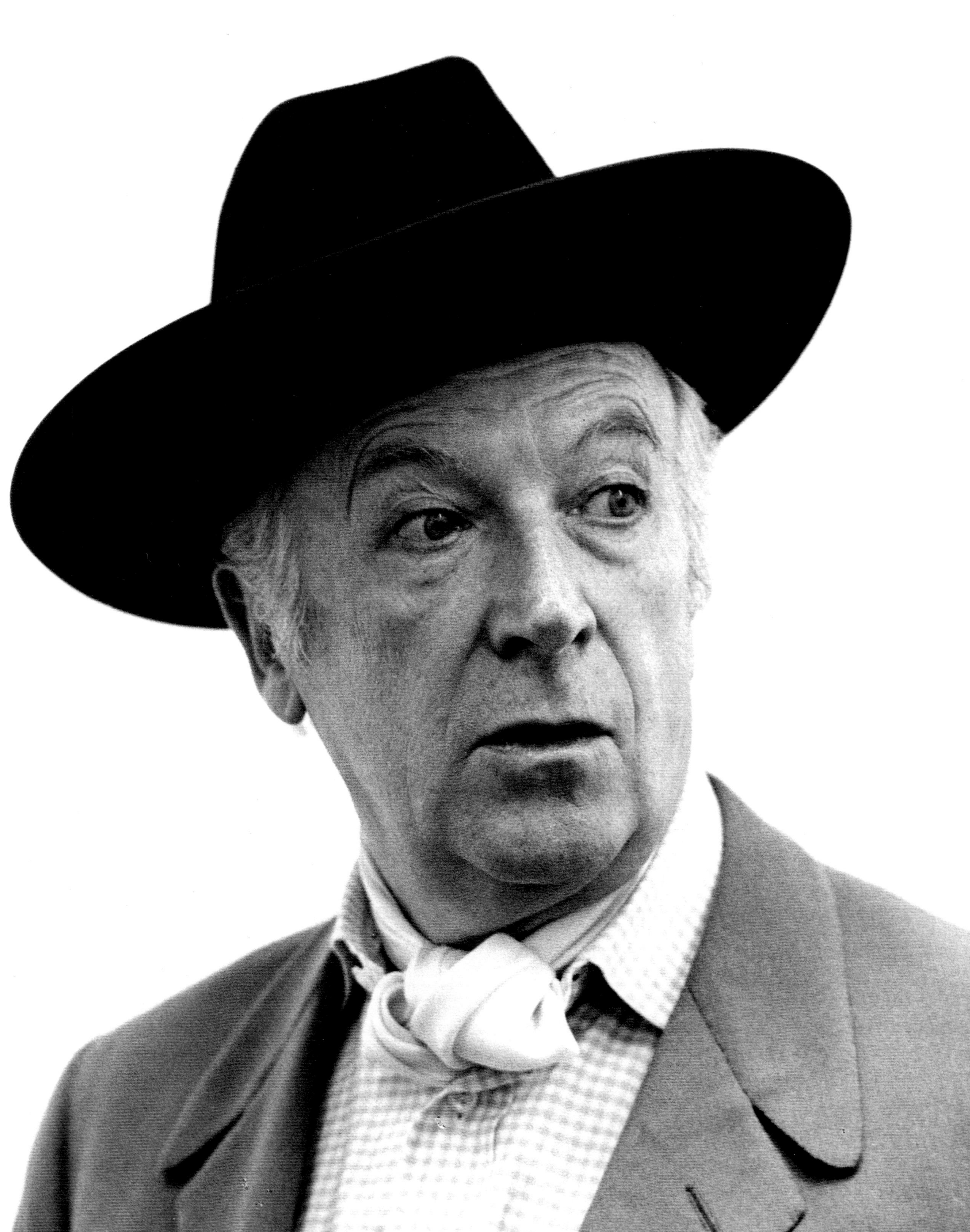

CECIL BEATON

CECIL BEATON, the great English photographer and stage designer, was visiting New York. I met him at someone's office for a photo session. He wore a black wide-brimmed hat which added a touch of the American West to his image. When he realized that I hadn't brought any strobe lights with me, but relied entirely on available light, he was very surprised.

"How can you work with available light?"

"I like to travel light and I work fast. It takes time to set up lights, and I wouldn't dare ask you to give me more than ten minutes."

"Good God," he said. "It takes me ten minutes just to load my camera."

When the photo was published, he wrote me a note, saying, "Thank you for the speediest, bestest likeness ever taken of me. I could never have done it myself. If it isn't too much to ask, I would appreciate a print." ◀

Index of Subjects

About the Author

BERNARD GOTFRYD WAS BORN IN RADOM, POLAND. Shortly after the start of World War II, he was hired as an apprentice photographer at a photo studio owned by a friend of his family. Nazi soldiers and members of the Gestapo brought film to the studio to be processed and the photos often showed atrocities that they had committed. At great risk to his life, he passed copies of the photos to the Polish Resistance. In late 1943, after an unsuccessful attempt to escape from the Radom ghetto made with the help of the Resistance, Gotfryd was captured by the Nazis and sent to the extermination camp in Maidanek.

By the time of his liberation in May 1945 from the Gusen II camp in Austria, Gotfryd had survived six concentration camps. In 1947 he emigrated to the United States and for the next two years worked as a photographer and studied photojournalism. In 1949 he was drafted into the U.S. Army and took basic training at Fort Benning, Georgia, where he was assigned as a combat photographer in the Signal Corps. In 1957 he joined the staff of *Newsweek* magazine and for more than thirty years he photographed prominent figures in art, literature, and politics.

In August 1990 his collection of twenty-one autobiographical short stories titled *Anton the Dove Fancier* was published by Simon and Schuster. In 1991 the book received the Christopher Award and the Pen/Martha Albrand Award for non-fiction by an American writer. It was later published in England and also translated into Dutch, Italian, Polish, and German. The New York Public Library selected *Anton the Dove Fancier* for its catalog of books aimed at 12- to 18-year-olds which reaches 3,000 libraries in the United States and abroad. In May 1996, a play based on *Anton the Dove Fancier* opened in Copenhagen, Denmark, to very favorable reviews. In 2000, an expanded edition with thirty stories was published by Johns Hopkins University Press.

Gotfryd is retired and divides his time between writing, lecturing, and gardening.